Best of the Best from the
DEEP SOUTH
Cookbook

Selected Recipes from the
Favorite Cookbooks of
Louisiana, Mississippi, and Alabama

Hostesses in period costumes welcome visitors to elegant, historic mansions during the Natchez Pilgrimages. Eighteen mansions are open to the public during the Fall Pilgrimage, and twenty-five mansions, some private residences, open their doors during the Spring Pilgrimage.

Best of the Best from the
DEEP SOUTH
Cookbook

Selected Recipes from the
Favorite Cookbooks of
Louisiana, Mississippi, and Alabama

EDITED BY
Gwen McKee
AND
Barbara Moseley

QUAIL RIDGE PRESS
Preserving America's Food Heritage

Recipe Collection ©2009 Quail Ridge Press, Inc.

Library of Congress Cataloging-in-Publication Data

Best of the best from the Deep South cookbook : selected recipes from the favorite
　　cookbooks of Louisiana, Mississippi, and Alabama / edited by Gwen McKee
　　and Barbara Moseley ; illustrated by Tupper England.
　　　　p. cm.. — (Best of the best regional cookbook series)
　　Includes index.
　　ISBN-13: 978-1-934193-41-9
　　ISBN-10: 1-934193-41-0
　　　　1. Cookery, American--Southern style. 2. Cookery—Louisiana. 3.
　　Cookery—Mississippi. 4. Cookery—Alabama. I. Moseley, Barbara. II. Title.
　　TX715.2.S68M3335 2009
　　641.5975--dc22　　　　　　　　　　　　　　　　　　　　　　　　　2009036226

ISBN-13: 978-1-934193-41-9 • ISBN-10: 1-934193-41-0

Book design by Cynthia Clark
Cover photo by Greg Campbell • Illustrated by Tupper England

Printed in the United States of America

First printing, January 2009 (paperbound) • Second. November 2009 (comb-bound)
Third, January 2011

On the cover: The Best Pecan Pie, page 249

QUAIL RIDGE PRESS
P. O. Box 123 • Brandon, MS 39043
info@quailridge.com• www.quailridge.com

CONTENTS

MISSISSIPPI DEVELOPMENT AUTHORITY, DIVISION OF TOURISM

Agriculture is Mississippi's number one industry, with the cotton industry ranking fifth. In 2007, Mississippi harvested approximately $434 million worth of cotton.

Quest for the Best
Regional Cooking

It seems that everywhere Barbara and I travel, we find that people love to talk about food. Invariably they mention specific dishes that have been an important part of their family's heritage and tradition, and do so with exuberance and pride.

"My mother always serves her fabulous cornbread dressing with our Thanksgiving turkey, and it is simply 'the best.'"

"Aunt Susan's famous pecan pie is always the first to go."

"No family occasion would be complete without Uncle Joe's chicken salad sandwiches."

Well, we heard, we researched, and we captured these bragged-about recipes so that people all over the country . . . and the world . . . could enjoy them.

My co-editor Barbara Moseley and I have been searching for the country's *best* recipes for three decades, and home cooks everywhere have learned to trust and rely on our cookbooks to bring them fabulous meals their friends and family will love! We always choose recipes based first and foremost on taste. In addition, the ingredients have to be readily available, and the recipes simple, with easy-to-follow instructions and never-fail results.

While touring the country and tasting the local fare, we delight in finding the little secrets that make the big difference. We have eaten buffalo in Wyoming, halibut in Alaska, lobster in Maine, gumbo in Louisiana, each prepared in a variety of creative ways. Finding out about conch in Florida and boysenberries in Oregon and poi in Hawaii. . . . No matter where we venture, this part of our job is always fun, often surprising, and definitely inspiring!

Though it is difficult to divide our country into specific regions according to cuisine, we chose to call the three states of Louisiana, Mississippi, and Alabama the Deep South, because, well, that's where and what it is. Deeply rooted in tradition and cultural cooking, there is much pride in who these people are and how they live and what they cook.

Hospitality, friendliness, and generosity seem to be one of the necessary ingredients in all their recipes. My Louisiana roots and Barbara's Mississippi roots make this region especially meaningful to us. We hope you enjoy our favorite recipe selections for the *Best of the Best from the Deep South Cookbook.*

Gwen McKee

Gwen McKee and Barbara Moseley, editors of
BEST OF THE BEST STATE COOKBOOK SERIES

BEVERAGES and APPETIZERS

Nottoway Plantation, completed in 1859, is the largest plantation home in the South. Emily Randolph, the wife of Nottoway's builder, confronted Union troops alone and kept them from ransacking her family's home on the Mississippi River, two miles north of White Castle, Louisiana.

Café Brûlot

1 orange
7 whole cloves
¼ cup sugar
3 cinnamon sticks, broken
  into pieces

¾ cup brandy
3 cups hot Louisiana coffee or
  dark-roast coffee

Remove orange peel in one continuous spiral, scraping off as much white pith as possible. Reserve orange for another use. Combine orange peel, cloves, cinnamon, and brandy in a bowl or 2-cup measure. Let stand 2–3 hours. Pour brandy with orange peel and spices over sugar in a chafing dish. Ignite brandy carefully. Pour in the hot coffee gradually to extinguish the flame. Ladle into demitasse cups. Yields 8 servings.

Simply Southern (Alabama)

Southern Tea

3 family-size tea bags
1 cup sugar
1 (12-ounce) can frozen
  lemonade

1 (12-ounce) can frozen
  pineapple juice

Place tea bags in a boiler of water and bring to a boil as usual. Put sugar in gallon pitcher; pour hot tea over and stir to dissolve. Add lemonade and pineapple juice. Finish filling pitcher with water. Serve chilled either in a punch bowl with a decorative ice ring, or in a pretty glass pitcher with ice. Serve with old-fashioned tea cakes.

Picnic in the Park (Mississippi)

Coffee Rum Punch

A big hit for a brunch or luncheon.

12 tablespoons instant coffee
2 cups sugar
2 cups water
3 (12-ounce) cans evaporated
   milk
3 cans whole milk

½ gallon coffee ice cream,
   softened
2 large bottles soda water
½ pint light rum
Whipped cream

Add sugar and coffee to water. Stir, heat, blend, remove from heat, and chill. Add remaining ingredients. Top with whipped cream and serve. Serves 30 cups.

The Gulf Gourmet (Mississippi)

Amaretto Punch

2 cups sugar
1 quart boiling water
1 (6-ounce) can frozen
   lemonade concentrate,
   thawed
1 (46-ounce) can unsweetened
   pineapple juice

2 quarts water
2 cups amaretto
1 (12-ounce) can frozen orange
   juice concentrate, thawed
2 tablespoons vanilla extract
1 tablespoon almond extract

Dissolve sugar in boiling water in a large container. Stir in remaining ingredients. Divide mixture among 6 heavy-duty sealable 1-quart plastic bags; seal. Freeze 12 hours or longer. Remove from freezer and let mixture stand until slushy before serving. Yields 6 quarts.

Beyond Cotton Country (Alabama)

Southern Champagne Punch

2 fifths champagne
1 fifth Chablis
1 pint vodka
1 (28-ounce) bottle soda water

1 (12-ounce) can frozen
lemonade concentrate,
undiluted

Chill ingredients and mix. A moderately strong punch can be made by using ½ pint vodka. Can be served from pitcher garnished with fresh fruits or from a punch bowl with an ice ring. If using an ice ring, do not use lemonade in punch, but dilute and make ring, adding fresh or canned fruit for decoration. Yields 15 servings.

The Alabama Heritage Cookbook (Alabama)

Mardi Gras Madness

1 ice ring
1 (40-ounce) bottle grape juice
1 (48-ounce) can unsweetened
pineapple juice
1 (2-liter) bottle lemon-lime
soft drink

1 fifth vodka or more, to taste
2 oranges or lemons, sliced
2 limes, sliced

Place ice ring in bottom of punch bowl. Add liquids in order given. Float slices of oranges and limes on top. Makes 8–9 quarts, about 65 (½-cup) servings.

Adds to the fun in true Carnival colors of purple, green, and gold!

Louisiana LEGACY (Louisiana)

Swamp Water

1 (3-ounce) package lime
gelatin (may use sugar-free)
1 cup hot water
2 liters carbonated water

1 (12-ounce) can frozen
unsweetened pineapple juice
concentrate

Mix lime gelatin with hot water to dissolve. Add carbonated water and frozen concentrate. Chill. Serve over ice. Yields 10 (12-ounce) servings.

Just for Kids (Louisiana)

Pappy's Hot Toddy

William Faulkner (1897–1962) was the author of The Sound and the Fury, As I Lay Dying, Absalom, Absalom! *and* Light in August. *He won the Nobel Prize for Literature in 1950. (The following recipe was submitted by his niece, Dean Faulkner Wells.)*

When grownups in the Faulkner family were sick, Pappy had an instant cure— his ever-popular Hot Toddy. It was guaranteed to cure or ease anything from the aches and pains of a bad spill from a horse to a bad cold, from a broken leg to a broken heart. Pappy alone decided when a Hot Toddy was needed, and he administered it to his patient with the best bedside manner of a country doctor.

He prepared it in the kitchen in the following way:

Take one heavy glass tumbler. Fill approximately half full with Heaven Hill bourbon (the Jack Daniel's was reserved for Pappy's aliments). Add one tablespoon of sugar. Squeeze ½ lemon and drop into glass. Stir until sugar dissolves. Fill glass with boiling water. Serve with potholder to protect patient's hands from the hot glass.

Pappy always made a small ceremony out of serving his Hot Toddy, bringing it upstairs on a silver tray, and admonishing his patient to drink it quickly before it cooled off.

The Great American Writer's Cookbook (Mississippi)

MISSISSIPPI DEVELOPMENT AUTHORITY, DIVISION OF TOURISM

William Faulkner, born in New Albany, Mississippi, is considered one of America's greatest writers. He won the Nobel Prize for Literature, two Pulitzer Prizes and the National Book Award. In his home, "Rowan Oak," (above) in Oxford, visitors may view Faulkner's study where an outline for A Fable *is written on the wall in the author's own handwriting.*

Bacon Tomato Dip

This may be placed in a hollowed round loaf, using bread for dippers, or served with chips.

10 slices bacon
1 (8-ounce) package cream
   cheese, softened
3 tablespoons prepared mustard
½ teaspoon celery salt

¼ cup finely chopped green
   pepper
1 medium tomato, peeled,
   seeded, finely chopped

Fry bacon until crisp. Drain and crumble. In bowl, combine cream cheese, mustard, and celery salt. Stir in bacon, pepper, and tomato. Chill at least 2 hours.

More Cultured Country Cooking (Alabama)

Corn Dip

1 (15-ounce) can Mexicorn,
   drained
1 (10-ounce) can Ro-Tel
   tomatoes, drained
½ (1-ounce) package dry
   ranch salad dressing mix

4–6 green onions, chopped
1 cup sour cream
1 cup mayonnaise

Mix well and serve cold with corn chips.

The Gift of Gracious Meals (Mississippi)

Mississippi State Sin

1 loaf French bread
1½ cups sour cream
2 cups shredded Cheddar
   cheese
1 (8-ounce) package cream
   cheese, softened

⅓ cup chopped green onions
½ cup chopped ham
⅓ cup chopped green chiles
Dash of Worcestershire

Slice off top of bread and hollow out inside (save pieces). Mix remaining ingredients. Pour into hollowed bread, and put top back on bread. Wrap in foil. Bake at 350° for one hour. Serve as a dip with hollowed out pieces of bread, crackers, or chips.

Bully's Best Bites (Mississippi)

Black-Eyed Pea Dip

1 (16-ounce) can black-eyed
  peas with jalapeño peppers,
  drained
½ cup margarine
5 green onions, finely chopped

6 slices bacon, cooked and
  crumbled
1 (8-ounce) package low-fat
  processed cheese, cubed
1 teaspoon garlic powder

Mash peas in large bowl until smooth. Add margarine and blend well. Stir in green onions, bacon, cheese spread, and garlic powder, mixing well. Pour mixture into 1-quart microwave-safe dish. Microwave at HIGH setting for 3–4 minutes or until cheese is melted. Stir well. Serve with tortilla chips or raw vegetables. Makes 1½ cups.

Cane River's Louisiana Living (Louisiana)

Montgomery Caviar

1 (16-ounce) can black-eyed
  peas, drained
6 green onions, sliced
½ teaspoon parsley
1 (15-ounce) can shoepeg
  corn, drained
½ teaspoon garlic powder

½ teaspoon onion salt
1 (10-ounce) can Ro-Tel
  tomatoes
½ (16-ounce) bottle Italian
  dressing
1 green pepper, diced
2–3 pear tomatoes, diced

Combine all ingredients; refrigerate until ready to serve. Serve with Tostitos or scoops.

Treasured Favorites (Alabama)

In early 1861, representatives from six of the states that had seceded from the Union gathered in Montgomery to form the government of the Confederate States of America, with Montgomery as the capital. On April 11, 1861, the telegraph was sent from the Winter Building in downtown Montgomery that ordered the fire on Fort Sumter, thus beginning the Civil War.

Jane's Broccoli Dip

1 cup chopped onion
1 stick margarine
2 packages frozen, chopped
  broccoli
1 (4-ounce) can sliced
  mushrooms

1 cup slivered almonds
1½ (6-ounce) rolls garlic cheese*
2 (10¾-ounce) cans cream of
  mushroom soup
Tabasco and Worcestershire to
  taste

Sauté onion in margarine. Add broccoli and simmer until tender.
Add remainder of ingredients and serve hot with corn chips.

*May substitute 6 ounces Velveeta and ½ teaspoon garlic powder.

Bell's Best (Mississippi)

Crockpot Crab Dip

¾ cup mayonnaise
1 (8-ounce) package cream
  cheese, softened
2 tablespoons apple juice

1 onion, minced
1 pound frozen lump crabmeat,
  thawed, carefully picked over

Mix mayonnaise, cream cheese, and apple juice in medium bowl
until blended. Place in 1- to 3-quart slow cooker. Stir in onions
and blend well. Gently stir in crabmeat. Cover and cook on LOW
heat 4 hours. Dip will hold for up to two hours.

The Cook's Book (Alabama)

Delicious Crawfish Dip

2 bunches green onions,
  chopped
¼ bunch parsley, chopped
1 stick margarine or butter
3 tablespoons flour
1 (12-ounce) can evaporated
  milk

1 egg yolk, beaten
Salt and pepper to taste
1 pound crawfish tails in a bag
  (add any fat in bag)
½ pound Mexican Velveeta
  cheese

Sauté onions and parsley in butter. Sprinkle in flour. Add evaporated milk. Stir over heat until thick. Remove from heat and stir
in egg yolk. Season. Add crawfish tails and cheese. Return to
heat and cook over low heat 10 minutes while stirring constantly.
Serve with good crackers or chips.

Kooking with the Krewe (Louisiana)

Shrimp Dip

This is better if made a day before serving.

¾ pound shrimp, cooked, deveined
¼ cup mayonnaise
1 teaspoon garlic powder
1 (8-ounce) package cream cheese, softened

½ teaspoon salt
½ teaspoon pepper
2 tablespoons grated onion
3–4 dashes Tabasco

Blend all ingredients well in a blender set at high speed. Serve with crackers or chips. Store in sealed container in refrigerator.

Gibson/Goree Family Favorites (Alabama)

Shrimp Balls

1 pound cooked shrimp
3 tablespoons cream cheese, softened
½ cup finely chopped celery
1 tablespoon grated onion
1 tablespoon finely chopped green bell pepper

1 boiled egg, chopped
1 teaspoon Worcestershire
2 teaspoons horseradish
¾ teaspoon salt
Garlic powder, black pepper, and red pepper to taste
Chopped parsley

Grind or cut up shrimp in small pieces. In bowl, place cream cheese; add all other ingredients to it, except parsley. Mix well. Roll into small balls. Place chopped parsley on wax paper and roll shrimp balls to coat with parsley. Chill until ready to serve. Makes 2–3 dozen.

From Mama to Me (Louisiana)

Creole Shrimp

2 cups cider vinegar
2 cups vegetable oil
2 tablespoons Creole mustard
1 cup finely chopped onion
3 cloves garlic, crushed

1 cup chili sauce
¼ teaspoon salt
4 tablespoons paprika
5 pounds shrimp, cooked, peeled, and deveined

In large bowl, blend vinegar, oil, mustard, onion, garlic, chili sauce, salt, and paprika. Add shrimp. Marinate, covered, in the refrigerator at least 4 hours.

Ambrosia (Mississippi)

Shrimp Mold

1 (10¾-ounce) can cream of
  mushroom soup
2 (8-ounce) packages cream
  cheese
2 envelopes gelatin
¼ cup water
2 (7-ounce) cans shrimp,
  drained

1 (7-ounce) can crabmeat,
  drained
1 bunch green onions, chopped
1 cup chopped celery
½ red bell pepper, chopped
1 tablespoon lemon juice
1 cup mayonnaise
Hot sauce to taste

Heat soup. Dissolve cream cheese in soup. Dissolve gelatin in
cold water. Add to soup. Add remaining ingredients. Place in
mold and refrigerate. Serve with crackers.

Sisters' Secrets (Louisiana)

Shrimp Mousse

2 envelopes unflavored gelatin
4 tablespoons water
4 cups Thousand Island
  dressing
½ cup diced celery

2 tablespoons lemon juice
3 (7-ounce) cans tiny shrimp,
  washed, or ½ cup chopped
  cooked shrimp

Soften gelatin in cold water and dissolve over hot water. Combine
with remaining ingredients, mixing well. Pour into an oiled 6-cup
mold and chill for 6–8 hours. Unmold on serving platter and serve
with wheat crackers. Yields 24–30 small servings.

Dining Under the Magnolia (Alabama)

Seafood Mousse

1 tablespoon unflavored
   gelatin, softened in ¼ cup
   cold water
1 cup hot sour cream (do not
   boil)
1 pound or 2 cups seafood
   mixture (crab and shrimp)
¼ cup mayonnaise

¼ cup chopped green onions
1 tablespoon grated onion
¼ cup finely chopped celery
1 cup whipping cream, whipped
Salt and pepper to taste
Few drops Tabasco and lemon
   juice

Add softened gelatin to hot sour cream; cool. Add seafood, mayonnaise, onions, and celery. When mixture begins to congeal, fold in whipped cream. Correct seasonings and pour into a wet mold. Chill.

Natchez Notebook of Cooking (Mississippi)

Creole Marinated Crab Claws

⅓ cup extra virgin olive oil
½ cup defatted chicken broth
½ cup wine vinegar
⅓ cup lemon juice
2 green onions, chopped
2 tablespoons minced garlic
1 tablespoon black pepper
1 teaspoon celery seeds or
   flakes

¼ cup parsley flakes
1 teaspoon light Creole
   seasoning
1 pound crab claws, rinsed,
   drained
Lettuce leaves, cherry tomatoes
   and black olives for garnish

Mix marinade and pour over crab claws in shallow dish. Refrigerate for at least 4 hours. Drain well and serve on a platter lined with lettuce leaves. Garnish with cherry tomatoes and black olives. Yields 6 servings.

River Road Recipes III (Louisiana)

 A Fais Do-Do is a Cajun party with music, dancing, and plenty of food. Lagniappe is a little something extra.

Margaret's Tangy Meatballs

Wonderful for open-house parties.

1 cup crushed cornflakes
2 pounds ground chuck
2 tablespoons onion flakes
2 tablespoons soy sauce
½ teaspoon pepper

½ teaspoon garlic powder
Dash of salt
2 eggs
½ cup ketchup

Mix all ingredients together for meatballs, shaping the size of a quarter. (Or make very small for more appetizers.) Place in one layer in large baking pan.

SAUCE:

1 (12-ounce) jar chili sauce
1 (16-ounce) can jellied
  cranberry sauce

2 tablespoons sugar
2 tablespoons lemon juice

Mix Sauce ingredients; pour over meatballs. Bake uncovered in 400° oven for 35 minutes. Meatballs may be made and frozen ahead of time. Serves 16–18.

A Samford Celebration Cookbook (Alabama)

Sweet and Sour Sausage

1 cup sugar
4 tablespoons cornstarch
4 tablespoons soy sauce
⅔ cup vinegar
1⅓ cups water
2 bell peppers, cut in pieces

1 (20-ounce) can pineapple
  chunks, drained
2½ pounds stuffed sausage, cut
  into bite-size pieces, cooked,
  and drained

Mix all ingredients except peppers, pineapple, and sausage in a large skillet. Cook over low heat until thick. Add bell peppers and continue to cook on low. Add pineapple chunks and sausage, and heat thoroughly. Serve hot in a chafing dish with party picks. Serves 12.

Southern Generations (Mississippi)

Pink Party Pinwheels

1 (8-ounce) can crushed
  pineapple
1 (8-ounce) package cream
  cheese, softened
1 small jar strawberry preserves

Red food coloring (optional)
1 loaf bread
Margarine, softened

Pour pineapple into a strainer or colander and drain juice, pressing with a fork. Combine well-drained pineapple, cream cheese, and preserves in a bowl and mix well. Add 1–2 drops of food coloring for desired tint. Trim crusts from bread, and roll slices flat with a rolling pin. Spread lightly with margarine, then a thin layer of cream cheese mixture. Roll each slice as for a jellyroll. Wrap in plastic wrap, and freeze until shortly before serving time. Slice thinly and arrange on a serving plate. Yields 6–7 dozen pinwheels.

Celebrations (Alabama)

Marie's Chocolate Chip Cheese Ball

1 (8-ounce) package cream
  cheese, softened
½ cup butter (no substitutes),
  softened
¼ teaspoon vanilla extract
¼ cup confectioners' sugar

2 tablespoons brown sugar
¾ cup miniature semisweet
  chocolate chips
Pecans, finely chopped
Graham crackers

Beat cream cheese, butter, and vanilla until fluffy. Gradually add confectioners' and brown sugars and beat just until combined. Stir in chocolate chips. Cover and refrigerate 2 hours.

Place mixture on a large piece of plastic wrap and shape into a ball. Refrigerate for at least one hour. Just before serving, roll cheese ball in pecans. Serve with graham crackers.

Heavenly Manna (Alabama)

Garlic Cheese Ball

2 (8-ounce) packages cream
  cheese
1 (16-ounce) package shredded
  sharp Cheddar cheese
1 clove garlic, crushed, or ½
  teaspoon garlic salt
¼ teaspoon red pepper

⅓ cup chopped olives
½ cup chopped nuts
1 (4-ounce) jar chopped
  pimentos
1 teaspoon Worcestershire
Paprika

Allow cream cheese to soften at room temperature. Blend with sharp cheese; mix well with other ingredients. Form into 2 balls and sprinkle well with paprika. Wrap in wax paper. Chill. These can be made ahead and frozen.

DOWN HOME in High Style (Alabama)

Dunleith Cheese Ring

2 pounds Cheddar cheese,
  shredded
2 cups chopped nuts
2 cups mayonnaise
2 small onions, grated

4 tablespoons Worcestershire
Salt, pepper, and cayenne to
  taste
Strawberry preserves

Mix all ingredients except preserves; mold with hands into desired shape (preferably a ring). Refrigerate or freeze. When ready to serve, fill center with strawberry preserves.

The Pilgrimage Garden Club Antiques Forum Cookbook
(Mississippi)

Jezebel Sauce

18 ounces pineapple preserves
18 ounces apple jelly
1 small can dry mustard

¾–1 jar horseradish
Approximately 1 teaspoon
  coarse black pepper

Serve over cream cheese, or ham, or with small slices of Cheddar cheese and crackers.

Top Rankin Recipes (Mississippi)

Homemade Boursin

1 (8-ounce) package cream
  cheese, softened
1 clove garlic, crushed
1 teaspoon basil

1 teaspoon caraway seeds
1 teaspoon dill weed
1 teaspoon chopped chives
Cracked black or lemon pepper

Blend cream cheese with garlic, basil, caraway, dill weed, and chives. Pat into a round flat shape. Roll on all sides (lightly) in cracked black pepper or lemon pepper. Make a few days ahead. Serve with assorted crackers.

The Country Mouse (Mississippi)

Spinach Cheese Pastries

PASTRY:

½ pound cream cheese,
  softened

1 cup salted butter, softened
2 cups all-purpose flour

Combine cream cheese and butter, using pastry blender. Cut in flour. Use hands to work dough until it holds together. Place on wax paper. Form into a ball and chill overnight.

  Roll dough to ⅓-inch thickness with floured rolling pin on a generously floured surface. Cut into 2-inch rounds with cutter.

FILLING:

1 medium onion, finely
  chopped
¼ cup olive oil
1 (10-ounce) package frozen
  spinach, thawed, drained
1¼ teaspoons salt

¼ teaspoon white pepper
1 cup feta cheese
½ cup pot cheese or cottage
  cheese
1 egg, beaten

Sauté onion in olive oil. Add spinach and seasonings, while cooking. Mix cheeses and egg. Combine spinach with egg mixture. Be sure to mix thoroughly. Cool to lukewarm. Place teaspoonful of Filling in center of each round of Pastry. Fold over to make crescent shape. Edges may be pressed with fork. Place on ungreased cookie sheet. Bake at 425° for 15–20 minutes. May be served warm or at room temperature. This is a great make-ahead-freeze-bake as needed.

Waddad's Kitchen (Mississippi)

Pepper Jelly Puffs

Puffs may be filled with jelly or preserves and dusted with confectioners' sugar for serving with morning coffee.

1 (5-ounce) jar Old English cheese	**1 cup flour**
½ cup butter	**2 tablespoons water**
	1 (4-ounce) jar hot pepper jelly

Cut cheese and butter into flour. Quickly stir in water and shape into a ball. Refrigerate overnight. Roll out dough very thin and cut with a biscuit cutter into 2-inch circles. Place ½ teaspoon pepper jelly in center of each circle. Fold over and crimp edges with fork. Bake at 350° for 10 minutes. Puffs may be frozen before or after baking. Reheat before serving. Yields 2–3 dozen.

Down Home in High Style (Alabama)

French Fried Pickles

1 quart dill pickles, thinly sliced	**2 teaspoons pepper**
1¾ cups all-purpose flour, divided	**2 teaspoons garlic salt**
	1 teaspoon salt
2 teaspoons red pepper	**3 dashes hot sauce**
2 teaspoons paprika	**1 cup beer**
	Vegetable oil

Dredge sliced pickles in 1 cup flour; set aside. Combine remaining ¾ cup flour with dry ingredients. Add hot sauce and beer, mixing well. Dip dredged pickles into batter. Deep-fry in hot oil (375°) until pickles float to surface and are golden brown. Drain on paper towels; serve immediately. Yields about 2½ dozen appetizer servings.

The Country Gourmet (Mississippi)

BREAD and BREAKFAST

Huntsville, Alabama, is home to the U.S. Space & Rocket Center, a museum whose large collection of missiles and space devices traces the history of U.S. aerospace development and space exploration. Huntsville, known as Rocket Capital of the World, is also home to Marshall Space Flight Center.

Spoon Yeast Rolls

1 package dry yeast	¼ cup sugar
2 cups warm water	1 egg
1½ sticks margarine, melted	4 cups unsifted self-rising flour

Dissolve yeast in warm water. Cream margarine and sugar. Add beaten egg. Add yeast to margarine mixture, then add flour. Stir until well mixed. Put in large bowl and refrigerate. To bake, drop by spoonfuls into greased muffin tins and bake at 425° until light brown. You do not have to wait for rolls to rise before refrigerating or after putting rolls in muffin pans.

Sumpthn' Yummy (Alabama)

Buttermilk Orange Rolls

2 cups sifted all-purpose flour	2 tablespoons melted butter
1 teaspoon sugar	Grated rind of 2 large oranges,
1 teaspoon salt	divided
1½ teaspoons baking powder	1 cup sugar, divided
½ teaspoon baking soda	¼ cup light corn syrup
⅓ cup shortening	¼ cup water
¾ cup buttermilk	½ teaspoon rum flavoring

Blend dry ingredients. Cut in shortening with a pastry blender. Add buttermilk all at once. Stir until dough forms a ball. Turn onto lightly floured surface and knead 15–20 times. Roll dough into a rectangle and spread with 2 tablespoons melted butter. Set aside 1 tablespoon grated orange peel. Mix remaining orange peel with ½ cup sugar. Sprinkle over rectangle of dough. Roll up jellyroll fashion beginning with the long side. Press edges together to seal. Cut into 1-inch slices. Place on greased baking sheet and bake at 450° for 10 minutes.

Combine remaining ½ cup sugar and reserved orange rind. Add corn syrup and water. Bring to a boil and boil for 2½ minutes over medium heat. Remove from heat and add rum flavoring. Cool slightly, then ice rolls while still hot.

The Alabama Heritage Cookbook (Alabama)

Orange Rolls

2 (8-count) cans crescent rolls
½ cup sugar
1 stick butter
1½ tablespoons grated
   orange rind

1 cup powdered sugar
2 tablespoons orange juice

Unroll rolls into 8 triangles. Cream sugar, butter, and orange rind. Spread creamed mixture on rolls; roll from short end. Cut each roll into 4 pieces. Place each one in a muffin liner. Place in muffin tins; bake at 350° for 10–15 minutes until lightly browned. Remove and glaze with a mixture of powdered sugar and orange juice. Yields 32.

Another Taste of Alabaster (Alabama)

Garlic Cheese Biscuits

2 cups buttermilk baking mix
⅔ cup milk
½ cup shredded cheese

¼ cup butter, melted
½ teaspoon garlic powder

Mix baking mix, milk, and cheese together. Drop by tablespoon onto baking pan. Bake for 20 minutes at 350°. Mix butter and garlic together and brush on biscuits after removing from oven.

The Five Star Family Book of Recipes (Alabama)

Sausage Cheese Biscuits

2 cups Pioneer biscuit mix
½ pound bulk pork sausage,
   browned
½ pound grated Cheddar
   cheese

½ teaspoon red pepper
   (optional)
1 egg

Mix all ingredients. Mix well; knead lightly. Pinch off dough and form into balls to make a biscuit about 1¾ inches in width. Place on greased baking sheet. Bake at 325° about 25 minutes or until golden brown.

Heart of the Home (Louisiana)

Buttercup Biscuits

This recipe won first prize in our Easter Brunch Contest.

2 sticks butter or margarine
1 (8-ounce) container sour
    cream

2 cups presifted self-rising
    flour

Blend butter and sour cream until creamy. Add flour; mix. Place by teaspoon into buttercup-size biscuit pans. Bake 30–35 minutes at 350° or until golden brown. Makes 4 dozen.

Kum' Ona' Granny's Table (Alabama)

Cheesy Corn Spoon Bread

1 medium onion, chopped
¼ cup (½ stick) butter or
    margarine
2 eggs
2 cups sour cream
1 (15-ounce) can whole-kernel
    corn, drained
1 (14-ounce) can cream-style
    corn

¼ teaspoon salt
¼ teaspoon pepper
1 (8-ounce) package cornbread
    muffin mix
1 medium jalapeño, minced
2 cups shredded Cheddar
    cheese, divided

Sauté onion in butter in a skillet until tender. Beat eggs in a bowl. Add sour cream, whole-kernel corn, cream-style corn, salt, and pepper to the eggs and mix well. Stir in cornbread mix just until combined. Fold in sautéed onion, jalapeño, and 1½ cups cheese. Spoon into a greased, shallow 3-quart baking dish. Sprinkle with remaining ½ cup cheese. Bake at 375° for 35–40 minutes or until a wooden pick inserted near center comes out clean. Cool slightly before serving. Yields 12–15 servings.

Savor the Spirit (Alabama)

 A Cajun fable: It is said some of the lobsters in Nova Scotia wanted to relocate with the Acadians to Louisiana, but the trip was so hard and long that they lost a lot of weight. Hence, crawfish! Breaux Bridge, Louisiana, is known as the "Crawfish Capital of the World."

Southern Cornbread

1½ cups self-rising cornmeal
½ cup self-rising flour

1 medium or large egg
1½ cups buttermilk

Lightly oil a black skillet. Place on center oven rack as the oven preheats to 450°. Combine ingredients in order given. Mix until all dry ingredients are moist and batter is smooth. Pour batter into hot skillet and bake for 25 minutes.

Recipes & Remembrances (Alabama)

Crackling Cornbread

2 cups plain cornmeal
1 cup self-rising flour
1 teaspoon salt
½ teaspoon baking soda

1 teaspoon sugar
1 egg
1 cup milk
2 cups pork cracklings

Preheat oven to 400°. Grease baking pan. Mix cornmeal, flour, salt, soda, sugar, egg, and milk. Stir in cracklings. Pour into prepared pan and bake for about 35 minutes or until golden brown on top.

Recipes from the Heart (Mississippi)

Cajun Crawfish Cornbread

2 cups cornmeal
1 teaspoon salt
1 teaspoon baking powder
6 eggs
2 medium onions, chopped
½ cup chopped jalapeño peppers

16 ounces Cheddar cheese, grated
⅔ cup oil
2 (15-ounce) cans cream corn
2 pounds crawfish tails

In bowl, combine cornmeal, salt, and baking powder. In medium bowl, beat eggs, onions, and jalapeño peppers. To grated cheese, add beaten eggs, onions, peppers, oil, corn, and crawfish tails. Combine this mixture with cornmeal; mix well. Pour into greased 4x12-inch baking dish. Bake at 375° for 55 minutes or until golden brown.

Family Favorites (Louisiana)

Educated Hush Puppies

1 cup cornmeal
1 teaspoon baking powder
½ teaspoon sugar
Red and black pepper to taste
1 egg
½ cup all-purpose flour

1 cup water
½ teaspoon salt
½ cup finely chopped green
  onions
Dash of Tabasco

Mix all ingredients well. Drop by teaspoonfuls into hot grease. Educated Hush Puppies will turn over by themselves.

Madison County Cookery (Mississippi)

Mama's Depression Fried Fritters

This recipe is over fifty years old. It was used for school lunches way-back-when.

Take leftover biscuit dough and shape into small fritters. Fry in hot grease and brown on both sides. Split open and fill with sugar while hot. The sugar melts and makes a delicious snack.

Kitchen Delights (Mississippi)

Frenchies

Lusty crusty munchies. Better make plenty.

1 (6-roll) package French
  mini-loaves
1¼ sticks butter or margarine
1 teaspoon garlic powder

1 teaspoon Tabasco
1 teaspoon water
1 tablespoon parsley flakes
  (optional)

Slice French bread into thin rounds (a generous ¼ inch). Melt butter; add remaining ingredients. Brush both sides of bread rounds very lightly with butter mixture. Bake on 2 cookie sheets in 225° oven 40–50 minutes till dry, but not brown. Turn heat off and leave in oven 30 minutes or more (or overnight). Store in tin or cookie jar.

Note: If you freeze the bread first and use a knife with a serrated edge (or electric knife), it will slice much easier and neater.

The Little New Orleans Cookbook (Louisiana)

Strawberry Bread

3 cups all-purpose flour
2 cups sugar
1 teaspoon ground cinnamon
1 teaspoon salt
1 teaspoon baking soda
4 eggs
1¼ cups Wesson oil
1 cup chopped pecans
2 (10-ounce) packages frozen
  strawberries, thawed

Preheat oven to 350°. In large mixing bowl, sift together flour, sugar, cinnamon, salt, and baking soda. Set aside. In small bowl, beat eggs and Wesson oil. Add pecans and strawberries. Add strawberry mixture to dry ingredients. Grease and flour 2 (9x5x3-inch) loaf pans; pour mixture in loaf pans and bake at 350° for 1 hour. (Bake 45–50 minutes for smaller pans.) Yields 2 large loaves or 4 small loaves.

Foods à la Louisiane (Louisiana)

Apricot Nut Bread

1 cup dried apricots
1 cup sugar
2 tablespoons shortening
1 egg
¼ cup water
2 cups all-purpose flour
¼ teaspoon baking soda
1 teaspoon salt
2 teaspoons baking powder
½ cup orange juice
½ cup chopped nuts

Chop apricots and soak in water for ½ hour. Mix together sugar, shortening, and egg. Stir in remaining ingredients except apricots and nuts and blend well. Stir in apricots and nuts last and let batter stand for 20 minutes. Bake in greased loaf pan for 1 hour at 350°.

Heirlooms from the Kitchen (Alabama)

Tiny Pecan Muffins

Delicious!

½ cup self-rising flour
1 cup light brown sugar
½ cup margarine, melted
1 teaspoon vanilla extract
1 cup chopped pecans
2 eggs, beaten

Mix all ingredients. Bake in well-greased miniature muffin tins in a 350° oven for 15 minutes. Do not bake longer than 15 minutes. Makes 3 dozen.

Shared Treasures (Louisiana)

Applesauce Muffins

2 cups biscuit mix
½ cup sugar, divided
1¼ teaspoons cinnamon,
  divided
½ cup applesauce

¼ cup milk
1 egg, slightly beaten
2 tablespoons oil
2 tablespoons margarine, melted

Combine biscuit mix, ¼ cup sugar, and 1 teaspoon cinnamon. Stir in applesauce, milk, egg, and oil. Beat vigorously for 30 seconds. Spoon into greased muffin tins. Bake at 400° for about 12 minutes. Remove from tins and dip tops in melted margarine, then in remaining cinnamon-sugar mixture. Makes 2 dozen.

I Promised a Cookbook (Mississippi)

Sweet Potato Muffins

½ cup margarine
1½ cups sugar
2 eggs, beaten slightly
1¼ cups mashed canned
  sweet potatoes
1½ cups all-purpose flour

2 teaspoons baking powder
¼ teaspoon salt
1 teaspoon cinnamon
1 cup milk
¼ cup chopped pecans
½ cup raisins

Cream margarine and sugar. Add eggs and potatoes. Sift together flour, baking powder, salt, and cinnamon. Add these dry ingredients alternately with milk. Fold in pecans and raisins. Fill greased miniature muffin tins ⅔ full. Bake 25 minutes at 400°. Yields 3½–4 dozen mini-muffins. May be frozen.

Come and Get It! (Alabama)

The Sweet Potato Queens love to parade.

Sausage Coffee Cake

1 pound bulk sausage	1½ teaspoons salt
½ cup chopped onions	2 tablespoons chopped parsley
¼ cup grated Parmesan cheese	2 cups Bisquick
	¾ cup milk
½ cup grated Swiss cheese	¼ cup mayonnaise
1 egg, beaten	1 egg yolk
¼ teaspoon Tabasco	1 tablespoon water

Brown sausage and onions; drain. Add next 6 ingredients. Make batter of Bisquick, milk, and mayonnaise. Spread half of batter in 9x9x2-inch greased pan. Pour in sausage mixture, then spread remaining batter on top. Mix egg yolk and water and brush top. Bake at 400° for 25–30 minutes or until cake leaves edges of pan. Cool 5 minutes before cutting into 3-inch squares. This recipe doubles easily in a 9x13-inch pan. Freezes well.

Louisiana Entertains (Louisiana)

Sour Cream Coffee Cake

1 (18¼-ounce) butter-flavored cake mix	¾ cup oil
	4 eggs
¼ cup sugar	1 cup sour cream

Mix all cake ingredients together to form batter.

TOPPING:

4 tablespoons brown sugar	¼ teaspoon cinnamon
1 cup chopped pecans	

Combine brown sugar, pecans, and cinnamon together. Put ⅓ Topping mixture in bottom of a greased tube or Bundt pan; add ½ batter; repeat with another ⅓ Topping mixture, then remaining cake batter. Top with last ⅓ Topping mixture. Bake at 325° for 55 minutes. Serves 8–12.

Bully's Best Bites (Mississippi)

Mal's St. Paddy's Day Parade has been a Jackson, Mississippi, tradition for over 25 years. The parade has grown each year and features the outrageous Sweet Potato Queens, along with an equally outrageous variety of "queens" that travel from all over America to be a part of this colorful event. Part of the proceeds go to the Blair E. Batson Hospital for Children.

King Cake

In New Orleans, this cake is served during Carnival season from the Feast of Epiphany (January 6) until Mardi Gras (the day before Ash Wednesday). The person receiving the baby (or the bean) is considered lucky; by custom that person must also supply the next King Cake.

CAKE:

1 stick plus 1 tablespoon butter, divided	⅓ cup warm water
⅔ cup 99% fat-free skim evaporated milk	4 eggs
	1 tablespoon grated lemon rind
½ cup sugar, divided	2 tablespoons grated orange rind
2 teaspoons salt	6 cups flour
2 packages dry yeast	

In a saucepan, melt 1 stick butter, milk, ⅓ cup sugar, and salt. Cool to lukewarm. In a large mixing bowl, combine 2 tablespoons sugar, yeast, and water. Let stand until foaming, about 5–10 minutes. Beat eggs into yeast, then add milk mixture and rinds. Stir in flour, ½ cup at a time, reserving 1 cup to flour kneading surface. Knead dough until smooth, about 5–10 minutes. Place in large mixing bowl greased with 1 tablespoon butter, turning dough once to grease top; cover and let rise in a warm place until doubled, about 1½–2 hours.

FILLING:

½ cup dark brown sugar, packed	1 tablespoon cinnamon
¾ cup granulated sugar	1 stick butter, melted, divided

For Filling, mix sugars and cinnamon. Set aside.

TOPPING:

1 cup sugar, colored (⅓ cup each of yellow, purple, and green)	1 egg, beaten
	2 (¾-inch) plastic babies, or 2 beans

For topping, tint sugar by mixing food coloring until desired color is reached. For purple, use equal amounts of blue and red. A food processor aids in mixing, and keeps the sugar from being too moist!

When dough has doubled, punch down and divide in half. On a floured surface, roll half into a 15x30-inch rectangle. Brush with half of melted butter and cut into 3 lengthwise strips. Sprinkle half of sugar mixture on strips, leaving a 1-inch lengthwise
(continued)

(King Cake continued)

strip free for sealing. Fold each strip lengthwise toward the center, sealing the seam. You will now have 3 (30-inch) strips with sugar mixture enclosed in each. Braid the 3 strips and make a circle by joining ends. Repeat with other half of dough. Place each cake on a (10x15-inch) baking sheet, cover with a damp cloth, and let rise until doubled, about 1 hour. Brush each with egg and sprinkle top with colored sugars, alternating colors. Preheat oven to 350°. Bake 20 minutes. Remove from pan immediately so sugar will not harden. While still warm, place 1 plastic baby* in each from underneath. Makes 2 (9x12-inch) cakes. Preparation time: 5½ hours. Freezes well.

To freeze: Wrap cooled cake tightly in plastic. Before serving, remove plastic and thaw.

Jambalaya (Louisiana)

Beignets

2 cups all-purpose flour
½ teaspoon salt
1 teaspoon baking powder
2 eggs, separated

⅔ cup milk
Oil, enough to deep-fry
½ cup powdered sugar or
    cinnamon sugar

Sift dry ingredients into a bowl. Add egg yolks to milk; mix well and add to dry ingredients. Beat egg whites until stiff and fold into batter. Heat oil until HOT. Drop by spoonfuls into deep fat. Beignets will float and pop over. Remove when light brown. Sprinkle with powdered sugar or cinnamon sugar.

Variation: Banana Pop-Overs: Dip 1 piece of banana into batter and drop into hot oil.

Cajun Cookin' (Louisiana)

The Café du Monde in the French Quarter of New Orleans, Louisiana, is where many tourists begin their morning or end their night, partaking of their famous beignets (a pastry made from deep-fried dough and sprinkled with confectioner's sugar) and café au lait (coffee made with milk and root chicory).

Pain Perdue
(Lost Bread or French Toast)

1 (5-ounce) can evaporated milk
2 eggs, well beaten
½ cup sugar
½ teaspoon vanilla
5 slices French bread
1 cup oil or butter
Powdered sugar

Mix together evaporated milk, eggs, sugar, and vanilla; dip each slice of bread into this mixture, coating well. Drain off excess batter and fry in hot oil or butter at 375° until brown; turn and brown other side. Drain on paper towels and sprinkle with powdered sugar. Yields 6 servings.

Cajun Cuisine (Louisiana)

Overnight Apple-French Toast

1 cup brown sugar
8 tablespoons butter
2 tablespoons light corn syrup
3–4 large tart apples such as
   Granny Smith, peeled and
   sliced
1 loaf French bread
3 eggs
1½ cups milk
1 teaspoon vanilla

Cook sugar, butter, and corn syrup at low temperature until thick. Pour into a 9x13x2-inch baking dish sprayed with nonstick cooking spray, or buttered well. Place apple slices on top. Cut bread in ¼-inch slices and place on top of apples, pressing bread together tightly. Whisk together remaining ingredients and pour over bread; cover and refrigerate overnight. Bake uncovered 40 minutes in 350° oven. Serve hot with Apple Syrup.

APPLE SYRUP:
1 cup applesauce
1 (10-ounce) jar apple jelly
½ teaspoon cinnamon
⅛ teaspoon ground cloves
Dash of salt

Cook over medium heat, stirring constantly until apple jelly melts and is consistency of syrup. Yields 8–10 servings.

Note: The French toast can be prepared ahead and freezes well.

Encore! Encore! (Mississippi)

Favorite Pancakes

Light as a feather.

1¼ cups all-purpose flour,
  sifted
2 teaspoons baking powder
½ teaspoon baking soda
1 tablespoon sugar

½ teaspoon salt
1 egg, beaten
1 cup buttermilk
2 tablespoons oil

Sift together dry ingredients. Combine egg, buttermilk, and oil. Add to dry ingredients, stirring until flour is moistened (batter will be lumpy). Bake on hot griddle. This can be made in a blender. For a variation, add a cup of blueberries. Makes 12 dollar-size pancakes or 8 (4-inch) ones.

When Dinnerbells Ring (Alabama)

Glazed Sausage and Apples

2 pounds sausage links
¼ cup brown sugar
2 large tart apples, peeled,
  cored and sliced

⅓ cup water
1 large onion, chopped

Brown sausage, remove from heat and drain drippings. Mix remaining ingredients and cook 8–10 minutes. Stir in sausage and continue to simmer until ready to serve. Glaze thickens as it cooks and coats the meat. Serves 8–10.

Lake Guntersville Bed & Breakfast Cookbook (Alabama)

Bacon Quiche

1 (9-inch) pie shell, unbaked
½ cup shredded Swiss cheese
¼ cup finely chopped onion
½ cup crumbled, crispy-fried
  bacon

1 (4-ounce) can sliced
  mushrooms, drained
4 eggs, beaten
2 cups half-and-half

Layer cheese, onion, bacon, and mushrooms in pie shell. Beat eggs and half-and-half together. Pour on top of mixture. Bake at 400° for 15 minutes and then turn oven to 350° and bake 45 minutes more or until set.

Scents from Heaven (Alabama)

Cajun Eggs

1½ teaspoons cooking oil
½ green bell pepper, chopped
2 jalapeño peppers, chopped
½ cup sliced fresh mushrooms
½ (10-ounce) can Ro-Tel
   tomatoes
3 stalks green onions, chopped

½ pound boiled crawfish tails,
   peeled
3 eggs
¼ cup shredded Cheddar
   cheese
¼ cup shredded Swiss cheese
3 dashes Tabasco

In a skillet with oil, sauté bell pepper and jalapeño peppers 2 minutes. Add mushrooms, tomatoes, green onions, and crawfish. Sauté 2 minutes. Crack 3 eggs over the vegetables, leaving them whole. Top with cheeses and Tabasco. Cover skillet and let eggs cook to desired doneness.

Roger's Lite Cajun Cookbook (Louisiana)

Eggs Gifford

10 eggs
½ cup flour
½ teaspoon salt
1 tablespoon baking powder
½ cup melted butter
1 (16-ounce) carton small curd
   cottage cheese

½ pound Monterey Jack
   cheese, shredded
½ pound Cheddar cheese,
   shredded
8 ounces diced green peppers
   (or jalapeños)

Beat eggs. Add remaining ingredients. Pour into 9x13-inch baking dish. Bake at 350° for 35 minutes. Let rest 5–10 minutes before cutting. Serve with a dollop of salsa, if desired.

Aliant Cooks for Education (Alabama)

Baseball great Hank Aaron was born in Mobile, Alabama, on February 5, 1934. His crowning moment was, of course, the home run that surpassed Babe Ruth's seemingly unbreakable record. That moment came on April 8, 1974, when he walloped home run #715 and trotted around the bases past the Babe and into history.

Ham and Eggs Breakfast

This is excellent to fix the night before for house guests.

8 slices white bread
2 or 3 (⅓-inch-thick) slices
  hickory smoked ham
Sliced cheese
7 eggs

3 cups milk
1½ teaspoons dry mustard
1 teaspoon salt
2 cups cornflakes
¼ cup butter, melted

Preheat oven to 300°. Trim crust from bread. Butter 9x13-inch casserole. Lay 4 slices bread in dish. Place ham slices on top. Top with slices of cheese and more bread. Beat together eggs, milk, mustard, and salt. Pour over bread. Refrigerate overnight. Crush cornflakes and sprinkle over top of casserole. Drizzle with butter. Bake for 1 hour.

The Country Gourmet (Mississippi)

Pepper Jelly

¾ cup ground green pepper
¼ cup ground hot peppers
6 cups sugar

1½ cups white vinegar
1 pouch Certo

Chop peppers fine and save juice. Combine peppers with juice, sugar, and vinegar in a large pot. Place over high heat and bring to a full boil. Boil one minute, stirring constantly. Remove from heat and stir in Certo. Let stand 5 minutes. Skim off foam and pour into hot jars. Seal.

Note: Handle hot peppers with care. The oils in the skins of hot peppers may burn your hands.

Great American Recipes from Southern 'n' Cajun Cook'n'
(Mississippi)

Breakfast Pizza

1 pound bulk pork sausage
1 (8-ounce) package
  refrigerated crescent rolls
1 cup frozen loose-pack hash
  brown potatoes, thawed
1 cup shredded Cheddar
  cheese
5 eggs, beaten

¼ cup milk
½ teaspoon salt
½ teaspoon pepper
2 tablespoons grated Parmesan
  cheese
Pimentos (optional)
Fresh oregano (optional)

Cook sausage in medium skillet until brown; drain and set aside. Separate crescent dough into 8 triangles. Place with elongated points toward center of greased 12-inch pizza pan. Press bottom and sides to form a crust. Seal perforations. Spoon sausage over dough. Sprinkle with hash brown potatoes and Cheddar cheese. Combine eggs, milk, salt, and pepper; pour over sausage mixture. Bake at 375° for 25 minutes. Sprinkle with Parmesan cheese and bake an additional 5 minutes. Garnish with pimentos and fresh oregano, if desired. Yields 6–8 servings.

Cooks and Company (Alabama)

Sausage-Grits Casserole

1 cup quick grits
3 cups undiluted beef bouillon
½ teaspoon salt
1 pound hot bulk sausage
2 sticks butter

4 eggs, beaten
1 cup milk
½ cup grated sharp cheese,
  divided

Cook grits in bouillon and salt until thick, about 3–4 minutes. In skillet, cook sausage until well done; drain on paper towels. Add sausage to cooked grits, mixing thoroughly. Add remainder of ingredients, using only half of the cheese, to grits and sausage, again mixing thoroughly. Pour into greased casserole. Sprinkle with remaining grated cheese before cooking. This looks very soupy before cooking; it thickens as it bakes. Bake for 30–45 minutes at 350°. Serves 8.

Gardeners' Gourmet II (Mississippi)

Grillades and Garlic Cheese Grits

Brunch, lunch, or dinner . . . delicious any time.

GARLIC CHEESE GRITS:

1 cup uncooked grits	2 tablespoons minced garlic
4 cups water, salted	2 eggs, beaten
½ cup (1 stick) butter	1+ cup shredded Cheddar cheese

Heat oven to 350°. Add grits to boiling water; reduce heat, stirring for 30 seconds. Cook as directed until thickened. Remove from heat. Add butter, garlic, eggs, and cheese. Pour into a greased casserole dish. Bake at 350° for one hour or until starting to brown slightly on top. Remove and let sit for 15 minutes. Serve with grillades or as a side dish.

1 pound round steak	3 tablespoons flour
1 teaspoon salt	2 cups water
½ teaspoon pepper	1 (15-ounce) can stewed
6 tablespoons flour, divided	tomatoes, or 2 tablespoons
4 tablespoons oil	tomato paste
2 medium onions	1 tablespoon parsley
4 cloves garlic, chopped	¼ teaspoon thyme
1 cup chopped bell pepper (optional)	

Cut round steak into small pieces of your choice (medallions or strips). Mix salt, pepper, and 3 tablespoons flour together. Dredge meat pieces in flour. In a heavy skillet, heat oil and brown meat. Set meat aside. In the same skillet, sauté onions, garlic, and bell pepper, if used. Set aside with meat. Add 3 tablespoons flour to drippings in pan (may have to add a little oil) and brown until a medium roux. Add water, stewed tomatoes or tomato paste, parsley, and thyme. Lower heat and add meat and vegetables, cover and simmer for 45 minutes or until meat is tender (may take longer). Serve with Garlic Cheese Grits.

Straight from the Galley Past & Present (Mississippi)

Creole Grits

1 medium onion, chopped
2 small bell peppers, chopped
¼ cup bacon grease
1 (16-ounce) can chopped
    tomatoes, undrained
¼ teaspoon sugar
1 teaspoon garlic salt
Dash of pepper
1½ cups uncooked grits

Sauté onion and bell peppers in bacon grease; stir in tomatoes, sugar, salt, and pepper. Simmer 30 minutes. (This can be made in advance up to this point.) Then add tomato mixture to grits that have been cooked according to package directions. Serves 10.

Heavenly Hostess (Alabama)

Blintz Soufflé

This is a wonderful brunch or morning bridge dish.

½ cup butter, softened
⅓ cup sugar
6 eggs
1½ cups sour cream
½ cup orange juice
1 cup all-purpose flour
2 teaspoons baking powder
Sour cream (for topping)
Blueberry syrup or assorted
    jams (for topping)

Preheat oven to 350°. Butter a 9x13-inch dish; set aside. In a large bowl, mix butter, sugar, eggs, sour cream, orange juice, flour, and baking powder until well blended. Pour ½ batter into 9x13-inch dish. Set remaining ½ aside. Prepare filling. Yields 8 servings.

BLINTZ FILLING:

1 (8-ounce) package cream
    cheese, softened
1 pint small curd cottage
    cheese
2 egg yolks
1 tablespoon sugar
1 teaspoon vanilla extract

In medium bowl or food processor fitted with metal blade, combine all ingredients. Mix until well blended. Drop filling by heaping spoonfuls over batter in dish. With a spatula or knife, spread filling evenly over batter; it will mix slightly with batter. Pour remaining batter over filling. Bake uncovered at 350° for 50–60 minutes or until puffed and golden. Serve immediately with sour cream and blueberry syrup or assorted jams.

Note: May be made a day ahead. Cover and refrigerate until ready to use. Before baking, bring to room temperature.

Vintage Vicksburg (Mississippi)

Cucumber Sandwiches

2 cucumbers
1 cup water
¾ cup cider vinegar
1 teaspoon salt (coarse kosher preferred)
1 loaf day-old white bread
½ stick butter or margarine, softened

1–1½ tablespoons mayonnaise
1 (8-ounce) package cream cheese, softened
Salt, pepper, and garlic salt to taste
½ teaspoon Worcestershire

Peel cucumbers and slice (not too thinly). Soak cucumbers in water, vinegar, and salt for 30 minutes ONLY (put 6 ice cubes on top of the mixture to chill). Drain cucumbers and pat dry. Cut bread rounds (a small liqueur glass is just the right size). Spread each round lightly with butter. Mix cream cheese with enough mayonnaise to make a spreadable consistency. Season lightly with salt, pepper, garlic salt, and Worcestershire. Spread on buttered side of each slice of bread. Place 1 cucumber slice on ½ of bread slices. Lightly salt, pepper, and garlic salt the cucumbers. Press another prepared bread round on top and press gently together. Continue until all sandwiches are completed.

Place on a cookie sheet that has been covered with a slightly damp towel. Cover with another slightly damp towel. Cover with plastic wrap. Chill for at least 3 hours before serving. These will keep for 2 days!

Variation: If cucumbers have large seeds, cut lengthwise, scrape out seeds and grate coarsely. Proceed as above through the soaking stage. Then mix with cream cheese mixture, adding finely diced canned water chestnuts for crunch. A dash of Louisiana Hot Sauce adds a new dimension. Makes a lot.

Critics' Choice (Mississippi)

In 1982 the United States Congress passed a Joint Resolution designating Jackson, Mississippi, as the official home of the International Ballet Competition. One of the world's most prestigious dance events, the IBC is a two-week "Olympic-style" competition for young dancers held at Thalia Mara Hall in Jackson every four years.

Fried Green Tomato Sandwich

Italian bread	Fried green tomatoes
Mayonnaise	Caramelized onions
Roasted red peppers	Provolone cheese

Slice and toast bread in oven. Mix mayonnaise and peppers together. On one slice of toast, spread mayonnaise mixture. Place a layer of tomatoes, next add a layer of onions, and top with cheese. Spread another slice of bread with mayonnaise mixture and place on top.

Recipes & Remembrances (Alabama)

Tomato Gravy

This was always an old standby when food was scarce during Depression days. Some of those "necessities" turned out to be favorite foods.

¼ cup Crisco	1½ cups stewed (canned)
6 level tablespoons flour	tomatoes
1 cup milk	1 teaspoon salt
1 cup water	

In large skillet, melt Crisco over high heat. Add flour and stir constantly until slightly brown. Remove from heat. Let cool. Mix together milk and water. Add to Crisco-flour mixture and stir until well blended. Add tomatoes. Put back on heat and stir until thickened. Add salt.

Variation: To make Old-Fashioned White Gravy, use the same recipe, but omit the tomatoes. Black pepper is also good in this gravy.

Kum' Ona' Granny's Table (Alabama)

SOUPS, CHILIS, and STEWS

Tupelo, Mississippi, is the birthplace of the Elvis Presley, the King of Rock and Roll. Visitors may tour the Elvis Presley Museum, chapel, and the two-room house where the King was born.

Creole Corn Soup

2 pounds ground chuck
2 medium onions, coarsely
  chopped
½ cup chopped celery
½ cup chopped green bell
  pepper
1 teaspoon Italian seasoning
½ teaspoon basil
2 teaspoons parsley flakes

2 (16-ounce) cans Italian-style
  tomatoes
1 (16-ounce) can tomato sauce
2 (16-ounce) cans whole-kernel
  corn
2 (16-ounce) cans cream-style
  corn
Salt and pepper to taste

Brown meat in Dutch oven or other heavy pot; drain off grease. Add onions, celery, and pepper; sauté about 5 minutes. Add seasonings, tomatoes, tomato sauce, and whole-kernel corn. Cook on medium heat about 30–45 minutes. Add cream-style corn and salt and pepper to taste. Continue to cook on low for another 20–30 minutes, stirring often as the cream-style corn causes ingredients to stick to bottom and is easy to scorch. The soup will be done at this point but you can continue to simmer for a few minutes. Check for seasoning to your taste.

Let's Say Grace Cookbook (Alabama)

Corn and Crabmeat Soup
(Acadian)

1 cup fresh yellow corn
¼ cup butter
¼ cup all-purpose flour
2 cups chicken stock

2 cups half-and-half cream
1 pound lump crabmeat
Salt and pepper to taste
Garlic powder to taste

Cut fresh corn from cob and save scrapings and milk. (Canned or frozen corn may be used.) Set aside. Melt butter in saucepan. Add flour and blend well. Add chicken stock, stirring constantly. Cook until thick and smooth. Stir in cream, crabmeat, corn, and seasonings. Cook over low fire until corn is tender.

The Best of South Louisiana Cooking (Louisiana)

Corn Soup

It is hard to believe this creamy soup is not full of heavy cream. You can garnish it with chopped green onions when serving.

1 onion, chopped
1 green bell pepper, seeded,
   chopped
½ teaspoon minced garlic
1 (16-ounce) bag frozen sweet
   corn
1 (8½-ounce) can cream-style
   corn

1 (10-ounce) can diced tomatoes
   and green chiles
1 (14½-ounce) can fat-free
   chicken broth
1 tablespoon Worcestershire
Salt and pepper to taste
2 cups low-fat milk
⅓ cup all-purpose flour

In a pot coated with nonstick cooking spray, sauté onion, green pepper, and garlic over medium-high heat until tender, about 5 minutes. Add frozen corn, cream-style corn, diced tomatoes and green chiles, chicken broth, Worcestershire, salt and pepper. In a separate bowl, blend together milk and flour. Gradually stir into corn mixture. Cook 15 minutes, until hot throughout. Makes 8 (1-cup) servings.

Trim & Terrific American Favorites (Louisiana)

Curried Chicken and Apple Soup

2 apples, peeled, cored, diced
2 onions, peeled, sliced
2 tablespoons butter
1 tablespoon curry powder
1 teaspoon flour
2 cups chicken stock

Salt to taste
⅛ teaspoon red pepper
½ cup white wine
1 cup half-and-half
½ chicken breast, cooked,
   diced

Sauté apples and onions in butter until onions are translucent. Stir in curry powder and flour, and cook 5 minutes. Add chicken stock, salt, and red pepper. Stir in wine and simmer 10 minutes. Strain and purée solids in food processor. Combine and chill mixture. Just before serving, add cream and chicken. Yields 4 servings.

Huntsville Entertains (Alabama)

Red Bean Soup

2 cups dried red kidney beans
¼ cup butter
1 medium onion, finely
  chopped
3 cloves garlic, finely chopped
2 ribs celery, finely chopped
1 tablespoon Worcestershire
1 bay leaf

1 teaspoon dried thyme leaves
½ pound ham, finely ground
Salt and pepper to taste
½ cup claret wine
2 hard-boiled eggs, finely
  chopped
1 lemon, thinly sliced

Soak the beans overnight in 1 quart of water. In a heavy Dutch oven melt the butter over medium heat. Add the onion, garlic, and celery, and sauté until brown. Add 2 quarts of water, beans, Worcestershire, bay leaf, and thyme. Simmer for 2 hours, or until the water has reduced to 1 quart. Strain the mixture and reserve the liquid. Force the beans through a sieve. Return the beans and liquid to the pot. Add the ham, salt, and pepper and simmer for 5–10 minutes. Pour the soup into a heated tureen. Stir in the wine, and garnish with the chopped egg and lemon slices. Serves 6–8.

La Bonne Cuisine (Louisiana)

Fresh Tomato-Rice Soup

1½ cups chopped onions
2 tablespoons bacon drippings
2 tablespoons butter or
  margarine
4 cups water

1½ pounds ripe tomatoes,
  peeled, cored, and chopped
⅓ cup raw white rice
½ teaspoon salt
¼ teaspoon pepper

Cook onions in drippings and margarine in a 3-quart saucepan, over medium heat, stirring often until browned, 6–7 minutes. Add water and tomatoes and bring to a boil. Stir in rice, salt, and pepper. Reduce heat and simmer, uncovered, 30 minutes or until rice is tender. Yields 6 servings.

Barbara's Been Cookin' (Mississippi)

Summer Cucumber Soup

This soup signals summer to me!

4–6 cucumbers*
6 tablespoons butter
  (unsalted is best)
2 medium onions, chopped
2 cups chicken broth
1 tablespoon minced fresh
  basil, or 1 teaspoon dried

2 tablespoons minced fresh
  mint, or 2 teaspoons dried
2 cups buttermilk
Salt and pepper to taste
Lemon for garnish

Stem, halve, seed, and roughly chop cucumbers. Melt butter in large, heavy saucepan. Add onions and cucumbers. Cover tightly and "sweat" the vegetables over medium heat for about 15 minutes. They should be soft, but not in the least brown. Stir in chicken broth and herbs. Remove from heat. Purée in small batches in blender. (Careful—hot liquids expand in the blender). Transfer purée to a large bowl; stir in buttermilk and salt and pepper to taste. Chill the soup for 4 hours minimum, and taste. Correct seasoning, if needed. Thin soup, if desired, with extra broth or buttermilk. Serve in chilled bowls with a thin lemon slice floating on top. Makes 6 servings.

*This is best with garden cucumbers. If you have to use the waxed grocery store variety, you must peel them as well, which makes the soup less green.

Best of Bayou Cuisine (Mississippi)

Chunky Baked Potato Soup with Cheese and Bacon

½ cup butter
½ cup chopped onion
½ cup chopped celery
¾ cup all-purpose flour
5 cups milk
1¼ cups chicken broth
¾ teaspoon salt
½ teaspoon pepper
1½ cups (6 ounces) shredded Cheddar cheese

4 large baking potatoes, baked, peeled, and cut into large chunks
12 bacon slices, cooked and crumbled
1 cup sour cream
Toppings: chopped green onions, shredded Cheddar cheese, crumbled cooked bacon

Melt butter in a large Dutch oven over medium heat; add onion and celery, and sauté until tender. Add flour to mixture and cook, whisking constantly, 3 minutes. Gradually add milk and broth, stirring until thickened. Stir in salt and pepper.

Add cheese to mixture and cook, stirring constantly, until melted. Stir in potatoes and bacon. Add sour cream and cook until thoroughly heated. Add desired toppings to each serving. Serves 10–12.

Absolutely à la Carte (Mississippi)

Quick Potato Soup

1 (16-ounce) bag frozen hash browns (square)
½ (16-ounce) bag frozen hash browns (shaved)
2 (14½-ounce) cans chicken broth
1 small onion, diced

2 (10¾-ounce) cans cream of chicken soup
2 cups skim milk
Salt and pepper to taste
Garlic salt (optional)
Grated cheese, chives, and real bacon bits for garnish

Bring hash browns, chicken broth, and onion to a slow boil. Simmer until potatoes are tender. Stir in cream of chicken soup and milk. (Add one can at a time, depending on how thick you like your soup.) Salt and pepper to taste. Add garlic salt, if desired. Let mixture simmer for 10–15 minutes, stirring occasionally. Top with grated cheese, chives, and real bacon bits.

Munchin' with the Methodists (Mississippi)

Broccoli-Cheese Soup

1 (10-ounce) package frozen
broccoli, chopped
1 (14½-ounce) can chicken
broth
2 teaspoons or 2 cubes chicken
bouillon
½ cup chopped onion
½ cup chopped celery

Pepper to taste
½ cup milk
2 tablespoons butter or
margarine
3 tablespoons cornstarch (with
enough milk to dissolve)
2½–3 cups shredded Cheddar
cheese (or Velveeta)

Boil first 5 ingredients until barely tender. Purée in blender for about 3 seconds. Add pepper. Return to heat. Add milk, butter, and cornstarch mixture. Blend and stir until hot. Add cheese. Cook until thickened, stirring constantly. Do not boil.

Bell's Best III: Savory Classics (Mississippi)

Cream of Broccoli Soup

1 bunch broccoli, trimmed
1½ cups chicken broth
½ cup butter
1 cup all-purpose flour

1 cup milk
Salt and pepper to taste
½ teaspoon cumin

Wash broccoli, and cut into bite-size pieces. Cook broccoli until just tender in boiling chicken broth in a medium-size boiler. Do not drain. Melt butter in a medium-size saucepan. Add flour to butter; whisk stirring constantly, for 3 minutes. Slowly add broth and broccoli to cooked roux (should be thick); thin out with milk, and add seasonings to taste. Serve hot. Yields 4 servings.

Dining Under the Magnolia (Alabama)

 Alabama has almost a million acres of recreational water; however, there are no natural lakes in the state. Four major artificial lakes—Guntersville, Wheeler, Martin, and Weiss—have been created by damming the Tennessee, Tallapoosa, and Coosa rivers.

Down-Home Cheddar Cheese Soup

The flavor is outstanding.

1 cup margarine, divided
½ cup each: finely chopped
  celery, green bell pepper,
  onion, carrot, cauliflower
1 tablespoon granulated
  chicken bouillon, or 2 cubes

2 cups water
⅔ cup all-purpose flour
4 cups milk
½ pound sharp Cheddar
  cheese, shredded

Heat ½ cup margarine over medium heat. Add vegetables; cook until tender, stirring often. Add chicken bouillon and water; heat to boiling. Cover; cook over low heat 10 minutes. Meanwhile, heat remaining ½ cup margarine in saucepan. Stir in flour; cook until bubbly. Remove from heat. Gradually stir in milk. Cook over medium heat, stirring often, until thickened, but do not boil. Stir in cheese till fully blended. Stir cheese mixture into vegetables and chicken broth mixture. Serves 8–10.

The Country Mouse (Mississippi)

Onion Soup

3 onions, sliced thinly
¼ cup margarine
2 (10½-ounce) cans beef
  broth
1 cup hot water

½ cup dry white wine
⅛ teaspoon cayenne pepper
¼ teaspoon black pepper
6 slices French bread
1 cup shredded Muenster cheese

Slice onions in bowl with margarine. Cover with stretch plastic wrap, vent, and microwave 10 minutes on HIGH. Add beef broth, hot water, wine, and peppers, and stir. Cook on HIGH again for 10 minutes, covered. Serve in individual bowls; top with French bread, then cheese, and serve. The heat of the soup will melt the cheese.

Kitchen Sampler (Alabama)

Roasted Garlic Soup

1 large head (bulb) garlic
½ teaspoon olive oil
¼ cup butter or margarine
½ onion, chopped
¼ cup all-purpose flour
2 medium baking potatoes,
   peeled, chopped

3 cups chicken broth
1 cup heavy cream
Salt and white pepper to taste
Chopped parsley for garnish

Preheat oven to 325°. Cut a small slice off top of whole garlic head to expose garlic cloves. Place in a garlic roaster or small baking dish, drizzle with olive oil, cover, and roast 30 minutes. Remove cover and roast 30 minutes more. When cool enough to handle, squeeze garlic pulp from peel.

In a large saucepan, heat butter over medium heat. Add onion and sauté until tender. Add flour and cook, stirring constantly, about 2 minutes, until lightly browned. Add roasted garlic, potatoes, and chicken broth. Bring to a boil, cover, and lower heat. Cook 15–20 minutes, stirring occasionally. Purée soup in food processor or blender until smooth. Return to saucepan and stir in cream, salt and white pepper. Heat thoroughly and taste for seasoning. Add more chicken broth if soup is too thick. Serve garnished with a little chopped parsley. Serves 6–8.

Kay Ewing's Cooking School Cookbook (Louisiana)

In 1803 the United States paid France $15 million for the Louisiana Territory— 828,000 square miles of land west of the Mississippi River. The lands acquired stretched from the Mississippi River to the Rocky Mountains and from the Gulf of Mexico to the Canadian border. Thirteen states were carved from the Louisiana Territory. The Louisiana Purchase nearly doubled the size of the United States.

Vegetable Beef Soup

1½ pounds stew meat (or
  ground chuck)
1 medium to large onion,
  chopped
1 (46-ounce) can tomato or
  V-8 juice
1 (16-ounce) package frozen
  green beans
1 (16-ounce) package frozen
  carrots
2 (16-ounce) packages frozen
  mixed vegetables

1 (16-ounce) package frozen
  whole-kernel corn
1 (16-ounce) can cream-style
  corn
½ gallon water
1 (16-ounce) package frozen
  green peas
1 cup small elbow macaroni
4 medium potatoes, diced
Seasonings to taste

Brown meat in large soup pot until uniform in color. Drain off
any excess fat. Add onion, tomato juice, beans, carrots, mixed
vegetables, corn, and water. Bring to boil and reduce heat to low.
Cook, stirring occasionally, until vegetables are done (approximately 1–1½ hours). Add peas and pasta to meat mixture.
Simmer approximately 30 minutes.

  In separate pot, bring potatoes to a boil; take off heat and allow
to stand. Add drained potatoes and any seasonings to soup pot,
and simmer until ready to serve. If container is crowded, wait
until the peas and pasta are added to add water, but bring soup to
high and heat thoroughly before returning to simmer. (You may
have to add more water when reheating.) Makes 18 (1½-cup)
servings.

Treasures from Our Kitchen (Mississippi)

Corn and Crawfish Chowder

1 stick margarine
2 tablespoons flour
1 onion, chopped
1 pound crawfish
1 quart milk
2 (15-ounce) cans cream-style
  corn
Tabasco to taste
1 (15-ounce) can whole-kernel
  corn

1 (10¾-ounce) can cream of
  potato soup
½ teaspoon Ac'cent
½ teaspoon Worcestershire
¼ cup grated provolone cheese
¼ cup chopped shallots
Seasoned salt to taste

Blend together margarine and flour over low heat. Add onion; sauté until wilted. Add remaining ingredients and cook on medium heat 40 minutes. Serves 7 or 8.

A Shower of Roses (Louisiana)

Red Pepper Bisque

8 red bell peppers
2 yellow onions, chopped
¼ cup butter (½ stick)
2 teaspoons minced garlic
½ cup minced basil leaves

6 cups rich chicken stock,
  divided
2 cups heavy cream
Salt and pepper to taste

Seed red peppers and cut into 1-inch pieces. Cook red peppers and onions in butter in a large skillet or saucepan over medium heat until onions are translucent, stirring frequently. Add garlic, basil, 2 cups chicken stock. Simmer about 10 minutes or until red peppers are tender, stirring occasionally. Process mixture in batches in blender or food processor until smooth. Strain into a soup pot and blend in remaining chicken stock. Simmer 10–15 minutes or until slightly thickened, stirring occasionally. Blend in heavy cream gradually. Add salt and pepper. Heat to serving temperature; do not boil. Ladle into soup bowls. Yields 2½ quarts.

Celebrations (Alabama)

Crabmeat or Crawfish Bisque

6 tablespoons butter or
margarine, divided
4 tablespoons finely chopped
onion
4 tablespoons finely chopped
green bell pepper
1 scallion (including top),
coarsely chopped
2 tablespoons chopped parsley
1 cup sliced fresh mushrooms
2 tablespoons flour

1½ cups milk
1 teaspoon salt
⅛ teaspoon pepper
¼ teaspoon ground mace
Dash of Tabasco
1 cup half-and-half
1½ cups cooked crabmeat, or 2
(6-ounce) packages frozen
crabmeat, thawed, or 1½
cups crawfish
3 tablespoons dry sherry

In a medium skillet, heat 4 tablespoons butter. Add onion, green pepper, scallion, parsley, and mushrooms. Sauté until soft, but not brown. Set aside.

In a large saucepan, heat remaining 2 tablespoons butter; remove from heat. Stir in flour. Gradually add milk. Cook, stirring constantly, until thickened and smooth. Stir in salt, pepper, mace, and Tabasco. Add sautéed vegetables and half-and-half. Bring to boiling stage, stirring. Reduce heat and add crabmeat or crawfish meat. Simmer, uncovered, 5 minutes. Just before serving, stir in sherry. Makes 4 servings.

The Country Gourmet (Mississippi)

MISSISSIPPI DEVELOPMENT AUTHORITY,
DIVISION OF TOURISM

Mississippi University for Women was the first public college for women in the nation. The college was established in Columbus by an act of the Mississippi Legislature on March 12, 1884. Pictured above is Callaway Hall, dormitory at MUW.

Catahoula Court-Bouillon

As with bouillabaisse, there are as many recipes for court-bouillon as there are Acadians and Creoles. Papa's version is a thick soup, much like a chowder, and can be made with either fresh or saltwater fish.

⅔ cup all-purpose flour
⅔ cup cooking oil
2 medium onions, chopped
1 sweet green bell pepper,
  chopped
2 stalks celery, chopped
3 cloves garlic, minced
  (optional)
1 (1-pound) can whole
  tomatoes, chopped,
  undrained

1 can Ro-Tel tomatoes
1 quart fish stock or water
1 tablespoon salt
1 teaspoon cayenne pepper
2½ pounds firm white fish, cut
  into fillets or steaks
1 bunch green onions, tops only,
  chopped
¼ cup finely chopped fresh
  parsley

In a large heavy pot, make a dark brown roux with flour and oil. Add onions, green pepper, celery, and garlic; cook 5 minutes. Add both cans of tomatoes and cook slowly over a low fire. Now, here's the secret to making a good court-bouillon—let it cook until the oil forms a thin layer, like paper, over the top of the mixture. You will have to stir occasionally, but after a half hour or so, the oil will rise to the top. Add warmed fish stock or water and seasonings, and let cook for 1 hour, stirring occasionally. Add fish and cook 15–20 minutes. Right before serving, add onion tops and parsley. Check seasonings and make any necessary adjustments. I usually put a bottle of Tabasco on the table for those who wish to make it hotter. Serve in deep bowls with rice, and of course, French bread. Serves 8.

Who's Your Mama, Are You Catholic, and Can You Make a Roux?
(Louisiana)

Roux

Louisiana State University's yearbook is named The Gumbo *for the state's most famous soup. Gumbo is more than a soup. It is a meal made of bits of either seafood, game, or fowl and Creole seasonings cooked together and served over rice. There are as many ways to make gumbo in Louisiana as there are cooks, but basically gumbo is of two types, depending upon whether it is thickened with okra or filé powder. Okra, an African vegetable, came to Louisiana with the Negro slaves. The Choctaw Indians, natives of the swamp land, ground sassafras leaves to make the filé powder. The settlers concocted the soups thickened with both ingredients. Perhaps you will want to try both, but first, you make a roux. Not only gumbos but many other Creole dishes begin with a roux. A recipe follows.*

3 tablespoons bacon
   drippings or shortening
3 tablespoons flour

Heavy black iron pot or heavy
   skillet

Melt fat in heavy skillet, and stir in flour. Continue to stir over low heat until flour is dark brown. (The slow dry heat fragments the starch molecules in the flour and develops a nut-like flavor that gives body to soups and stews. It also reduces thickening power of the flour.) A roux is used as a base for most Creole dishes. The quantity of fat and oil may vary from recipe to recipe, but the method of cooking remains the same.

'Tiger Bait' Recipes (Louisiana)

Microwave Roux

Frozen chopped vegetables work just fine—they just sizzle a bit more and require a few more seconds cooking time. Grandmother would even be fooled by this one!

⅔ cup vegetable oil
⅔ cup flour
⅔ cup chopped onion
⅔ cup chopped celery
⅔ teaspoon minced garlic

⅔ cup chopped green bell
   pepper
⅔ cup chopped green onions
   (optional)
⅔ cup hot water

Mix oil with flour in a 4-cup measuring bowl. Microwave uncovered on HIGH for 6 minutes. Stir and cook another 30–60 seconds on HIGH till the color of mahogany.

Now you can add your chopped vegetables, stir well, and "sauté" them on HIGH for another 5 minutes till soft but not brown.

Now, before stirring, pour oil off top. Add hot tap water, stirring till smooth. Beautiful! And it freezes for later use.

The Little Gumbo Book (Louisiana)

Seafood Gumbo II

½ cup vegetable oil
½ cup flour
1 large onion, chopped
2–3 garlic cloves, minced
1 (1-pound) can tomatoes,
 undrained
1½ pounds frozen okra or
 equivalent fresh
Oil for frying okra
2 quarts hot water
3½ tablespoons salt

¾ teaspoon red pepper
1 large bay leaf
¼ teaspoon thyme
8–10 allspice berries
Few grains chile pepper
2 pounds headless raw shrimp,
 peeled
1 pound claw crabmeat, picked
1 pint oysters
½ cup chopped green onions
½ cup chopped parsley

Make a very dark roux with oil and flour in a large heavy pot. Add onion and garlic. Cook slowly until onions are transparent. Add tomatoes, and cook on low heat until oil rises to the top (about 30 minutes), stirring frequently. In separate skillet, fry okra in oil on moderately high heat, stirring constantly until okra is no longer stringy. Add the okra to the other mixture; stir and simmer about 10 minutes. Add water, salt and pepper. Simmer partially covered for 45 minutes. Add other seasonings and simmer an additional 20 minutes, then add shrimp and simmer 15 minutes; then add crabmeat, simmering 15 minutes more. Add the oysters the last 5 minutes of cooking. Taste carefully for seasoning, adding more if necessary. Remove from fire and stir in green onions and parsley. Serve over rice. Variations may be made by adding different seafoods, sausages, or poultry. Serves 8–10.

River Road Recipes II (Louisiana)

Louisiana is a fisherman's paradise. Lakes, rivers, streams, bayous, and the Gulf of Mexico are all abounding with fish that seem anxious to jump onto your hook! The Atchafalaya Basin is a magnificent 800,000-plus-acre natural swampland, and Toledo Bend Reservoir is a 186,000-acre bass fishing paradise. One cannot go very far in Louisiana without coming upon a great place to fish.

The Grand Dining Room's
Uncle Bud's Seafood Gumbo

1 cup chopped onions
1 cup chopped celery
1 cup chopped green pepper
⅛ cup bacon fat
1 bay leaf
1 teaspoon oregano leaves
1 teaspoon thyme leaves
⅛ teaspoon cayenne pepper
1 tablespoon gumbo filé
2 cups water

1 (14½-ounce) can diced
  tomatoes in juice
1 (8-ounce) can tomato sauce
⅓ cup brown roux
½ pound medium shrimp
4 ounces shucked oysters,
  including liquid
½ pound claw crabmeat
¾ cup cut okra
Salt and pepper to taste

Sauce onions, celery, and green pepper in bacon fat until onions are translucent. Add spices. Add water, tomatoes, and tomato sauce. Bring to a boil, add roux, and cook until mixture thickens. Add shrimp, oysters, crabmeat, and okra and simmer until cooked. Add salt and pepper. Serves 10–12.

Recipe from the Grand Dining Room,
Grand Hotel Marriott Resort, Golf Club & Spa, Point Clear
Alabama's Historic Restaurants and Their Recipes (Alabama)

 Both freshwater and saltwater fishing waters are located within a quarter mile of each other at Gulf Shores, Alabama. Seafood booths and outdoor activities highlight the National Shrimp Festival held there each October.

Blue Ribbon Chili

2 pounds chili ground meat
(brown, just to get red out)
1 large onion, chopped
1 large green bell pepper,
chopped
3 ribs celery, chopped
1 (10-ounce) can Ro-Tel
tomatoes, diced
3 heaping tablespoons chili
powder
1 heaping tablespoon paprika
2 teaspoons Ac'cent (optional)
1 (8-ounce) can tomato sauce
1 can water or more
1 teaspoon cayenne pepper
1 teaspoon salt
3 (16-ounce) cans cream-style
red kidney beans

Cook all but beans together with meat for about 45 minutes. Add
kidney beans and cook another 15 minutes.

A Shower of Roses (Louisiana)

Quicky Chili

1 pound ground beef
1 large onion, chopped
1 tablespoon minced garlic
½ small can (2–3 tablespoons)
chili powder
1½ tablespoons ground cumin
1 (14½-ounce) can stewed
tomatoes
½ (46-ounce) can tomato juice
3 (15-ounce) cans kidney beans

Brown beef, onion, garlic, and chili powder. Add cumin, tomatoes,
and tomato juice. Add kidney beans and simmer 30 minutes.

Blue Mountain College Cookbook (Mississippi)

Oven Beef Stew

2 tablespoons flour
1½ teaspoons salt
Dash of pepper
2 tablespoon shortening
1½ pounds beef chuck, cut in
   1-inch chunks
2 (10¾-ounce) cans
   condensed tomato soup
2½ cups water

1½ cups chopped onion
½ teaspoon dried, crushed
   basil
4 medium potatoes, pared,
   cubed
4 medium carrots, cut in 1-inch
   pieces
½ cup dry red wine (or water)

Combine flour, salt, and pepper; coat meat cubes and brown in hot shortening in a Dutch oven. Add soup, water, onion, and basil. Cover and bake at 375° for 1 hour. Add potatoes, carrots, and wine. Cover and bake 1 hour longer, or until tender.

The Pick of the Crop (Mississippi)

SALADS

Fat-bottomed cypress trees growing in shallow lakes and bayous are a familiar sight in Louisiana. The Louisiana Bald Cypress can grow to 80 feet in height and 40 feet in circumference.

Spinach-Strawberry Salad

1 pint fresh strawberries
12 ounces fresh spinach
¼ cup safflower oil
1–2 tablespoons sugar
2 tablespoons minced green
  onion

1 teaspoon salt
Dash of Tabasco
2 tablespoons salad vinegar
2 tablespoons sesame seeds,
  toasted

Slice strawberries. Tear spinach into bite-size pieces. Combine safflower oil, sugar, onion, salt, Tabasco, and salad vinegar to make dressing. Add sesame seeds. Gently toss in strawberries and spinach.

Tasteful Treasures (Mississippi)

Twenty-Four Hour Spinach Salad

1 pound fresh spinach,
  washed, dried, torn
Salt and pepper to taste
4 hard-cooked eggs, sliced
1 pound bacon, cooked,
  crumbled
1 small head iceberg lettuce,
  shredded

2 Bermuda onions, thinly sliced
1 large bag frozen English peas
½ cup mayonnaise
½ cup Miracle Whip
12 ounces baby Swiss cheese,
  shredded

Place spinach into large glass salad bowl so layers may be seen. Sprinkle with salt and pepper. Add layer of eggs, crumbled bacon, lettuce, and another sprinkle of salt and pepper. Add a layer of onions and uncooked frozen peas. Repeat process until bowl is filled. Cover and refrigerate overnight.

Early in the morning of the day the salad is to be used, mix mayonnaise and Miracle Whip; spoon over top of salad. This topping should penetrate through salad. Sprinkle shredded Swiss cheese over top and refrigerate until serving time. Serves 12.

The Gulf Gourmet (Mississippi)

Romaine Salad

SWEET AND SOUR DRESSING:

1 cup vegetable oil
1 cup sugar
½ cup red wine garlic vinegar

1½ tablespoons soy sauce
Salt and pepper to taste

Blend all ingredients. Yields 2½ cups.

SALAD:

1 cup chopped walnuts
1 (3-ounce) package oriental
  noodle soup, uncooked,
  broken (discard flavor
  packet)
4 tablespoons unsalted butter

1 bunch broccoli, coarsely
  chopped
1 head romaine lettuce, washed
  and broken into pieces
4 green onions, chopped
1 cup Sweet and Sour Dressing

Brown walnuts and noodles in butter; cool on paper towels. Combine noodles and walnuts with broccoli, romaine, and onions. Pour on dressing and toss to coat just before serving. Serves 8.

Down Home Dining in Mississippi (Mississippi)

Butter Churn Croutons

Children love these—a good way to introduce them to salads is to include these.

4 tablespoons butter
Dashes of seasoned salt,
  garlic salt, red pepper,
  and lemon pepper

6 slices stale bread, cubed

Melt butter in large skillet. Add seasonings, then add bread cubes all at once and stir to coat evenly. Spread on cookie sheet and bake 10 minutes in 325° oven, then turn it off and leave in oven for several hours.

A Salad a Day (Mississippi)

Sensation Salad Dressing

6 tablespoons grated
  Romano cheese
2 tablespoons grated
  bleu cheese
Juice of 1 lemon, more if
  desired

2 cloves garlic, pressed
⅓ cup olive oil
⅔ cup vegetable oil
¼ teaspoon black pepper
½ teaspoon salt

Grate cheeses and mix together. Set aside. Combine remaining ingredients. For each individual serving of tossed green salad, sprinkle with 1 tablespoon of the mixed cheeses and 3 tablespoons dressing.

Hint: Freeze bleu cheese to grate.

'Tiger Bait' Recipes (Louisiana)

Green Goddess Salad Dressing
(Assaisonnement à la Déesse Verte)

1 clove garlic, crushed
2 tablespoons chopped green
  onion
2 tablespoons lemon juice
3 tablespoons tarragon wine
  vinegar

½ cup low-fat sour cream
1 cup low-fat mayonnaise
½ cup chopped parsley
Salad and coarse black pepper
  to taste

Mix in the order given, and chill. Serve over your favorite vegetable salad. Yields 18 (2-tablespoon) servings.

Cooking for Love and Life (Louisiana)

In 1700 B.C., when Ramses II sat on Egypt's throne, a sophisticated Indian civilization flourished in northeastern Louisiana. They built vast earthworks that may have taken generations to complete, including a bird-shaped ceremonial mound one-third the size of the great pyramids. Named Poverty Point after a struggling plantation that once stood on the grounds near Pioneer, this is one of the nation's major archaeological sites.

Kum-Back Salad Dressing

1 teaspoon mustard
2 cloves garlic, minced
Dash of Tabasco
Juice of 1 lemon
1 pint mayonnaise

1 tablespoon Worcestershire
Dash of paprika
1 (12-ounce) bottle chili sauce
1 teaspoon black pepper
¼ onion, grated

Mix all ingredients together with electric mixer and chill. Serve over green tossed salad.

Calling All Cooks (Alabama)

Celery Seed Dressing for Fruit Salad

½ cup Karo
1 heaping tablespoon
  cornstarch
½ cup vinegar
¾ cup Wesson oil

1 teaspoon salt
1 teaspoon dry mustard
1 teaspoon celery seeds
1 tablespoon onion juice

Mix Karo with cornstarch until smooth. Add vinegar and cook in top of double boiler over boiling water until thick. Let cool, then add slowly, beating constantly, oil and seasonings.

Gourmet of the Delta (Mississippi)

Sweet and Sour Slaw

1 large cabbage, shredded
3 stalks celery, chopped
1 bell pepper, chopped
1 (4-ounce) jar chopped
  pimentos
1 large red onion, shredded

½ cup red wine vinegar
½ cup white vinegar
¾ cup sugar
1½ teaspoons salt
¾ cup oil
Coarsely ground black pepper

Layer cabbage, celery, bell pepper, pimentos, and onion in bowl. Boil vinegars, sugar, and salt for 2 minutes. Remove from heat; add oil and black pepper; return to heat and bring to a boil. Pour over vegetables while hot. Cover tightly. Refrigerate overnight. If refrigerated, this will keep indefinitely. Serves 10–12.

When Dinnerbells Ring (Alabama)

Race Track Slaw

1 (5-ounce) package sliced
  almonds
¼ cup sesame seeds
2 (3-ounce) packages ramen
  noodles
1 (16-ounce) package slaw mix
1 bunch green onions, chopped

1 cup vegetable oil
6 tablespoons rice wine vinegar
¼ cup sugar
1 teaspoon salt
1 teaspoon pepper
1 teaspoon MSG (optional)

Toast almonds and sesame seeds on a baking sheet in 350° oven 5
minutes or just until brown. Discard ramen noodles seasoning
packets. Combine slaw mix, green onions, uncooked ramen noodles, almonds, and sesame seeds in a large bowl and mix well.

Combine oil, vinegar, sugar, salt, pepper, and MSG in a small
bowl and mix well. Pour over slaw mixture just before serving,
tossing to mix. Yields 8–10 servings.

Calling All Cooks, Four (Alabama)

Skillet Salad

4 slices bacon
¼ cup vinegar
1 tablespoon brown sugar
1 teaspoon salt

1 tablespoon finely chopped
  onion
4 cups shredded cabbage
½ cup finely chopped parsley

Cook bacon until crisp; remove from skillet and crumble. Add
vinegar, sugar, salt, and onion to fat in skillet. Add crumbled
bacon; heat thoroughly. Remove from stove and toss cabbage and
parsley in hot dressing. Makes 6–8 servings.

Favorite Flavors of First (Alabama)

Nutty Broccoli Salad

½ pound bacon
4 cups chopped tender broccoli
1 (2-ounce) package sliced
  almonds
1 cup white raisins

1 medium red onion, chopped
1 (4-ounce) package salted
  sunflower seeds, or 1 cup
  unsalted roasted peanuts

Fry bacon and crumble. Combine all ingredients and refrigerate.
One hour before serving, add Dressing.

DRESSING:
2 tablespoons red wine vinegar   1 cup mayonnaise
2 tablespoons sugar

Mix and pour over salad.

Golden Moments (Mississippi)

Marinated Broccoli and Cauliflower Salad

1 (8-ounce) bottle Italian salad
  dressing
1 cup mayonnaise
1 cup grated Parmesan cheese
2 bunches fresh broccoli, raw
1 head fresh cauliflower, raw
1 pound bacon, fried crisp,
  crumbled

6 hard-cooked eggs, chopped
¼–½ cup finely chopped
  green onions
1 (8-ounce) jar pimento-stuffed
  olives, drained

Mix Italian dressing, mayonnaise, and cheese; set aside. Wash
broccoli and cauliflower; break into flowerets and place in large
bowl. Add bacon, eggs, onions, and olives; toss lightly. Add dressing and toss gently to coat all ingredients. Cover tightly and marinate in refrigerator several hours before serving.

Sisters' Secrets (Louisiana)

Comes the Sun

Scrumptious and sunny!

VINAIGRETTE:

1 clove garlic	1 cup salad oil
1½ teaspoons salt	5 tablespoons vinegar, or 3
1½ teaspoons mustard	tablespoons vinegar plus 2
½ teaspoon pepper	tablespoons lemon juice

Crush garlic with salt. Add mustard and pepper. Beat in oil by tablespoons alternately with vinegar. Refrigerate overnight. Remove garlic, if milder flavor is desired.

1 (1-pound) can whole green beans, drained	2 eggs, hard-cooked
	2 tablespoons mayonnaise
4 strips bacon	1 teaspoon lemon juice

Marinate beans in Vinaigrette and chill. Fry bacon until crisp; crumble. Chop egg whites and mix with mayonnaise and lemon juice. Arrange beans like spokes around center of egg white mixture. Sprinkle bacon onto beans, and sieve the egg yolks over all.

A Salad a Day (Mississippi)

Bean Salad

1 (16-ounce) can cut green beans	1 medium onion, sliced thin
	½ cup cider vinegar
1 (16-ounce) can cut yellow wax beans	⅔ cup cooking oil
	½ cup sugar
1 (16-ounce) can red kidney beans	1 teaspoon salt
	1 teaspoon pepper
¼ cup chopped green pepper	

Drain beans, rinse well, and drain again. Add green pepper and sliced onion to beans. Mix other ingredients and add to bean mixture. Mix well and marinate overnight in refrigerator. Serves 6.

Recipes and Reminiscences of New Orleans I (Louisiana)

Tailgate Vegetable Salad

1 (11-ounce) can shoepeg corn
1 (15-ounce) can tiny English
  peas
1 (14½-ounce) French-style
  green beans
1 (2-ounce) jar diced pimento
½ cup finely chopped bell
  pepper
½ cup finely chopped onion
½ cup finely chopped celery

Drain corn, peas, beans, and pimento. Combine with chopped pepper, onion, and celery.

DRESSING:

½ cup sugar
¾ cup vinegar
½ cup oil
1 teaspoon salt
1 teaspoon pepper
1 tablespoon water

Mix all ingredients in saucepan and bring to a boil. Cool and pour over vegetables. Chill and serve.

Cooking with Gilmore (Mississippi)

English Pea Salad

2 (15-ounce) cans English peas
1 bell pepper, chopped
½ purple onion, chopped
1 cup mayonnaise
1 cup (8 ounces) sour cream
1 (1-ounce) package ranch
  dressing mix
Shredded Cheddar cheese
Bacon bits

Combine peas, bell pepper, and onion. Mix mayonnaise and sour cream with ranch dressing mix. Combine dressing with peas and mix well. Just before serving, toss with cheese and bacon bits; serve on lettuce leaves.

Editor's Extra: Add chopped fresh tomatoes, and you're in heaven!

Barbara's Been Cookin' (Mississippi)

Corn Salad

2 (12-ounce) cans shoepeg
  corn, drained
2 tomatoes, seeded, drained,
  and chopped but not peeled
1 bell pepper, seeded and
  chopped
1 purple onion, chopped
1 cucumber, peeled, seeded,
  and chopped

½ cup sour cream
4 tablespoons mayonnaise
2 tablespoons white vinegar
½ teaspoon celery seed
½ teaspoon dry mustard
½ teaspoon black pepper
2 teaspoons salt

Mix all vegetables. Combine sour cream, mayonnaise, vinegar, and seasonings. Pour over vegetables. Cover and refrigerate overnight. Good with barbeque, hamburgers, or stuffed in a tomato. Serves 10–12. Recipe can easily be doubled.

Note: May use a box of cherry tomatoes, cut in half, in place of regular tomatoes.

Magic (Alabama)

Cornbread Salad

1 (10-inch) skillet of cornbread,
  baked, cooled, crumbled
1 cup chopped celery
1 cup chopped pecans
2 ripe tomatoes, chopped

1 cup chopped green bell pepper
2 bunches green onions,
  chopped
1 pint mayonnaise

Toss all together and refrigerate overnight.

Family Traditions (Louisiana)

 Florence, Alabama-native Sam Phillips discovered and produced records by the legendary Elvis Presley, Johnny Cash, Jerry Lee Lewis, and Carl Perkins among many others after opening Sun Studios in Memphis, Tennessee.

Rice Salad

2 (6-ounce) packages
  chicken-flavored rice
¾ cup chopped green bell
  pepper
16 pimento-stuffed olives,
  sliced

8 green onions, chopped
  (use tops, if not too strong)
2 (6-ounce) jars marinated
  artichoke hearts, sliced
⅔ cup mayonnaise
1 teaspoon curry powder

Cook rice as directed on package, omitting butter. Cool. Add pepper, olives, and onions. Drain artichoke hearts and save marinade. Add sliced artichokes. Mix marinade, mayonnaise, and curry powder. Add to salad; toss and chill. Serves 12.

The Cook's Book (Mississippi)

Spaghetti Salad

1 (12-ounce) package vermicelli
2 tablespoons seasoned salt
1 tablespoon Ac'cent
4 tablespoons Wesson oil
3 tablespoons lemon juice
1 medium onion, finely
  chopped
1 large green pepper, finely
  chopped

1 cup finely chopped celery
1 (4½-ounce) can chopped
  black olives
1 (5-ounce) jar chopped green
  olives
1 (2-ounce) jar chopped
  pimentos
1 cup mayonnaise

Break up, cook, drain and rinse vermicelli. Mix together seasoned salt, Ac'cent, oil, and lemon juice. Pour over vermicelli, cover and refrigerate overnight.

Mix onion, green pepper, celery, black olives, green olives, pimentos, and mayonnaise. Add to vermicelli mixture. Will keep for a week or two, refrigerated.

Variation: Boiled shrimp or cooked chopped chicken breasts may be added.

Treasures from Our Kitchen (Mississippi)

"Bears" Special Salad

1 large box corkscrew colored
  noodles (rotini)
1 large bunch broccoli with
  florets, cut small
2 cucumbers, seeded, cut in
  bite-size pieces
2 packages imitation crabmeat
2 packages fresh mushrooms,
  chopped

5 tomatoes, cubed
1 large purple onion, cut in
  rings
3 stalks celery, cut in bite-size
  pieces
3 green bell peppers, cubed
3 large bottles Zesty Italian
  dressing

Boil rotini noodles until tender; drain. In large bowl, mix noodles and all other ingredients, except salad dressing. Mix vegetables and crabmeat well. Pour salad dressing over vegetables and rotini, and toss gently. Chill.

Recipes from Bayou Pierre Country (Louisiana)

A Mississippi bear hunt inspired the "Teddy Bear." In 1902, President Theodore Roosevelt visited Mississippi to settle a border dispute between Mississippi and Louisiana. During his visit, he went bear hunting near Onward, Mississippi. After a while with no success, a member of the hunting party located a bear and offered the President the opportunity to shoot the bear. Roosevelt refused to shoot the helpless bear that was exhausted and possibly injured. News of the president's actions became national news and inspired Morris Michtom, a New York merchant, to create a stuffed toy bear and name it "Teddy's Bear." The rest is history.

Black-Eyed Pea Salad

2 (15-ounce) cans black-eyed
  peas with jalapeños,
  undrained
½ cup chopped celery

½ cup chopped purple onion
1 large tomato, chopped
1 large avocado, chopped
1 small bottle Catalina dressing

Mix ingredients together and marinate overnight.

Recipes & Remembrances (Alabama)

Vidalia Onion Potato Salad

This is so good and different from regular potato salad.

1½ cups mayonnaise
½ cup oil
¼ cup cider vinegar
3 pounds new potatoes, boiled
  and sliced

2 or 3 medium Vidalia onions,
  sliced
Salt and pepper
Fresh parsley for garnish

Beat mayonnaise, oil, and vinegar with a fork until well mixed.
Pour over potatoes and onions which have been layered in a bowl
and each layer sprinkled with salt and pepper. Refrigerate several hours before serving. Garnish with fresh parsley.

Gran's Gems (Mississippi)

Baked Potato Salad

10 ounces cream cheese,
  softened
2 cups sour cream
1½ cups mayonnaise
1½ pounds bacon, cooked and
  crumbled
⅓ cup chopped green onions

½ cup creamy Italian dressing
Dash of Worcestershire
1 teaspoon pepper
½ teaspoon salt
1 teaspoon garlic powder
6 large baking potatoes,
  unpeeled, baked, and cooled

Combine cream cheese and sour cream in a large bowl, stirring
well. Add mayonnaise, bacon, green onions, dressing, Worcestershire sauce, pepper, salt, and garlic powder; stir well. Slice potatoes into ½-inch pieces and stir into mayonnaise mixture. Serves
8–10.

Absolutely à la Carte (Mississippi)

My Potato Salad

2–2½ pounds red potatoes,
    peeled, cooked, drained
1 medium onion, diced
1 (2-ounce) can pimentos,
    drained, mashed
2 teaspoons mustard
5 boiled eggs, mashed
½–¾ cup diced sweet pickles
½ cup salad dressing or
    mayonnaise
Salt and pepper to taste
Lettuce cups

Partially mash potatoes with potato masher or fork. Add onion, pimento, mustard, mashed boiled eggs, pickles, mayonnaise, and salt and pepper. You may need more mayonnaise; you want it smooth and not dry. It is better to make this salad when potatoes are hot. Let cool and serve in lettuce cups.

Seasoned with Love Too (Mississippi)

Bacon-And-Egg Stuffed Tomatoes

6 large tomatoes
Salt and pepper
6 hard-cooked eggs, chopped
¾ cup diced celery
⅓ cup mayonnaise
6 slices bacon, cooked and
    crumbled
2 tablespoons chopped fresh
    parsley
¼ teaspoon salt
¼ teaspoon pepper
Paprika

Wash tomatoes. Cut top from tomatoes; scoop out pulp, leaving shells intact. Chop tomato pulp. Drain tomato shells and sprinkle cavities with salt and pepper. Combine tomato pulp, eggs, celery, mayonnaise, bacon, parsley, salt and pepper; stir well. Fill tomato shells with mixture. Sprinkle with paprika. Makes 6 servings.

Favorite Recipes from First Baptist Church of Columbiana
(Alabama)

Eloise's Tomato Aspic

You will like this tomato aspic even if you think you don't like tomato aspic.

2 cups tomato cocktail juice
1 teaspoon powdered sugar
1 tablespoon celery salt
1 bay leaf
2 packages unflavored gelatin
½ cup cold water

2 teaspoons lemon juice
1 teaspoon onion juice
Salt, Worcestershire, and
   Tabasco to taste
Olives (green or black) chopped
Celery, finely chopped

Combine and simmer juice, sugar, celery salt, and bay leaf 10 minutes. Dissolve gelatin in ½ cup cold water. Remove bay leaf from juice and add lemon, onion juice, salt, Worcestershire, and Tabasco. Add gelatin and mix thoroughly. Add olives and celery and gel in refrigerator.

The Tastes & Traditions of Troy State University (Alabama)

Crunchy Hot Chicken Salad

3 cups diced cooked chicken
1 cup finely chopped celery
2 teaspoons chopped onion
½ cup sliced almonds
1 (10¾-ounce) can cream of
   chicken soup, undiluted
1½ cups cooked rice
1 tablespoon lemon juice

½ teaspoon salt
¼ teaspoon pepper
¾ cup mayonnaise
¼ cup water
3 hard-cooked eggs, sliced
2 cups crushed potato chips
¾ cup shredded Cheddar
   cheese

Combine first 9 ingredients; toss gently and set aside. Combine mayonnaise and water; beat with a wire whisk until smooth. Pour over chicken mixture; stir well. Add eggs, and toss gently. Spoon into greased, 2-quart shallow baking dish; cover and refrigerate 8 hours or overnight.

Bake at 450° for 10–15 minutes or until thoroughly heated. Sprinkle with potato chips and cheese; bake an additional 5 minutes. Yields 6–8 servings.

Treasured Tastes (Alabama)

Chicken Salad in Raspberry Ring

Serve this on a large silver platter surrounded with fruit. So pretty.

CREAMY MAYONNAISE:

1 cup mayonnaise	½ cup heavy cream, whipped

Combine mayonnaise and whipped cream. Makes 1⅔ cups.

2 cups cubed cooked or	¾ cup sliced celery
canned chicken	1 teaspoon lemon juice
1 teaspoon salt	½ cup Creamy Mayonnaise
2 hard-cooked eggs, chopped	

Lightly toss ingredients together. Chill. Serve in Raspberry Ring.

RASPBERRY RING:

3 (10-ounce) packages frozen	1¼ cups boiling water
red raspberries	¾ cup sugar
2 envelopes plain gelatin	¼ teaspoon salt
½ cup lemon juice	¾ cup cantaloupe balls

Thaw raspberries. Drain, reserving 2 cups syrup (use berries for garnish). Soften gelatin in lemon juice. Dissolve in boiling water. Stir in sugar, salt, and reserved raspberry syrup. Chill till partially set. Add cantaloupe balls. Pour into 5-cup ring mold. Chill till firm. Pass additional Creamy Mayonnaise.

Old Mobile Recipes (Alabama)

Waldorf Chicken Salad

3 cups medium diced, cooked	½ cup golden raisins
chicken	½ cup small diced celery
¾ cup coarsely chopped	2 scallions, finely sliced
walnuts	Salt and pepper to taste
¾ cup small diced Granny	
Smith apples	

In large bowl combine all ingredients.

DRESSING:

1 cup mayonnaise	¼ cup apple cider vinegar
½ cup sour cream	1 tablespoon honey

Whisk ingredients together and pour over salad in large bowl; cover and refrigerate until ready to serve on fresh green lettuce leaves.

Let's Say Grace Cookbook (Alabama)

Chicken Salad Supreme

1 (2½- to 3-pound) cooked hen	1½ cups mayonnaise
1 cup seedless white or red grapes	1½ teaspoons curry powder
	1 tablespoon lemon juice
1 (8-ounce) can water chestnuts (optional)	1 tablespoon soy sauce
	Pineapple slices or crisp lettuce leaves
1 cup diced celery	Additional mayonnaise
1 cup slivered almonds	½ cup toasted slivered almonds

Remove chicken from bone and cut in bite-size pieces. Mix chicken, grapes, chestnuts, if desired, celery, and 1 cup slivered almonds. Mix mayonnaise, curry powder, lemon juice, and soy sauce; add to chicken mixture. Mix well. Serve on pineapple slices or crisp lettuce leaves. Top with additional mayonnaise and ½ cup toasted slivered almonds. Serves 12–15.

The Mississippi Cookbook (Mississippi)

Shrimp and Caper Salad

This is better if made the night before.

2 pounds shrimp, peeled, deveined	½ cup oil and vinegar salad dressing
Liquid crab boil	¾ cup mayonnaise
2 tablespoons fresh lemon juice	1 tablespoon celery seed
¾ cup chopped green onions	Crisp salad greens
1½ cups chopped celery	Tomato wedges and hard-cooked egg wedges for garnish
3 tablespoons capers, drained	
1 cup sliced black olives	

Boil shrimp in water, adding liquid crab boil and lemon juice. Drain shrimp, discarding liquid. Combine all ingredients and chill. Serve on crisp salad greens and garnish with tomato wedges and hard-cooked egg wedges. Serves 6.

One of a Kind (Alabama)

Treasures

A true epicurean treasure!

2 cups mayonnaise
½ cup horseradish, drained
½ teaspoon MSG (optional)
2 teaspoons dry mustard
2 teaspoons lemon juice
½ teaspoon salt
1 pound medium shrimp,
  cooked, peeled

1 pint box cherry tomatoes
1 (6-ounce) can black olives,
  drained
1 (8-ounce) can water chestnuts,
  drained
1 (6-ounce) can whole
  mushrooms, drained
½ head cauliflower florets

Combine first 6 ingredients; mix well. In a large bowl, combine remaining ingredients, including cauliflower. Pour mayonnaise sauce over shrimp and vegetables; refrigerate. Before serving, add cauliflower florets.

Great Flavors of Mississippi (Mississippi)

Shrimp Salad Stretched

SALAD:

1 pound well-seasoned boiled
  shrimp, peeled
3 small red potatoes, peeled,
  boiled in shrimp water

2 hard-boiled eggs, peeled and
  chopped
2 tablespoons chopped onion
¼ cup chopped celery

Save the shrimp water to boil the potatoes in. If using crab boil bag to season shrimp, remove before boiling potatoes. Cube the potatoes. Mix all ingredients and add the Dressing. Chill until ready to serve. Serve on crisp lettuce leaf.

DRESSING:

¼ cup (heaping) mayonnaise
3 teaspoons Durkee's dressing
  (more according to taste)
½ teaspoon salt

¼ teaspoon black pepper
Sprinkling of red pepper
Sprinkling of dill weed

Combine ingredients. Mix. Check seasonings for taste.

Turnip Greens in the Bathtub (Louisiana)

Seafood Salad

2 pounds cooked seafood
  (shrimp, crawfish, crabmeat,
  tuna, or a combination)
½ cup French dressing
1½ tablespoons finely grated
  onion
½ cup finely grated green
  pepper

½ cup finely grated celery
1 teaspoon salt
½ teaspoon pepper
1 teaspoon Tabasco
1 teaspoon Worcestershire
1 cup mayonnaise
2 hard-boiled eggs, chopped

In a large bowl, combine seafood with all ingredients except mayonnaise and eggs. Mix well and refrigerate 30 minutes. Fold in mayonnaise and eggs. Best if made ahead. Serves 6–8.

Jambalaya (Louisiana)

Horseradish Salad

1 (3-ounce) package lemon
  Jell-O
1 (3-ounce) package lime Jell-O
2 cups boiling water
1 cup mayonnaise
3 tablespoons prepared
  horseradish

1 (15-ounce) can crushed
  pineapple, undrained
1 (2-ounce) jar diced pimentos,
  undrained

Dissolve Jell-O in boiling water. Combine Jell-O mixture, mayonnaise, and horseradish in blender until smooth. Stir in pineapple and pimentos. Lightly oil or spray a 7x11-inch pan, or use mold. Chill until firm.

Shared Treasures (Louisiana)

 Metairie, Louisiana, is home to the longest bridge over water in the world, the Lake Pontchartrain causeway. The causeway connects Metairie with St. Tammany Parish on the North Shore. The causeway is 24 miles long.

Coca Cola Salad

1 (15½-ounce) can crushed
  pineapple, drained, reserve
  juice
1 (10-ounce) bottle maraschino
  cherries, drained, reserve
  juice

2 (3-ounce) packages cherry
  Jell-O
1 (12-ounce) can Coca Cola, cold
1 (3-ounce) package cream
  cheese
1 cup chopped pecans

Heat reserved fruit juices to dissolve Jell-O. Let the mixture cool, and add cold Coca Cola. Put mixture into refrigerator until it begins to thicken. Then fold in chopped cream cheese, chopped nuts, and cold fruit. Pour in molds which have been rinsed in cold water, and place in the refrigerator to congeal.

Unmold on lettuce leaves, dipping molds in heated water (not boiling) as nearly the depth of the mold as possible. Loosen carefully around the top with tip of small knife. Center the serving dish on top of mold, holding the dish and mold firmly together, and turn upside down. Garnish with a bit of mayonnaise or salad dressing.

Variation: Strawberries may be substituted for cherries.

Feeding His Flock (Mississippi)

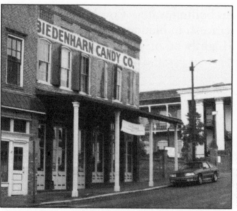

VICKSBURG CONVENTION & VISITORS BUREAU

The Biedenharn Candy Company Museum in Vicksburg, Mississippi, commemorates the site where the soft drink, Coca-Cola, was first bottled in 1894.

Sue's Hot Mixed Fruit

1 (20-ounce) can pineapple
  chunks
1 (16-ounce) can sliced pears
1 (16-ounce) can sliced peaches
1 (16-ounce) can Queen Anne
  or Royal cherries (green)

¼ cup white raisins
3 oranges, sliced with rind
  left on
¼ stick butter
2 tablespoons flour
¾ cup sugar

Drain fruit well, and reserve juices. Place fruits in baking dish. Heat butter in saucepan. Stir in flour, then add 1 cup reserved fruit juices. Sprinkle sugar over drained fruit, then pour butter mixture over all. Mix well. Bake at 350° for 30 minutes.

Mountain Laurel Inn and Mentone Memories (Alabama)

Easy Ambrosia Salad

1 (20-ounce) can crushed
  pineapple with juice
1 (6-ounce) box orange Jell-O
2 cups buttermilk

1 cup flaked coconut
½ cup chopped pecans
1 (8-ounce) carton Cool Whip,
  thawed

Combine pineapple and Jell-O in saucepan. Heat just until Jell-O is dissolved. Remove from heat; stir in buttermilk, coconut and pecans. Fold in Cool Whip. Pour into 9x13-inch pan. Chill until firm. Serves 12–15.

Bell's Best III: Savory Classics (Mississippi)

Bing Cherry Salad

1 (16-ounce) can Bing cherries
1 (3-ounce) package lemon
  Jell-O

½ envelope Knox gelatin
½ pint sour cream
1 cup chopped pecans

Drain cherries and reserve juice. Dissolve Jell-O in 1 cup hot cherry juice. If not enough juice to make 1 cup, add water. Dissolve gelatin in ¼ cup cold water and mix with hot Jell-O. Chill until nearly thick, then add sour cream and blend. Add cherries and nuts and pour into slightly oiled mold. Serve on lettuce with mayonnaise.

Inverness Cook Book (Mississippi)

Apricot Pineapple Salad

1 (15-ounce) can apricots,
  drained, chopped
1 (15-ounce) can crushed
  pineapple, drained
2 (3-ounce) packages orange
  Jell-O

2 cups boiling water
1 cup combined apricot and
  pineapple juice
¾ cup miniature
  marshmallows

Drain and chill fruit, reserving all juices. Dissolve Jell-O in boiling water. Add 1 cup juice, reserving rest for Topping. Chill until mixture has congealed slightly. Fold in fruit and marshmallows. Pour into 9x11-inch shallow dish. Chill until firm, then spread with Topping.

TOPPING:
½ cup sugar
3 tablespoons flour
1 egg, slightly beaten
1 cup reserved juices

2 tablespoons butter
1 cup whipped cream or Cool
  Whip
¾ cup grated Cheddar cheese

Combine sugar and flour; blend in egg, then gradually stir in juice. Cook over low heat until thickened, stirring constantly. Remove from heat; stir in butter. Cool. Fold in whipped cream and spread over gelatin mixture. Sprinkle with grated cheese. Cut in squares and serve on lettuce.

A Bouquet of Recipes (Louisiana)

Blueberry Salad

2 cups water and/or drained
  juice from fruit
2 (3-ounce) packages
  blackberry Jell-O

1 (16-ounce) can blueberries,
  drained (reserve juice)
1 (20-ounce) can crushed
  pineapple, drained

Heat juice/water to boiling and add to Jell-O. Add other ingredients. Allow to congeal.

TOPPING:
1 (8-ounce) package cream
  cheese, softened
½ cup sugar

½ pint sour cream
1 teaspoon vanilla

Cream ingredients together and spread on top of salad when congealed.

Scents from Heaven (Alabama)

Orange Almond Salad

A great combination of flavors with a sweet and tangy dressing.

¾ cup sugar
1 teaspoon dry mustard
1 teaspoon salt
⅓ cup cider vinegar
1 cup vegetable oil
Leaf lettuce

1 (11-ounce) can Mandarin
 oranges, chilled, drained
½ cup chopped green onions
½ cup slivered almonds,
 toasted

Combine sugar, mustard, salt, and vinegar in a food processor. With machine running, add oil through feed tube until combined. Chill.

To serve, prepare individual plates of lettuce, oranges, green onions, and almonds. Spoon dressing over salads. Serves 6.

Kay Ewing's Cooking School Cookbook (Louisiana)

Strawberry Pretzel Salad

¾ cup butter or margarine,
 softened
3 tablespoons plus 1 cup sugar,
 divided
1⅔ cups finely broken stick
 pretzels
1 (9-ounce) carton Cool Whip

1 (8-ounce) package cream
 cheese, softened
1 (6-ounce) package strawberry
 Jell-O
2 cups boiling water
1 pint frozen strawberries,
 thawed

Cream butter and 3 tablespoons sugar; add pretzels. Press dough into a 9x13-inch pan. Bake for 10 minutes at 350°. Let cool completely.

Mix together Cool Whip, cream cheese, and remaining 1 cup sugar. Spread on top of cooled pretzel mixture.

Dissolve Jell-O in water. Mix with strawberries when partially set, then spread on top of cream cheese layer. Refrigerate till firm.

Tasting Tea Treasures (Mississippi)

Hot Pepper Jelly Salad

1 (3-ounce) box lemon Jell-O
1 (10-ounce) jar green hot
  pepper jelly
1 (8-ounce) can crushed
  pineapple (with juice)
1 (2-ounce) jar pimentos,
  chopped

1 (3-ounce) package cream
  cheese, softened
Dash of Tabasco
2 tablespoons half-and-half
2 tablespoons mayonnaise
¼ cup chopped pecans

Follow directions on Jell-O box, dissolving in hot water and using ½ the water called for. Dissolve hot pepper jelly in hot Jell-O. Add crushed pineapple, juice, and pimentos. Mash cream cheese and add Tabasco, half-and-half, mayonnaise, and pecans. Grease muffin cups with oil. Add small amount Jell-O mixture. Put in spoonful of cream cheese mixture. Fill with remaining Jell-O mixture. Refrigerate till set.

Natchez Notebook of Cooking (Mississippi)

VEGETABLES

PHOTO COURTESY OF BELLINGRATH GARDENS AND HOME

Located south of Mobile, Alabama, the Charm of the Deep South—otherwise known as Bellingrath Gardens and Home—offers year-round strolls of sensual delight on its many natural pathways.

New Year's Black-Eyed Peas

3 pounds dried black-eyed
  peas
2 ribs celery, chopped
3 large onions, chopped
6 large carrots, peeled,
  chopped
2 large green bell peppers,
  chopped
3 pounds cooked ham, cut
  into bite-size pieces

7 cloves garlic, crushed
4 small red peppers, chopped
  (optional)
½ teaspoon thyme
5 bay leaves
2 teaspoons salt
1 teaspoon black pepper
1 teaspoon sugar
Additional salt and black pepper
  to taste

Soak peas in water to cover for 8–10 hours and drain. Place peas in large saucepan. Add celery, onions, carrots, green peppers, ham, garlic, red peppers, thyme, bay leaves, salt, black pepper, and sugar and mix well. Add enough water to cover the peas by 2 inches. Bring to a boil over high heat. Reduce heat to low. Cook, covered, for 8–10 hours. Season with additional salt and black pepper to taste. Serve with cornbread, turnip greens, and pepper sauce. May serve over rice. Yields 30 servings.

Bay Tables (Alabama)

Southern-Style Greens

3½–4 pounds collard, turnip
  or mustard greens, or a
  mixture
½ pound lean salt pork or
  smoked ham hock

1 tablespoon sugar
3 beef bouillon cubes
8 cups water
1 tablespoon margarine
Salt and pepper to taste

Wash greens in a sink full of water. Swish greens to remove any grit. Drain and rinse sink. Repeat washing. Lift greens out of water. Remove and discard all large stems. Combine pork, sugar, bouillon cubes, water, and margarine in a large soup pot. Bring to a boil over medium-high heat. Boil for 5–10 minutes. Add greens. Reduce heat and simmer, covered, for 1½ hours or until greens are tender. Add salt and pepper to taste. You may peel and quarter turnip roots and add to the soup pot for the last 30 minutes of cooking. Makes 8–10 servings.

Cooking Wild Game & Fish Southern Style (Mississippi)

Squash Dressing

2 cups cooked, mashed
 squash, well drained
2 cups bread crumbs
½ cup chopped onion
3 eggs, beaten

1 (10¾-ounce) can cream of
 chicken soup
¾ stick margarine, melted
½ teaspoon celery seed
Salt and pepper to taste

Combine all ingredients; bake in greased casserole dish at 350°
until done, approximately 30 minutes.

The Cook's Book (Alabama)

Squash Morelle

An interesting and tasty dish for dinner parties.

2 pounds yellow squash,
 sliced
1 cup chopped onion
1 teaspoon butter
2 eggs, beaten
½ cup sour cream

2 tablespoons butter, softened
1 tablespoon sugar
1½ teaspoons salt
½ cup shredded mozzarella
 cheese
½ cup ground almonds

Place squash and onion in a 2-quart glass or ceramic casserole
dish. Dot with butter and cover tightly with plastic wrap.
Microwave on HIGH (100%) 16 minutes. Shake dish once or twice
to rearrange contents. (Shaking eliminates removing the cover.)
Drain and mash.

Mix together eggs, sour cream, butter, sugar, salt, and cheese
and stir into squash. Microwave on HIGH (100%) 4 minutes.

Sprinkle with ground almonds and microwave on HIGH (100%)
4 minutes more. Yields 6 servings.

Tout de Suite à la Microwave II (Louisiana)

Country Club Squash

6 or 8 tender, small squash
Salt and pepper to taste
2 tablespoons butter
1 chicken or beef bouillon
   cube (or 1 teaspoon
   granules)

1 tablespoon grated onion
1 egg, well beaten
1 cup sour cream
¾ cup bread crumbs
½ cup grated cheese
Dash of paprika

Cut and cook squash until tender; drain and mash. Add salt, pepper, butter, bouillon cube, and onion. Add well beaten egg and sour cream. Pour into a 1-quart casserole dish. Combine bread crumbs, grated cheese, and paprika, and sprinkle on top of squash. Bake at 350° for 30 minutes. Serves 6.

The Mississippi Cookbook (Mississippi)

Stuffed Baked Eggplant or Mirlitons

3 large mirlitons or medium-
   size eggplants
¼ cup chopped celery
1 tablespoon chopped pimento
½ cup chopped onion
¼ cup chopped bell pepper

½ cup butter
1 cup cooked chopped shrimp
1 cup white crabmeat
Salt, pepper, and garlic powder
½ cup bread crumbs
¼ cup chopped green onions

Cut eggplants in half and steam until tender. Cool, scoop out, and keep shells intact, reserving pulp. Brown vegetables in melted butter. Add shrimp, crabmeat, and pulp of eggplant. Season well. Stir together and cook 10 minutes. Add bread crumbs and green onions. Add more melted butter, if too dry. Stuff shells of eggplant. Sprinkle top with bread crumbs. Bake at 350° until hot.

The Best of South Louisiana Cooking (Louisiana)

Crispy Eggplant

½ cup mayonnaise
1 tablespoon instant minced
  onion
½ teaspoon salt
⅓ cup fine dry bread crumbs

⅓ cup grated Parmesan cheese
½ teaspoon dried Italian
  seasoning
1 eggplant (about 1 pound), cut
  crosswise into ½-inch slices

In small bowl, stir together first 3 ingredients. In shallow dish, or on sheet of wax paper, combine bread crumbs, Parmesan, and Italian seasoning. Brush both sides of eggplant slices with mayonnaise mixture; dip in crumb mixture and coat well. Place in shallow, greased baking pan or on a baking sheet. Bake at 425° for 15–17 minutes or until crisp and browned. Serves 4.

Loaves and Fishes (Alabama)

Delmonico Baked Creole Eggplant

2 eggplants, peeled, diced
1 onion, chopped
2 stalks celery, chopped
1 cup small shrimp
Butter

1 tomato, chopped
Dash of Tabasco
Dash of Worcestershire
1 bay leaf
¼ cup seasoned bread crumbs

Parboil eggplant. Sauté onion, celery, and shrimp in butter. Add tomato. Cook for several minutes. Add Tabasco, Worcester-shire, and bay leaf. Cook until desired consistency. Fold in eggplant. Place in greased baking dish. Top with seasoned bread crumbs. Bake at 350° for approximately 20 minutes.

Going Wild in Mississippi (Mississippi)

Ratatouille

2 small eggplants
3 medium-size tomatoes
2 green bell peppers
3 small zucchini squash
2 onions

2 yellow squash
3 tablespoons olive oil, divided
Salt and pepper to taste
1 teaspoon garlic powder
¼ cup water

Slice eggplants, tomatoes, peppers, zucchini, onions, and squash about ¼- to ½-inch thick. Layer vegetables in casserole that has been oiled with 1 tablespoon olive oil, starting with onions, bell pepper, and vegetables as desired. Repeat until all vegetables are used. Sprinkle salt and pepper, remaining olive oil, and garlic powder over vegetables. Pour ¼ cup water over casserole. Cover and bake in 275° oven for 1½ hours. Test vegetables for tenderness. Good cold or hot. Serves 8–10.

Waddad's Kitchen (Mississippi)

Succotash

¼ pound salt pork, cut up
1 tablespoon shortening
1 large onion, chopped
1 small green bell pepper, chopped
1 cup sliced fresh or frozen okra

1 (8-ounce) can tomato sauce
1 (16-ounce) can whole-kernel or cream-style corn
1 (16-ounce) can lima beans
1 tablespoon sugar

Bring salt pork to a boil in water and scald; drain and fry well in shortening. Add onion and fry lightly; add bell pepper, okra, and tomato sauce; cook at medium heat for about 15 minutes. Add corn, lima beans, and sugar; cook ½ hour on low heat. If mixture becomes too thick, add water as needed.

Cajun Cooking (Louisiana)

Cabbage Casserole

1 pound ground beef
1 pound bulk seasoned sausage
1 medium onion, diced
1 medium bell pepper, diced
1 stalk celery, thinly sliced
2 cloves garlic, crushed
1 cup rice
¼ cup water

2 (10-ounce) cans Ro-Tel diced
   tomatoes with green chiles
1 medium head cabbage,
   coarsely shredded
16 ounces Velveeta cheese
½ stick margarine
1 tablespoon flour
1 cup milk

Brown meat and sausage in Dutch oven. Drain fat; add onion, pepper, celery, garlic, and rice. Cook 5 minutes. Add water, tomatoes, and cabbage; cook 10 minutes. Pour into a 9x13-inch baking dish.

In separate bowl, microwave cheese and butter until melted. Stir in flour and milk. Pour over meat mixture. Bake at 350° for 45 minutes. Uncover, and bake 15 minutes more. Serve with corn bread. This recipe freezes well.

Treasures from Our Kitchen (Mississippi)

Hot and Spicy Cabbage

2 ounces center-cut smoked
   ham
½ cup chopped onion
½ cup chopped green bell
   pepper
Olive-oil-flavored cooking spray

1 (10-ounce) can chopped Ro-Tel
   tomatoes
½ teaspoon sugar
4 cups sliced cabbage
⅛ teaspoon each: white and
   black pepper

Stir-fry ham, onion, and bell pepper in cooking spray. Add Ro-Tel tomatoes and sugar; simmer 2–3 minutes. Add cabbage and peppers. Simmer 15 minutes. Yields 8 servings.

Southern But Lite (Louisiana)

 Louisiana is the only state in the Union that does not have counties. Its political subdivisions are called parishes.

Zucchini-Corn Casserole

1½ pounds zucchini or yellow
  crookneck squash
1 medium onion, finely
  chopped
½ green pepper, finely
  chopped
2 tablespoons vegetable oil
2 eggs, beaten
½ cup grated Cheddar cheese
½ teaspoon salt
½ teaspoon garlic salt
¼ teaspoon pepper
¼ teaspoon dried rosemary
1 (16-ounce) can cream-style
  white shoepeg corn

Slice zucchini and steam until just tender. Let cool. Sauté onion
and pepper in oil until limp. Add eggs, cheese, and seasonings to
corn. Fold into zucchini along with sautéed onion and pepper.
Pour into buttered casserole and place in pan of hot water. Bake
at 350° for 45 minutes or until firm. Crumbled bacon or cubed
ham makes a nice addition. Serves 6–8.

Revel (Louisiana)

Corn Casserole

1 (17-ounce) can whole-kernel
  corn, drained
1 (17-ounce) can cream-style
  corn
1 box Jiffy Corn Muffin Mix
1 stick margarine
1 medium to large onion,
  chopped
1 green pepper, chopped
1 (8-ounce) carton sour cream
2 cups grated sharp Cheddar
  cheese

Mix corns and dry Jiffy mix together. Melt margarine; sauté onion
and pepper. Place corn mixture in 9x13-inch greased baking pan.
Spoon onion mixture over corn. Spoon sour cream over onion
mixture. Top with cheese. Bake at 350° for 30 minutes.

Note: Better if made the night before. Can be frozen.

Gibson/Goree Family Favorites (Alabama)

Kay's Corn Casserole

½ stick butter
3 tablespoons flour
1 cup whipping cream

2 (11-ounce) cans white corn
1 (3½-ounce) can French-fried
  onion rings

Melt butter in saucepan. Add flour, stirring over low heat; add cream and stir until thickened. Drain corn and stir into sauce. Place in greased casserole and top with onions. Bake at 350° for 15 minutes.

Take Five, A Cookbook (Mississippi)

White Corn Casserole

10 strips bacon
1 medium onion, chopped
2 (12-ounce) cans white corn,
  drained

1 (8-ounce) carton sour cream

Fry bacon crisp. Sauté onion in bacon grease. Combine 8 strips bacon, corn, sour cream, and onion. Cook at 350° for 20 minutes or until bubbly. Top with remaining bacon. Yields 5–6 servings.

Kitchen Sampler (Alabama)

Fried Green Tomato Casserole

6 medium green tomatoes,
  sliced in rounds
Salt and pepper to taste
1 cup Ritz Cracker crumbs,
  divided

1 cup grated sharp Cheddar
  cheese
6 tablespoons butter, divided

Layer half the tomatoes in a greased shallow dish. Sprinkle with salt and pepper. Add ½ cracker crumbs and ½ cheese. Top with ½ butter (in small pieces). Layer remaining tomatoes, add seasonings, and cheese. Add remaining crumbs and butter. Bake, covered, at 350° for 30 minutes. Uncover and bake 10 minutes or until brown.

Aliant Cooks for Education (Alabama)

Fried Green Tomatoes

Green tomatoes
Sweet milk
Vegetable oil
Fish-fry made with corn flour
Salt and black pepper

Slice tomatoes into approximately ⅛-inch rounds (2 or 3 slices equal 1 serving). Soak slices for one hour in enough milk to cover completely. Remove and coat generously with fish-fry. Pat fish-fry down on both sides of slices.

Put enough oil in skillet to cover bottom completely and generously, but not enough to lap over sides of slices. Heat oil in skillet to medium high. Oil is properly heated when a pinch of fish-fry sizzles, but does not burn. Add tomato slices in one layer so that sides do not touch. Salt and pepper the top sides. When coating is barely brown on bottom side, turn slices. Salt and pepper the top sides. Continue turning slices until coating is golden brown. Remove and drain on paper towels. Serve immediately.

Variations: Coating may also be made of 2 parts flour to 1 part fine-grind cornmeal. Finely grated Parmesan cheese and/or paprika may be added to coating.

The Southern Cook's Handbook (Mississippi)

Southern Tomato Pie

2–3 good-size tomatoes,
  sliced
1 tablespoon Italian seasoning,
  or to taste
1 tablespoon oregano, or
  to taste
1½ teaspoons chives, or to
  taste
Salt and pepper to taste
1 (9-inch) pie crust, cooked until
  light brown
1 cup grated sharp Cheddar
  cheese
1 cup mayonnaise

Sprinkle tomato slices with seasonings; place slices in pie crust. Combine cheese and mayonnaise to make a thick paste; cover tomatoes with paste. Bake at 350° until paste is bubbly and crust is a deep, golden brown.

Great Flavors of Mississippi (Mississippi)

Okra and Tomatoes Creole

½ small onion, chopped
1 tablespoon bacon grease
  or oil
½ cup washed and sliced
  fresh okra

1 teaspoon flour
1 tomato, cut in pieces
½ teaspoon sugar
Salt and pepper to taste

In heavy medium-size saucepan or skillet, slightly brown onion in bacon grease, about 1 minute on medium heat. Dredge okra in flour and add to onion. Continue cooking until okra is slightly brown, about 5 minutes. Add tomato to mixture. Add sugar. Cook partly covered over slow heat about 25 minutes, stirring occasionally to keep from sticking. Add seasoning. Serves 1–2.

Quickies for Singles (Louisiana)

Asparagus and Tomato Slices

An easy, colorful dish for luncheons or buffet dinners.

4 medium, firm ripe tomatoes
1 (15-ounce) can asparagus
  spears, drained
½ cup mayonnaise
3 tablespoons grated onion

Tabasco to taste
½ teaspoon Worcestershire
2 cups grated sharp Cheddar
  cheese

Preheat oven to 350°. Cut stem ends off tomatoes and slice each into 3 thick slices. Cut asparagus spears in half and arrange on top of tomato slices in a buttered, shallow baking dish. Combine remaining ingredients and spoon over asparagus. Bake 10–15 minutes or until cheese melts. Do not overbake. Tomatoes may be prepared early in the day and refrigerated before baking. Serves 6–8.

Magic (Alabama)

On April 15, 1866, the world's first electric trolley streetcars began in Montgomery, Alabama. Many people assume the trolley system began in San Francisco, but it's not so. The Lightening Route, as it was called, continued to operate until 1936 when the city replaced it with buses.

Asparagus Supreme

1 (10¾-ounce) can asparagus
  and juice
4 hard-boiled eggs, sliced
Cracker crumbs
1 (10¾-ounce) can cream of
  mushroom soup
2 tablespoons butter, melted
3 tablespoons Sauterne wine
3 or 4 dashes Tabasco

1 teaspoon Worcestershire
Garlic salt (optional), salt,
  pepper, and sugar to taste
1 cup grated New York State
  cheese
1 slice bread, crust trimmed
½ cup slivered almonds,
  blanched

Into buttered casserole, alternate layers of asparagus, eggs, cracker crumbs, and soup that has been mixed with asparagus juice, butter, wine, and seasonings. Top with cheese, small pieces of bread, and almonds. Bake at 350° for about 20 minutes. Serves 6–8.

Gourmet of the Delta (Mississippi)

Creamy Scalloped Potatoes

2 pounds potatoes (about 6
  medium)
4 tablespoons butter, divided
3 tablespoons all-purpose flour

1 teaspoon salt
¼ teaspoon pepper
2½ cups milk
1 small onion, finely chopped

Pare and cut potatoes into enough thin slices to measure about 4 cups. Heat 3 tablespoons butter in saucepan over low heat until melted. Blend in flour, salt, and pepper. Cook over low heat, stirring constantly, until mixture is smooth and bubbly; remove from heat. Stir in milk; heat to boiling, stirring constantly. Boil and stir 1 minute.

Arrange potatoes in greased 2-quart dish in 3 layers, topping each of the first 2 with ½ the onion and ⅓ the white sauce. Top with remaining potatoes and sauce. Dot with remaining 1 tablespoon butter. Cover and bake at 325° for 40 minutes, or 350° for 30 minutes. Uncover and bake until potatoes are tender, 60–70 minutes longer. Let stand 5–10 minutes before serving. Yields 6 servings.

Once Upon a Stove (Alabama)

Hash Brown Potato Casserole

1 (2-pound) package frozen
  hash brown potatoes
1 stick butter or margarine
½ cup finely chopped onion
1 (10¾-ounce) can cream of
  chicken soup, undiluted

2 cups sour cream
1 teaspoon salt
1 teaspoon pepper
1 (8-ounce) package grated
  sharp cheese
2 cups crushed cornflakes

Pour frozen hash brown potatoes in a large shallow casserole dish to defrost. In a saucepan, melt butter or margarine. Add chopped onion, soup, and sour cream. Remove from heat. Add salt and pepper. Mix this mixture well with potatoes. Top with grated cheese, then with crushed cornflakes. Bake at 350° for about 1 hour—until hot and bubbly. Do not overbake. May divide in half and freeze part.

The Pick of the Crop (Mississippi)

Skillet Potato Pie

1 pound potatoes, cooked,
  cooled
3 tablespoons snipped chives
1 teaspoon salt, divided
3 eggs, beaten

¼ cup light cream
¼ cup grated Parmesan cheese
Dash of pepper
4 tablespoons butter or
  margarine, divided

Peel and shred potatoes. Add chives (reserve some for garnish) and ½ teaspoon salt. Mix eggs, cream, cheese, remaining ½ teaspoon salt, and pepper; reserve. Heat 2 tablespoons butter in a 10-inch nonstick skillet over medium heat. Add potatoes, shaping into a pattie. Pour egg mixture over the potato pattie, and reduce heat to low. Cook about 10 minutes, or until potatoes are brown. Invert potato pattie onto a platter. Heat remaining butter in skillet until hot. Slide potato pattie back into skillet, and cook 8 more minutes, or until brown. Cut into wedges and garnish with chives. Yields 4–6 servings.

Come and Dine (Mississippi)

Caroline's Mashed Potatoes

5 pounds potatoes
1 (8-ounce) package cream
  cheese, softened
1 (8-ounce) carton sour cream

1 stick butter, softened
2 tablespoons onion salt
Salt and pepper to taste
Grated cheese

Boil and mash potatoes. Add next 5 ingredients and mix well. Put into a 9x13-inch pan. Top with grated cheese. Bake 30 minutes at 350° until bubbly.

Bethany's Best Bites (Alabama)

Onioned Potatoes

4 medium baking potatoes
¼ cup butter or margarine,
  softened

¼ envelope (3 tablespoons)
  onion soup mix

Scrub potatoes (do not pare). Cut each lengthwise in ¼-inch slices. Blend butter and onion soup mix; spread on one side of each potato slice. Reassemble potatoes; wrap each in foil, sealing securely. Bake on grill top over coals for one hour, or until done, turning once. Makes 4 servings.

Editor's Extra: May bake wrapped potatoes in 350° oven for 1 hour.

Pigging Out with the Cotton Patch Cooks (Louisiana)

Stewed Fresh Potatoes

8–10 small new potatoes,
  or 4 large cobbler potatoes
1 teaspoon salt
½ stick margarine

1 teaspoon pepper
4 tablespoons flour
1 cup water

Peel potatoes; wash and cut into chunks (cut small potatoes in half; cut larger ones into 5–8 pieces). Place in saucepan, and cover with water. Add salt; cook 25–30 minutes. When potatoes are tender, add margarine and pepper. Combine flour and water; blend well, add to potato mixture, stirring well so mixture does not lump. Yields 8–10 servings.

Irondale Cafe Original WhistleStop Cookbook (Alabama)

Oven-Roasted Sweet Potatoes and Onions

4 medium sweet potatoes,
  peeled and cut into 2-inch
  pieces (about 2½ pounds)
2 medium Vidalia or other
  sweet onions, sliced

2 tablespoons extra virgin olive
  oil
¾ teaspoon garlic-pepper blend
½ teaspoon salt

Preheat oven to 425°. Combine all ingredients in a 9x13-inch baking dish, tossing to coat. Bake at 425° for 35 minutes or until tender, stirring occasionally. Yields 6 servings.

Beyond the Grill (Mississippi)

Sweet Potato Soufflé

3 pounds sweet potatoes
½ cup margarine, softened
½ cup brown sugar
¼ cup granulated sugar

2 teaspoons vanilla
½ teaspoon ground cinnamon
½ teaspoon ground nutmeg
Large marshmallows

Wash and scrub sweet potatoes; place them in a saucepan. Cover potatoes with water; bring to a boil; reduce heat to medium-high and cook about 40 minutes. Stick the potatoes with a sharp knife to test for doneness; the potatoes need to be cooked a little longer for soufflé than for candied yams.

When potatoes are done, drain and rinse with cold water until cool enough to handle. Peel and place in mixing bowl. Add margarine and mash with a potato masher. Add brown sugar, granulated sugar, vanilla, cinnamon, and nutmeg; mix with an electric mixer until smooth. Pour into baking dish and bake at 350° for 15–20 minutes or until hot. Remove from oven and cover with marshmallows, return to oven long enough for marshmallows to start melting and brown slightly. Yields 10–12 servings.

Note: If the potatoes are cold when you put them into the oven, you might want to cover them with foil while heating to prevent overcooking.

Irondale Cafe Original WhistleStop Cookbook (Alabama)

Sweet Potato Casserole

3 (16-ounce) cans sweet
   potatoes, drained, mashed
⅓ cup sugar
1¾ sticks margarine, melted,
   divided
2 eggs, well beaten

1 tablespoon vanilla
¾ cup brown sugar
⅓ cup milk
⅓ cup all-purpose flour
1 cup very coarsely chopped
   pecans

Mix potatoes, ⅓ cup sugar, 1 stick melted margarine, eggs, and vanilla well and pour into a 9x13-inch pan. Mix remaining ingredients and slowly pour on top of sweet potato mixture; spread evenly without disturbing sweet potato mixture. Bake at 350° for 1 hour, or until topping is set as a pecan pie would be. Makes approximately 12 servings.

Cajun Cookin' (Louisiana)

Glazed Sweet Potatoes

3 pounds sweet potatoes
1 cup brown sugar
1½ tablespoons cornstarch
¼ teaspoon salt
⅛ teaspoon cinnamon

1 cup apricot nectar
½ cup hot water
2 teaspoons grated orange rind
2 tablespoons butter
½ cup chopped nuts

Boil potatoes in skins until tender but not mushy. Drain and cool. Peel and slice; place in 9x13-inch baking dish. Combine sugar, cornstarch, salt, and cinnamon in medium sauce pot. Stir in nectar, hot water, and orange peel. Bring to a full rolling boil, stirring constantly. Remove from heat; add butter and nuts. Pour over potatoes. Bake at 350° for 25 minutes or until sauce is bubbling.

Gibson/Goree Family Favorites (Alabama)

Arthur Guyton, who lived in Jackson, Mississippi, was a physician and the author of Textbook of Medical Physiology, the most widely used text of physiology in the world. He also designed a special leg brace, a hoist for moving patients from bed to chair to bathtub, and a motorized wheelchair. For inventing these devices, he received a Presidential Citation. All ten of his children are doctors.

Candied Carrots

1 pound carrots, peeled,
  steamed
1 cup peach preserves
¼ cup butter, melted

Cut carrots in slices. Add peach preserves and butter in shallow pan. Bake 30 minutes at 325°. Serves 6.

A Samford Celebration Cookbook (Alabama)

Cousin Patty's Carrot Soufflé

Extra good and colorful.

¾ cup sugar
3 tablespoons flour
¼ teaspoon salt
¼ teaspoon black pepper
1 teaspoon baking powder
1 stick butter, softened
1 teaspoon vanilla
2 tablespoons rum (optional)
1 (16-ounce) can carrots,
  drained
3 eggs

Preheat oven to 350°. Whisk together sugar, flour, salt, pepper, and baking powder. Combine all ingredients in blender and blend thoroughly. Pour into casserole and bake 45 minutes. Serve hot. Serves 4–6 hungry hogs!

The Hungry Hog (Louisiana)

Broccoli Casserole

1 package frozen broccoli
1 cup grated Cheddar cheese
1 (10¾-ounce) can cream of
  chicken soup
1½ cups cooked rice
1 cup chopped onion
½ cup chopped green onions
½ cup chopped celery
¼ pound butter
Salt and cayenne pepper to taste
Seasoned Italian bread crumbs

In a medium-size pot, cook broccoli according to directions. Drain well. Mix broccoli with cheese and soup. Stir in rice; set aside. In a large skillet, sauté onions and celery in butter until done, 5 minutes. Add to broccoli-rice mixture. Season to taste. Place all ingredients in a greased casserole dish. Top with bread crumbs. Bake at 325° for 1 hour.

The Encyclopedia of Cajun and Creole Cuisine (Louisiana)

Spinach Pauline

2 (10-ounce) packages frozen
  chopped spinach, cooked
  and well drained
6 tablespoons finely minced
  onion
¼ cup margarine, melted
1 teaspoon salt
¾ teaspoon black pepper

6 tablespoons heavy cream or
  evaporated milk
6 tablespoons grated Parmesan
  cheese
2 tablespoons cream cheese,
  softened
Tabasco (optional)
Italian bread crumbs

Cook spinach according to package directions in unsalted water. Drain. Sauté onion in margarine. Add drained spinach, salt and pepper to taste. Pour in milk. Add cheeses and Tabasco. Mix well. Before serving, place in baking dish and top with buttered Italian bread crumbs and bake at 375° for 10–15 minutes. Freezes well. Serves 4–6.

River Road Recipes II (Louisiana)

Spinach Casserole

This usually appeals even to "spinach haters."

2 (10-ounce) packages frozen
  chopped spinach
1 (8-ounce) package cream
  cheese, softened

1 stick butter, softened, divided
Salt and cayenne pepper to taste
1 cup Pepperidge Farm Herb
  Stuffing

Cook spinach according to directions on package. Drain and add softened cream cheese and ½ stick butter. Mix well and season in casserole; cover with herb stuffing to form a top crust. Pour on remaining ½ stick melted butter. Bake in 350° oven 20–30 minutes, until thoroughly hot. Serves 6.

Old Mobile Recipes (Alabama)

Creamy Spinach Casserole

2 cups bite-size, crispy rice
  cereal squares
1 teaspoon onion powder
3 tablespoons melted butter
1 (8-ounce) package cream
  cheese
1 (5-ounce) can evaporated
  milk
2 teaspoons lemon juice

¾ teaspoon seasoning salt
Dash of pepper
1 egg, beaten
1 (8-ounce) can sliced
  mushrooms, reserve ¼ of
  liquid
2 (10-ounce) packages frozen
  spinach, cooked and drained

Preheat oven to 350°. Combine cereal, onion powder, and butter, and set aside. In a saucepan, combine cream cheese, milk, lemon juice, seasoning salt, pepper, and liquid reserved from mushrooms. Cook and stir on low until smooth. Add egg; cook and stir constantly until thickened. Stir in mushrooms and spinach. Pour into 1½-quart casserole. Add cereal topping. Bake for 15–20 minutes. Serves 8.

Sterling Service (Alabama)

Sautéed Mushrooms

1½ pounds mushrooms, sliced
4 cloves garlic, chopped
3 tablespoons whole basil
1 tablespoon ground thyme
½ cup chopped fresh parsley

4 tablespoons olive oil
½ cup port wine
½ cup heavy cream
Salt and pepper to taste

In a large bowl, thoroughly mix mushrooms, garlic, basil, thyme, and parsley. Cover bowl with plastic wrap and refrigerate 2 hours.

Using a skillet large enough to hold the mushroom mixture, heat olive oil over medium-high heat. Add mushroom mixture and cook 6 minutes, stirring constantly. Add wine, lower heat to medium-low, and cook 4 more minutes. Add cream and continue to cook 5–7 minutes. Remember to stir constantly to prevent sticking and keep the sauce smooth. Season to taste.

Editor's Extra: We like to serve this over grilled steaks.

Pass the Meatballs, Please! (Louisiana)

Onion Casserole

The secret is that you can make this ahead and refrigerate it until needed. Men especially like it.

4 large mild onions, sliced
5 tablespoons butter
1 loaf French bread, cut in
  ½-inch slices

1 pound Swiss cheese, sliced
1 (10¾-ounce) can cream of
  mushroom soup
1 soup can milk

Sauté onions in butter until clear; remove from heat. In a buttered 9x13x2-inch casserole dish, place a layer of French bread; cover with half the onions and half the cheese. Repeat layers. Combine soup and milk; pour over casserole. Refrigerate overnight or longer (will keep 2 or 3 days).

To serve, bake in a 350° oven for 30 minutes or until bubbly and only slightly brown. Yields 8–10 servings.

Family Secrets (Alabama)

Onion Pie

May be used as a main dish if hungry men are not to be fed.

CRUST:
1 cup saltine cracker crumbs   ¼ cup butter, melted

Mix together and press into a 9-inch pie pan. You may use regular pie crust if you prefer.

FILLING:
3 cups diced onions
¼ cup butter
½ pound Swiss cheese, finely
  grated
1 tablespoon flour

1 teaspoon salt
¼ teaspoon cayenne pepper
3 eggs, beaten well
1 cup scalded milk

Sauté onions in butter slowly, stirring constantly until golden. Remove from fire, drain, and put into pie shell. Combine cheese, flour, salt, and cayenne; stir in eggs and milk. Pour over onions and bake in 350° oven for 40 minutes. Cut into small wedges and serve. Yields 8 or more servings.

The Gulf Gourmet (Mississippi)

Easy English Pea Casserole

2 (16-ounce) packages frozen
green peas
1 pound sliced mushrooms
(or canned)
1 (8-ounce) can sliced water
chestnuts

1 (¾-ounce) package Italian
seasoning mix
½ stick butter, melted

Mix all ingredients, except butter, and place in a large, oblong baking dish. Pour butter on top. Cover and bake at 350° for 45 minutes. Serves 6.

Southern Generations (Mississippi)

Crispy Fried Okra

1 pound fresh okra, stemmed,
cut into ½-inch slices, or
1 (10-ounce) package frozen
cut okra, thawed and dried
1 or 2 egg whites, slightly
beaten

½ heaping cup white cornmeal
½–¾ teaspoon onion powder
½ teaspoon salt, or to taste
¼ teaspoon freshly ground
pepper, or to taste
Corn oil

Add okra slices to egg whites and toss until well coated. Combine cornmeal, onion powder, salt, and pepper in a plastic bag. Add okra slices a handful at a time to the cornmeal mixture, shaking until thoroughly coated. Remove from bag and place on a baking sheet. Okra can be refrigerated at this point. Heat oil and fry a small batch of okra at a time. If too much is added at one time, okra will smother rather than fry. Remove from oil, drain on a paper towel, and place in a warm oven until all okra is prepared. Serve immediately. Serves 3–4.

Taste of the South (Mississippi)

At age 27, Bob Pittman of Brookhaven, Mississippi, created the programming for the music television network MTV, launched in 1981. He founded Quantum Media in 1987, became president and CEO of Time Warner Cable in 1990, CEO and managing partner of Century 21 Real Estate Corporation in 1995, and finally, in 1996, he became the president and CEO of AOL, where he retired as COO in 2001.

Old Settlers Baked Beans

½ pound ground beef
½ pound bacon, diced
1 medium onion, chopped
⅓ cup sugar
½ cup brown sugar
¼ cup ketchup
¼ cup barbecue sauce
1 tablespoon prepared
  mustard

½ teaspoon pepper
½ teaspoon chili powder
1 (16-ounce) can pork and
  beans, undrained
1 (16-ounce) can kidney beans,
  rinsed and drained
1 (16-ounce) can northern
  beans, rinsed and drained

In a large skillet, cook beef, bacon, and onion until meat is done and onion is tender. Drain; combine all remaining ingredients, except beans. Add to meat mixture; mix well. Stir in beans. Place in greased 2½-quart casserole. Bake uncovered for 1 hour at 350°. Makes 8–10 servings.

Golden Moments (Mississippi)

Barbecued Baked Beans

1 (31-ounce) can baked beans
1 tablespoon Worcestershire
1 teaspoon prepared mustard
½ cup white sugar

½ cup barbecue sauce with
  onions
¼ cup chopped onions
3 slices bacon

Mix all ingredients except bacon; place in 1¾-quart casserole dish. Top with bacon. Bake at 350° for 1 hour. Serves 6.

The Mississippi Cookbook (Mississippi)

JESSEOWENS.COM

In addition to setting seven world records, track star Jesse Owens of Oakville, Alabama, was also the winner of four gold medals at the 1936 Summer Olympics held in Berlin, Germany: one each in the 100 meters, the 200 meters, the long jump, and as part of the 4x100 meter relay team. His birthplace in Oakville dedicated a park in his honor in 1996, at the same time the Olympic Torch came through the community, 60 years after his Olympic triumph. In 2008, Adidas released the ZX800 Jesse Owens shoe to honor his tremendous accomplishments. The sneaker, which boasts a very patriotic color scheme, features a portrait of Owens on the inside.

Green Beans and Stewed Potatoes

3 slices bacon
3 cups fresh green beans,
  snapped
4 cups water
1 teaspoon salt

½ teaspoon pepper
4 small fresh potatoes, scraped
3 tablespoons margarine, melted
2 tablespoons flour

Brown bacon in large saucepan. Add green beans, water, salt, pepper, and potatoes. Cover and simmer 40–50 minutes or until potatoes are tender. (Gently stir at 10-minute intervals to prevent sticking. Additional water may be added, if needed.) After potatoes are cooked, remove ½ cup hot liquid from beans and potatoes. Combine with margarine and flour to make creamy paste. Stir paste into beans and potatoes while still cooking. Simmer 10 minutes, or long enough to thicken liquid. Serves 4.

Dinner on the Ground (Louisiana)

My Granny's Green Beans

¼ cup bacon drippings, or
  vegetable oil
3–4 cloves garlic
1–2 onions, whole
1 pint green beans, canned
  or fresh

1 bay leaf
Salt and pepper to taste
Crushed red pepper flakes
  or paprika

Fill a large pot with about 1–2 inches of water. Add bacon drippings or oil. Add garlic and onions. Bring this to a slow boil and simmer. Add green beans, bay leaf, salt and pepper. Bring to another slow simmer. Simmer until green beans glisten with the oil, and seasonings have married. Garnish with sprinklings of crushed red pepper flakes or paprika, and serve with freshly made corn muffins.

Another Taste of Alabaster (Alabama)

Green Beans Wrapped in Bacon

3 (15-ounce) cans whole green
  beans
1 pound bacon

1 cup brown sugar
½ cup vinegar
Salt and pepper to taste

Put 8–10 beans together in a bundle and wrap with a strip of bacon. Secure with a toothpick. Place bundles in a casserole dish. Mix brown sugar, vinegar, and seasonings together. Pour mixture over beans, and bake about 50 minutes at 350°.

Recipes from the Heart of Branch (Mississippi)

Lois' Apricot Casserole

Delightful with any meats.

1 (29-ounce) can peeled
  apricots
½ (1-pound) box light brown
  sugar

3 tablespoons lemon juice
½ box Cheese Ritz Crackers
½ stick butter or margarine

Remove seeds from apricots and drain in colander for 1–1½ hours. Turn apricot cavities up in glass baking dish and sprinkle with sugar and lemon juice to marinate overnight in refrigerator. Just before baking, coarsely crumble crackers over apricots; drizzle with butter, and bake at 350° for 40–45 minutes. Serves 8.

The Cook's Book (Mississippi)

Sweet and Sour Beets

1 tablespoon cornstarch
3 tablespoons vinegar
3 tablespoons sugar or sugar
  substitute

1 teaspoon salt
½ cup beet juice
1 (16-ounce) can beets

Combine all ingredients except beets in a medium saucepan. Heat until thickened. Cool. Add beets. Serve warm or cold.

L'Heritage Du Bayou Lafourche (Louisiana)

PASTA, RICE, ETC.

Legend has it that the crossroads of Highways 61 and 49 outside Clarksdale, Mississippi—now marked by three huge guitars—is where bluesman Robert Johnson sold his soul to the devil in exchange for his guitar-playing genius.

Chicketti

2 cups bite-size spaghetti
  pieces, cooked, drained
2 cups chopped cooked chicken
1 cup chicken broth
1 (10¾-ounce) can cream of
  mushroom soup
1 cup shredded Cheddar
  cheese, divided

½ onion, chopped
¼ cup pimentos, drained
¼ cup chopped green bell
  pepper
½ teaspoon salt
¼ teaspoon pepper

Combine pasta, chicken, broth, soup, ½ cup cheese, onion, pimentos, green pepper, salt, and pepper in a large bowl and mix well. Spoon into a greased 3-quart baking dish. Sprinkle with remaining ½ cup cheese. Bake at 325° for 45–60 minutes or until cooked through. Yields 8 servings.

Celebrations (Alabama)

Baked Spaghetti

1 cup chopped onion
1 cup chopped green bell
  pepper
1 tablespoon margarine, or
  butter
1 (28-ounce) can chopped
  tomatoes with juice
1 (4-ounce) can sliced ripe
  olives, drained
1 (4-ounce) can mushrooms,
  drained

2 teaspoons oregano
2 pounds ground chuck, cooked
  and drained
12 ounces thin spaghetti,
  broken, cooked, drained
2 cups shredded Cheddar cheese
1 (10¾-ounce) can cream of
  mushroom soup
¼ cup water
¼ cup grated Parmesan cheese

Sauté onion and green pepper in butter in a large skillet. Add tomatoes, olives, mushrooms, oregano, and ground beef. Bring to a boil, reduce heat and simmer, uncovered, 10 minutes. Place half of spaghetti in a greased 9x13-inch baking dish. Top with half of tomato mixture and sprinkle with half Cheddar cheese. Repeat layers. Mix soup and water until smooth. Pour over casserole and sprinkle with Parmesan cheese. Bake, uncovered, in pre-heated 350° oven 30–35 minutes. Yields 12 servings.

Simple Pleasures from Our Table to Yours (Alabama)

Spaghetti Carbonara

1 (8-ounce) package spaghetti	½ cup sliced mushrooms
½ stick butter	Salt and pepper to taste
1 cup chopped ham or bacon	1 egg, beaten
⅓ cup sliced onion	½ cup half-and-half
⅓ cup chopped bell pepper	½ cup grated Parmesan cheese

Boil spaghetti in large pot of salted water. Drain. Melt butter and sauté ham, onion, bell pepper, and mushrooms until tender. Add drained spaghetti. Salt and pepper to taste. Mix egg with half - and-half and add. Toss in Parmesan cheese and stir until heated through. Remove from heat and serve. Serves 4.

Magic (Alabama)

Creole Shrimp Spaghetti

4 tablespoons chopped onion	4 cups cooked tomatoes
½ cup sliced celery	1 cup sliced fresh mushrooms
2 tablespoons butter, melted	1 teaspoon sugar
¼ cup all-purpose flour	1 pound cooked shrimp
1 teaspoon salt	8 ounces spaghetti, cooked
¼ teaspoon pepper	

Cook onion and celery in butter until tender. Stir in flour, salt, and pepper. Add juice from tomatoes (2 cups) and stir until smooth. Crush tomatoes and add to sauce along with mushrooms and sugar. Simmer over low heat 40 minutes. Add cooked shrimp. Serve over cooked spaghetti. Best if prepared ahead of time. May be frozen. Cook ½ hour to reheat. Add water, if necessary.

A Cook's Tour of Shreveport (Louisiana)

The Atchafalaya Basin, cutting a 15-mile-wide path across south Louisiana, is the largest and last great river-basin swamp. It comprises an area of 860,000 acres of swamps, lakes and water prairies.

Oyster Spaghetti

6 dozen oysters
1 clove garlic
1 bunch green onions
1 cup chopped parsley
¼ cup olive oil
1 cup sliced mushrooms
  (optional)

½ teaspoon basil
1 pound spaghetti, cooked
½ cup Parmesan cheese
Salt and pepper to taste

Drain oysters well. Reserve liquid. You may need it if spaghetti is too dry. Sauté garlic, onions, and parsley in olive oil. Add mushrooms and oysters. Cook over low heat until oysters curl. Add basil. Toss oyster mixture with cooked spaghetti and Parmesan cheese. Season with salt and pepper. If spaghetti is too dry, you may add olive oil or oyster liquid. If spaghetti has too much liquid, you could add Italian bread crumbs and/or more Parmesan cheese. Serves 6 generously.

Talk About Good II (Louisiana)

Seagrove Shrimp

Great with sourdough bread and salad.

8 ounces pasta of choice
1 red bell pepper
1 yellow bell pepper
1 small onion, chopped
1 tablespoon olive oil
1 tablespoon minced garlic
1 cup half-and-half

1 cup chicken stock
Cayenne pepper to taste
1 teaspoon chopped basil
1 pound peeled shrimp
1 cup shredded Parmesan
  cheese

Cook pasta according to package directions. Rinse in cool water and set aside. Cut peppers in strips and sauté with onion in olive oil and garlic. Add half-and-half and chicken stock. Add seasonings and cook down quickly over hot heat. Add shrimp and cook until pink. Stir in pasta and Parmesan cheese.

Kitchen Keepsakes (Alabama)

Sunday Night Show-off

1 (16-ounce) package
  vermicelli or thin spaghetti
½ cup butter or margarine
½ cup flour
1 cup chicken broth
1 cup heavy cream
1 cup shredded Swiss cheese
4 tablespoons sherry

White pepper to taste
1 (16-ounce) can sliced
  mushrooms, drained
3 pounds shrimp, cooked and
  peeled
½ cup fresh grated Parmesan
¼ cup slivered almonds

Cook pasta and drain. Make cream sauce out of butter, flour, broth, and cream over low heat, stirring constantly until sauce thickens. Blend in cheese, sherry, and white pepper; heat and stir until cheese melts; add mushrooms. Remove from heat. Add shrimp. Add spaghetti to sauce. Turn into large, shallow casserole. Sprinkle with Parmesan cheese and slivered almonds. Heat under broiler 5–7 minutes until lightly brown. Serve immediately. Makes 12 servings.

Best of Bayou Cuisine (Mississippi)

Crawfish Fettuccine

3 sticks butter
3 onions, chopped
2 green peppers, chopped
3 stalks celery, chopped
3 pounds crawfish tails
3 cloves garlic, minced

1 tablespoon chopped parsley
½ cup flour
1 pint half-and-half
1 pound jalapeño cheese, cubed
12 ounces fettuccine

In a saucepan, melt butter and sauté onions, bell peppers, and celery until tender. Add crawfish and simmer 10 minutes, stirring occasionally. Add garlic, parsley, flour, and half-and-half; mix well. Simmer on low heat for 30 minutes, stirring occasionally. Add cheese and stir until melted. Meanwhile, cook noodles; drain and cool. Combine noodles and sauce. Pour into a greased 6-quart casserole, or 2 greased 3-quart casseroles. Bake, uncovered, in a 300° oven for 20 minutes or until heated thoroughly. Freezes well. Serves 12.

Straight from the Galley Past & Present (Mississippi)

Spicy Crawfish Pasta

Great dish served with garlic bread and salad.

1 package rotini (spiral) pasta
1 stick butter or margarine
1 bunch green onions, chopped
1 medium yellow onion, chopped
1 teaspoon minced garlic
1 (1-pound) package crawfish tails
1 pint half-and-half
6–8 ounces jalapeño-Jack cheese
Salt, black pepper, and red pepper to taste
Parmesan cheese (optional)

Prepare pasta according to package directions. Drain and set aside to cool. In a large nonstick skillet, melt butter. Add onions and garlic; sauté approximately 3 minutes. Add crawfish and sauté another 3 minutes. Reduce heat to medium and add half-and-half. Reduce heat to low and add slices of jalapeño-Jack cheese to the sauce. Stir sauce frequently until cheese is thoroughly melted (sauce will be slightly lumpy). Season to taste, but go lightly with pepper; the jalapeños in the cheese make the sauce very spicy.

In a large casserole dish, combine drained, cooked pasta and crawfish sauce. Sprinkle with Parmesan cheese and serve while hot. (Can be prepared ahead and reheated in oven at 350°.) Serves 4 or 5.

Fiftieth Anniversary Cookbook (Louisiana)

Crab and Shrimp Lasagna

A show stopper! Well worth the trouble.

3 tablespoons butter
3 tablespoons all-purpose flour
2 cups milk
2 (10¾-ounce) cans cream of
 shrimp soup
1⅓ cups grated Parmesan
 cheese, divided
¼ cup sherry
1 (8-ounce) package lasagna
 noodles
1 tablespoon olive oil
2 cups cottage cheese
1 (8-ounce) package cream
 cheese, softened

2 eggs, beaten
1 large white onion, chopped
4 tablespoons fresh basil, or
 2 tablespoons dried basil
2 tablespoons chopped, fresh
 parsley or 1 tablespoon dried
Salt and pepper to taste
1 pound shrimp, cooked and
 peeled
1 pound fresh crabmeat
Juice of 1 lemon
2 cups grated Swiss cheese,
 divided
3 tomatoes, sliced

Make a white sauce by melting butter in saucepan and stirring in flour. Cook until smooth, stirring constantly, over very low heat. Add milk slowly, stirring until thickened. Add soup, 6 tablespoons Parmesan cheese, and sherry. Set aside.

Cook lasagna noodles, adding 1 tablespoon olive oil to cooking water. Cook noodles to al dente stage and drain. Combine cottage cheese, cream cheese, eggs, onion, basil, parsley, salt and pepper. In another bowl, combine shrimp, crabmeat, lemon juice, and 1½ cups of the soup sauce.

In a 9x13-inch casserole, layer the lasagna in the following order: ½ cup soup sauce, lasagna noodles, ½ shrimp and crabmeat sauce, ½ cottage cheese mixture, ½ remaining soup sauce, and 1 cup Swiss cheese. Repeat layers. Top with 1 cup Parmesan cheese. Bake at 350° for 45 minutes. Place sliced tomatoes on top, and bake an additional 10–15 minutes. Allow lasagna to sit 10 minutes before serving. Serves 10–12.

Great Performances (Mississippi)

Lasagna

SAUCE:

10 ounces lasagna or wide
  noodles, cooked, drained
½ pound bulk sausage
1½ pounds lean ground meat
1 clove garlic, minced
1 tablespoon whole basil

1½ teaspoons salt
2 cups tomatoes
2 (6-ounce) cans tomato paste
2 (6-ounce) cans water
1 pound pepperoni sausage,
  sliced (optional)

Mix sausage, ground meat, garlic, basil, salt, tomatoes, tomato paste, and water.

CHEESE FILLING:

3 cups Ricotta or creamy
  cottage cheese
½ cup grated Parmesan or
  Romano cheese
2 tablespoons parsley flakes

2 eggs, beaten
2 teaspoons salt
½ teaspoon pepper
1 pound grated mozzarella
  cheese

Mix ingredients together, except mozzarella. Spoon a few table-spoons of Sauce on bottom of dish, then a layer of noodles. Spread a layer of Cheese Filling, sprinkle with mozzarella cheese, then top with Sauce. Repeat layers. Bake in 375° oven for 30 minutes. Let stand a few minutes before cutting into squares. Serves 12.

Treasured Tastes (Alabama)

MISSISSIPPI DEVELOPMENT AUTHORITY,
DIVISION OF TOURISM

Columbus, Mississippi-born Thomas Lanier Williams, known as Tennessee Williams, was a novelist, short story writer, poet, play-wright, and winner of two Pulitzer Prizes (for Streetcar Named Desire *and* Cat on a Hot Tin Roof*). His home, now a welcome center, is open to the public.*

Gourmet Noodles

Great with steak or roast.

¼ pound butter
½ pound sliced mushrooms
¼ cup chopped onion
¼ cup sliced almonds
1 clove garlic, minced

1 tablespoon lemon juice
1 (10-ounce) can beef
  consommé
4 ounces medium egg noodles

Melt butter. Add mushrooms, onion, almonds, and garlic, and cook about 10 minutes on low heat. Add remaining ingredients and cook till noodles are tender, about 10 minutes. Serves 4.

Best of Bayou Cuisine (Mississippi)

Spinach Stuffed Manicotti

1 pound ground meat
1 onion, chopped
1 teaspoon chopped garlic
½ green bell pepper, chopped
14 ounces chopped spinach
Salt and pepper to taste
¼ cup cottage cheese

2 eggs, well beaten
14 cooked manicotti shells
1 (26-ounce) jar spaghetti sauce
½ cup grated Parmesan cheese
1 cup shredded mozzarella
  cheese

Cook ground meat, onion, garlic, and bell pepper; season to taste. Drain well and set aside to cool. Cook and drain spinach, cool; add cottage cheese and eggs; mix well. Add to meat mixture. Stuff shells with mixture and place in oiled 9x13-inch pan. Pour spaghetti sauce over manicotti shells. Sprinkle with Parmesan cheese, then sprinkle with mozzarella. Preheat oven to 350° and bake 30 minutes.

Sisters' Secrets (Louisiana)

Manicotti

SAUCE:

1½ cups chopped onions
½–1 teaspoon garlic powder
2 pounds ground beef
1 (35-ounce) can tomatoes, undrained
1 (8-ounce) can tomato sauce
2 tablespoons chopped parsley
1 tablespoon salt
2 tablespoons sugar
1 tablespoon Italian seasonings
¼ teaspoon pepper
1 (4-ounce) can sliced mushrooms (optional)
1½ cups water

Sauté onions, garlic, and ground beef—may use a little oil if necessary. Add other ingredients, mashing tomatoes with fork. Bring to a boil and reduce heat. Simmer, covered, stirring occasionally, for 1 hour.

FILLING:

2 pounds ricotta cheese
1 (8-ounce) package mozzarella cheese, diced
⅓ cup grated Parmesan cheese
2 eggs
1 teaspoon salt
¼ teaspoon pepper
1 tablespoon chopped parsley
¼ cup grated Parmesan, divided
1 package manicotti noodles, cooked

Combine all ingredients except ¼ cup Parmesan and noodles. Blend well. Spread about ¼ cup Filling down each manicotti noodle. Spoon a little sauce in casserole dishes, then place noodles on top. Cover with rest of sauce and sprinkle with remaining Parmesan. Bake at 350°, uncovered, ½ hour.

Giant Houseparty Cookbook (Mississippi)

Football Casserole

Keep one of these in the freezer for after the game.

1 pound ground beef
2 tablespoons shortening
1 medium onion, chopped
1 medium bell pepper, chopped
2 cups canned tomatoes
1 tablespoon ketchup
1 tablespoon steak sauce

2 tablespoons chopped parsley
1 (5-ounce) package elbow
   macaroni
Salt and pepper to taste
1 (10¾-ounce) can cream of
   mushroom soup
1 cup grated Cheddar cheese

Brown beef in shortening. Add onion, bell pepper, tomatoes, ketchup, steak sauce, and parsley. Simmer 30 minutes. Cook macaroni according to package directions. Drain. Combine macaroni and ground beef mixture in casserole dish. Season to taste. Gently spoon mushroom soup into mixture. Mix lightly. Sprinkle with grated cheese. Bake at 350° for 30 minutes or until bubbling and brown.

When Dinnerbells Ring (Alabama)

Coach Paul William "Bear" Bryant is remembered for revitalizing University of Alabama's Crimson Tide football program into the nation's top-ranked college team. His 1961, 1964, 1965, 1973, 1978, and 1979 teams all won National Championships. In 37 years as a head football coach, he won 323 games, lost just 85, and tied 17. He was the winningest Division 1 football coach in history, until Penn State's Joe Paterno broke his record during the 2001 season. Coach Bryant retired from university in 1982 and died less than a year later. His nickname stemmed from his having agreed to wrestle a captive bear during a theater promotion when he was 13 years old. He was also known for his trademark houndstooth hat.

Catahoula Dirty Rice

3 onions, diced
2 bell peppers, diced
1 tablespoon chopped garlic
2 bunches green onion, diced
5 cups water, divided
1 quart canned whole tomatoes
1 pound smoked sausage,
  cut up
1 pound ground beef
1 medium-size chicken, cut in
  pieces
3 cups cooked rice
1 teaspoon salt
1 teaspoon pepper sauce or to
  taste

Place onions, peppers, garlic, and green onions in large pot. Add 2 cups water and canned tomatoes. Cook approximately 45 minutes. Brown sausage and drain. In same pan, brown ground beef and drain. In separate pan, place a small amount of oil, (enough to cover bottom of pan) and brown lightly floured chicken pieces in oil. When brown, add 1 cup water and cook on low heat until chicken is tender (about 30 minutes.) Add sausage and ground beef to chicken and gravy. Add rice and meat to tomato mixture with remaining 2 cups of water. Cook about 45 minutes over medium-low heat. Add salt and pepper sauce. Freezes well, prepared in advance.

The Tastes & Traditions of Troy State University (Alabama)

Shrimp and Rice Casserole

2 (6-ounce) packages Uncle
  Ben's wild and white rice
2 tablespoons butter
1 cup celery, bias cut
½ cup sliced green onions
½ green bell pepper, chopped
2 (2½-ounce) jars sliced
  mushrooms, drained

2 tablespoons chopped pimentos
½ teaspoon salt
1 teaspoon pepper
1½ teaspoons Ac'cent
2 cups shrimp, cooked, cleaned

Cook rice according to directions. Sauté in butter, the celery, onions, and green pepper. Stir in mushrooms, pimentos, seasonings, and shrimp. Fold into cooked rice. Put in buttered 2-quart casserole. Add Topping. Serves 8–10.

TOPPING:

1 (10¾-ounce) can cream of
  celery soup
1⅓ cups sour cream
⅔ cup bread crumbs

2 tablespoons butter
2 tablespoons freshly snipped
  parsley

Combine soup and sour cream. Spoon over casserole. Toss bread crumbs in butter and add to top, then add parsley. Bake in 325° oven for 40 minutes.

Try Me (Alabama)

PHOTO COURTESY OF U.S. STATE DEPT.

Condoleezza Rice

Born November 14, 1954, in Birmingham, Alabama, Condoleezza Rice has become one of the most acclaimed women in America and the world. She was a professor of political science at Stanford University and later the first female provost of Stanford. As a child, Rice was a gifted student and a prodigy on the piano. She entered college at the age of 15 with the intention of becoming a concert pianist. Rice changed her plans and studied international politics. At age thirty-four she became the expert on the Soviet Union for President George H. Bush's administration. President George W. Bush was so impressed with Rice's abilities, he appointed her National Security Advisor, and on November 16, 2004, Bush nominated Rice to replace Colin Powell as Secretary of State. Dr. Condoleezza Rice became the 66th Secretary of State on January 26, 2005.

Stuffed Peppers
with Shrimp and Rice

6 medium bell peppers
½ cup rice
½ cup butter or margarine
1 pound small or medium
  shrimp, peeled
1 large onion, chopped
1 clove garlic, chopped

½ teaspoon cayenne pepper
½ teaspoon salt
½ teaspoon pepper
1 (20-ounce) can diced tomatoes
1 cup Pepperidge Farm
  seasoned dressing

Prepare bell peppers for stuffing by cutting bottom out and cleaning seeds from inside. Boil peppers 5 minutes. Remove and drain. Cook rice; set aside. Melt butter or margarine in saucepan. Place shrimp, onion, garlic, cayenne pepper, salt, and pepper in pan of melted butter; cook for 5 minutes. Pour tomatoes in same pan and cook 5 more minutes. Remove from heat and mix cooked rice with all ingredients in same pan.

Place peppers in baking dish. Fill each with rice mixture, then top with seasoned dressing. Cover dish and place in 350° oven 30 minutes. Serves 3–6.

Calling All Cooks, Two (Alabama)

Beauvoir (circa 1848-1851), located in Biloxi, Mississippi, is the retirement home of Jefferson Davis, President of the Confederate States of America. The compound consisted of approximately 608 acres when Davis lived there (today, the site is approximately 52 acres in size). The name "Beauvoir" means "beautiful to view." The home faces the Gulf of Mexico and Spanish moss hangs from many of the large old trees on the property.

Beauvoir and the Jefferson Davis Presidential Library suffered heavy damage from Hurricane Katrina on August 29, 2005. These two structures can and will be restored given time and funding. However, the Library pavilion (where Jefferson Davis penned "The Rise and Fall of the Confederate Government"), the Hayes cottage, Soldier's Home Barracks replica, Confederate Soldier's Museum, Giftshop, and director's home were totally destroyed. Replicas of those buildings totally destroyed will be built after the restoration of Beauvoir House and Presidential Library are complete. Prior to Katrina, the Jefferson Davis Presidential Library maintained a collection of 12,000 books on United States history, southern history, and history of the American Civil War. The library also maintained collections of photographs, personal letters, manuscripts, envelopes, postcards, newspaper clippings, records of Confederate heritage organizations such as the United Confederate Veterans and the Sons of Confederate Veterans, and records from the Veterans home that once was present on the grounds. Many of these records survived, and the salvageability of the collections stands at about sixty percent.

Stuffed Bell Peppers

4 large green peppers
½ pound butter
2 cups chopped onions
½ cup chopped celery
½ cup chopped parsley
½ pound ground beef
½ loaf fresh bread

½ pound shrimp, peeled and
 deveined
3 eggs
Salt and pepper to taste
1 clove garlic
½ cup bread crumbs

Preheat oven to 350°. Cut peppers lengthwise, removing seeds and stems, and wash. Boil in slightly salted water; do not over-cook. Remove and drain well. In a large sauté pan, melt butter. Add onions, celery, parsley, and garlic, and sauté for 15 minutes, or until done. Add ground meat and shrimp and cook for 20 minutes longer.

Wet bread under faucet, squeeze out all liquid and add to sautéed ingredients. Add eggs, salt and pepper; stir well to blend bread into meat. Remove and fill peppers with mixture; top with bread crumbs, and place on a baking dish. Add ½ cup water at bottom of dish and bake until brown.

The Encyclopedia of Cajun and Creole Cuisine (Louisiana)

MISSISSIPPI DEVELOPMENT AUTHORITY, DIVISION OF TOURISM

Beauvoir (prior to Hurricane Katrina)

Stir-Fry Chicken, Broccoli, and Rice

It is best to have all ingredients ready before you begin the cooking process.

4 tablespoons corn oil, divided
2 cups broccoli florets
1 cup carrots, cut into
  matchsticks
½ cup coarsely chopped
  walnuts
Garlic powder
4 chicken breast halves,
  deboned and cut into strips

2 tablespoons soy sauce
1 teaspoon ginger (optional)
½ teaspoon sugar
2 cups chicken broth
¼ cup sliced green onions
1 cup Uncle Ben's Converted
  Rice

Put 2 tablespoons corn oil in skillet or wok over medium heat. Add broccoli, carrots, walnuts, and garlic powder; stir-fry for 2 minutes. Remove vegetables. Add remaining 2 tablespoons corn oil; add chicken. Stir-fry until chicken turns white. Add soy sauce, ginger, and sugar, and stir-fry 2 more minutes.

Take out chicken, and put into bowl with vegetables. Add broth and green onions to skillet, and bring to boil. Stir in rice and cover tightly. Simmer 20 minutes. Remove from heat and stir in vegetables. Let stand until liquid is absorbed.

Blue Mountain College Cookbook (Mississippi)

First Place Chicken Casserole

Superlatives are definitely in order for this make-ahead dish that came to us already aptly named. We suggest cooking the rice in the broth left from the chicken. We promise rave reviews, too!

2–3 cups cooked, diced chicken
4 hard-boiled eggs, chopped
2 cups cooked rice
1½ cups chopped celery
1 small onion, chopped
1 cup mayonnaise
2 (10¾-ounce) cans cream of
　mushroom soup

1 (3-ounce) package slivered
　almonds
1 teaspoon salt
2 tablespoons lemon juice
1 cup bread crumbs
2 tablespoons margarine

Mix all ingredients except bread crumbs and margarine. Place mixture in buttered 9x12-inch pan or casserole. Brown bread crumbs lightly in margarine. Sprinkle over casserole. Refrigerate overnight.

Remove from refrigerator 1 hour before cooking. Bake 40–45 minutes at 350°. Serves 8.

Cotton Country Cooking (Alabama)

Chicken and Sausage Casserole

10 chicken breasts
9 cups boiling water
3 envelopes dry chicken noodle
　soup mix
2 cups raw rice
1 pound hot sausage
1 green bell pepper, chopped
1 large onion, chopped

1 cup chopped celery
Salt to taste
Curry powder to taste
2 (10¾-ounce) cans cream of
　mushroom soup
½ cup blanched almonds,
　toasted in melted butter

Boil chicken breasts until tender. Let cool. Debone chicken and cut into small pieces; set aside.

To boiling water add soup mix and rice. Boil 9 minutes, uncovered. · Fry sausage; remove from skillet and drain. In sausage drippings sauté bell pepper, onion, and celery. Add this and sausage to soup mix. Season to taste with salt and curry powder. Add mushroom soup and chicken pieces.

Place mixture in large casserole dish and bake 45 minutes at 350°. Top with blanched, toasted almonds and bake an additional 15 minutes. Serves 16. Can be prepared ahead, frozen, thawed and baked.

Hospitality Heirlooms (Mississippi)

Chicken and Sausage Jambalaya

1 small fryer	1 cup chopped yellow onion
1 rib celery with leaves	¾ cup chopped green pepper
1 onion, halved	¼ cup chopped fresh parsley
1 clove garlic	2 cloves garlic, minced
2 cups converted long-grain rice	1 (6-ounce) can tomato paste
	1 large bay leaf
1 pound smoked sausage, sliced into ½-inch pieces	¼ teaspoon thyme
	2 teaspoons salt
1 pound ham, cubed	½ teaspoon pepper
½ stick butter	¼ teaspoon Tabasco

In a large pot, cover chicken with water; add celery, onion, 1 clove garlic; boil until tender, about 1 hour. Reserve stock. Remove meat from bones. In 5 cups stock, cook rice until all liquid is absorbed, about 25 minutes.

In a Dutch oven, fry sausage and ham until lightly browned, 3–5 minutes. Remove meat. Add butter to pan and sauté onion, pepper, and parsley until tender, about 3 minutes. Add chicken, sausage, and ham; stir in minced garlic, tomato paste, bay leaf, thyme, salt, pepper, and Tabasco. Add rice and mix thoroughly. Cook over low heat 15 minutes, stirring frequently. Remove bay leaf and serve. Serves 8–10.

Jambalaya (Louisiana)

The tallest capitol building in the United States (34 floors), the Louisiana State Capitol in Baton Rouge, was completed in 1932 in a mere fourteen months. Governor Huey Long was assassinated there in 1935. His statue and grave face the building he worked hard to have built.

J. C.'s Creole Jambalaya

I know you'll enjoy this one!

2 chicken bouillon cubes
1 cup hot water
1 cup chopped onion
¼ cup chopped green bell
  pepper
¼ cup chopped celery
1 teaspoon chopped garlic
¼ cup vegetable oil
1 cup chopped ham
1¼ cups short-grain rice

1 pound chopped shrimp
⅓ cup peeled, chopped
  tomatoes
1 teaspoon salt
¼ teaspoon black pepper
1 teaspoon Tabasco
1 tablespoon Tabasco jalapeño
  sauce
2 tablespoons chopped parsley

Dissolve bouillon cubes in hot water. Over medium heat, sauté onion, bell pepper, celery, and garlic in oil until wilted. Add ham and rice and stir-fry 5 minutes. Add shrimp, tomatoes, bouillon water, salt, black pepper, and Tabasco sauces, and bring to a boil. Lower heat, cover, and cook 30 minutes. Stir in parsley. Serve hot. Serves 4–6 hungry hogs!

The Hungry Hog (Louisiana)

Red Beans and Rice

2 pounds red kidney beans
2 cups chopped onions
½ cup chopped green bell
  pepper
1½ cloves garlic, mashed
2 tablespoons chopped parsley
1 pound cured ham, cubed
1 pound smoked sausage,
  sliced

1 ham bone (optional)
1 tablespoon salt
½ teaspoon pepper
½ teaspoon cayenne
2 bay leaves
½ teaspoon thyme
2 quarts water
2 cups raw rice, cooked

Soak beans overnight in water to cover.

Add remaining ingredients, except rice. Cook on low heat 3 hours. Stir the mixture only once every half hour. Remove bay leaves. Serve over fluffy rice.

The Pick of the Crop (Mississippi)

Sausage, Red Beans, and Rice Casserole

1 pound ground beef	2 teaspoons salt
1 tablespoon oil	1 tablespoon chili powder
1 large onion, chopped	Dash of black pepper
¼ bell pepper, chopped	1 cup raw rice
1 (14½-ounce) can chopped	1 (15-ounce) can kidney beans
tomatoes	¾ pound smoked sausage
1 cup water	

Brown meat in oil; add onion and bell pepper. Cook until transparent, stirring constantly. Add tomatoes, water, salt, chili powder, and black pepper. Simmer 10 minutes. Remove from fire; add raw rice and beans. Pour into buttered dish. Slice half of sausage over top, and cover with foil. Bake at 350° for 1 hour. Stir slightly, slice remainder of sausage over top, cover, and bake ½ hour longer.

Treasured Tastes (Alabama)

Broccoli-Chicken-Ham Pizza

1 ready-made pizza crust	1 (10-ounce) can white chicken
1 (10¾-ounce) can chicken,	meat, drained
mushroom, or celery soup	½ cup finely sliced or diced bell
1 pound fresh broccoli,	pepper
chopped	Chopped mushrooms (optional)
5–10 ounces chopped, thinly	1 cup grated sharp Cheddar or
sliced ham, or Canadian	mozzarella cheese
bacon	

Place prepared crust on baking stone, lightly greased pizza pan, or cookie sheet. Spread ½–¾ can of soup onto crust. Add broccoli, ham, chicken, bell pepper, and mushrooms, if desired. You can mix all together and spread evenly over crust or just sprinkle evenly over crust. Top with cheese. Bake for 20–25 minutes at 375° until golden brown.

The Tastes & Traditions of Troy State University II (Alabama)

MEATS

Cajun and zydeco music is as much a part of Louisiana's landscape as bayous and moss-draped oaks. Perhaps the most distinctive instrument of zydeco (besides the accordion) is the "frottoir" (metal washboard). Zydeco combines French dance melodies, elements of Caribbean music, and the blues.

Marinated Pepper-Crusted Beef Tenderloin

1 cup port
1 cup soy sauce
½ cup olive oil
1½ teaspoons pepper
1 teaspoon dried whole thyme
½ teaspoon Tabasco
4 cloves garlic, crushed
1 bay leaf
1 (5- to 6-pound) beef
 tenderloin, trimmed
2 tablespoons coarsely ground
 pepper

Combine port, soy sauce, olive oil, 1½ teaspoons pepper, thyme, Tabasco, garlic, and bay leaf in a bowl; mix well. Place beef in a large shallow dish. Pour port mixture over beef. Marinate, tightly covered, for 8–10 hours, turning occasionally. Drain beef, reserving marinade. Bring reserved marinade to a boil in a saucepan. Boil 3 minutes and remove from heat. Discard bay leaf.

Coat beef with 2 tablespoons coarsely ground black pepper. Place beef on a rack in a roasting pan. Insert meat thermometer into beef. Bake at 425° for 45–60 minutes or until meat thermometer registers 140° for medium-rare or 150° for medium, brushing frequently with heated reserved marinade. Garnish with fresh parsley. Yields 12 servings.

Bay Tables (Alabama)

Beef Tips with Wine

It's so easy and very good.

2 pounds beef tips or beef stew
1 (10¾-ounce) can cream of
 mushroom soup
1 soup can red wine
1 package dry onion soup mix
1 (1-pound) carton whole
 mushrooms, washed and left
 whole

Spray deep casserole dish with cooking spray. Add meat and layer with mushroom soup, wine, onion soup mix, and mushrooms. Bake at 300° for 3 hours. Good to serve with rice or egg noodles.

Mama Couldn't Cook (Alabama)

Best Brisket Ever

I have never tasted meat like this, and the gravy is good enough to drink. Try it! You won't be disappointed. This is a "must do" recipe.

1 (4- to 5-pound) brisket
  (point end), trimmed
Tony Chachere's Creole
  Seasoning
Cracked black pepper

Garlic powder
1 (10¾-ounce) can cream of
  mushroom soup
1 (10¾-ounce) can French
  onion soup

Heavily season brisket on both sides, using Tony's and lots of pepper and garlic powder. Do not use salt because there is sufficient salt in Tony's. Spoon out mushroom soup into heavy, oven-proof cooking utensil with tightly fitting lid. Place seasoned brisket fat-side-up on flat rack so it won't be directly on the bottom of whatever you are using. Place rack with brisket on top of soup. Spoon a can of French onion soup over and around the brisket. Cook covered in preheated, 350° oven for 1 hour. Lower temperature to 200° and continue to cook covered for 3 more hours. Do not remove cover during cooking. Cool. Slice cross grain with electric knife. Absolutely to die for! The gravy is so good you will want to comb it through your hair. For party buffet, serves 20–25; for family, serves 8.

Note: May add 1 can consomme for additional gravy.

Too Good To Be True (Louisiana)

Noccalula Falls, which drops a spectacular 90 feet over a Lookout Mountain ledge in Gadsden, Alabama, is named after Cherokee Princess Noccalula, who, as legend has it, threw herself from a rock ledge into the falls and died, rather than marry a wealthy neighboring chief, as arranged by her father. A statue of the legendary Princess Noccalula looks over the edge of the bluff near Noccalula Falls in Gadsden.

PHOTO COURTESY OF NORTH ALABAMA TOURISM

Barbecued Brisket

1 (5- to 6-pound) beef brisket
3 ounces liquid smoke
Garlic salt, onion salt, celery
   salt to taste
5 tablespoons Worcestershire

Salt and pepper to taste
6 ounces barbecue sauce
2 tablespoons all-purpose flour
½ cup water

In a baking dish sprayed with nonstick cooking spray, place brisket. Sprinkle with liquid smoke and 3 salts; refrigerate overnight.

When ready to bake, sprinkle with Worcestershire and salt and pepper to taste. Place foil loosely on top. Cook at 250° for 5 hours; uncover and pour barbecue sauce over meat. Cook uncovered for another hour. Remove to platter and let cool before slicing. Remove fat from sauce remaining in dish. Add flour and water to sauce and stir. Cook until sauce thickens. Serve sauce hot with brisket. Makes 10 servings.

Note: Great with rice or on sandwiches with slaw.

Temptations (Mississippi)

Pot Roast

6 green onion tops, chopped
   fine, divided
2 onions, chopped, divided
3 stalks celery, chopped fine
5 cloves garlic, chopped fine

Salt and pepper to taste
1 tablespoon Worcestershire
1 (6- to 8-pound) beef or pork
   roast
6 Irish potatoes

Mix 4 green onions, 1 chopped onion, 1 stalk celery, garlic, salt and pepper, and Worcestershire. Make deep slits in roast and stuff mixture into slits until all mixture has been used. Let set in refrigerator overnight. Put roast in roasting pan. Brown at 350°. Turn meat occasionally, adding a little water from time to time as needed. When roast is a deep dark brown all around, add water to fill half your pan. Cover and let cook about 2 hours or until meat is cooked. Add potatoes and remaining onions and celery for gravy, and let cook with roast until done. When serving, cut meat in thin slices and put potatoes around the roast. Makes a pretty dish.

Nun Better (Louisiana)

Rump Roast with Gravy

1 (3½-pound) rump roast	½ cup plain flour
3½ cups water, divided	
2 envelopes Lipton Beefy Onion Soup	

Pour a little oil or spray in bottom of heated iron skillet. Sear the roast on all exposed surfaces, being careful not to puncture the roast. It is not necessary to brown the roast; searing seals in the juices.

Place the roast in an enamel roasting pan. Pour 2 cups water in skillet and sprinkle with soup. Stir with a metal spatula. Pour mixture over the roast and put cover on pan. Place in 350° oven and cook for approximately 2½ hours (about 45 minutes per pound) or until fork-tender. Remove roast to platter or serving plate, reserving the juices.

With a wire whisk, gradually add remaining 1½ cups water to flour, and mix until smooth. Pour reserved juices from roasting pan into a saucepan. Slowly add flour/water mixture, stirring rapidly to prevent lumping. Heat. It may be necessary to add more water if gravy is too thick. You may add a little Kitchen Bouquet to the gravy for a richer color (usually not necessary).

The roast will cut more evenly if it has cooled for 20–30 minutes. Carve roast across the grain for maximum tenderness.

More Cultured Country Cooking (Alabama)

RANDOM HOUSE.COM

John Grisham once called Oxford, Mississippi, home. It was there that he wrote many of his best-selling novels. His novels include: *A Time to Kill, The Firm, The Pelican Brief, The Client, The Chamber, The Rainmaker, The Runaway Jury, The Partner, The Street Lawyer, The Testament, The Brethren, A Painted House, Skipping Christmas, The Summons, The King of Torts, Bleachers, The Last Juror, The Broker, The Appeal, Playing for Pizza,* and *The Associate* . Eight of his novels have been made into films: *The Firm, The Pelican Brief, The Client, A Time to Kill, The Rainmaker, The Chamber, A Painted House,* and *Runaway Jury.* In 1983, he was elected to the Mississippi House of Representatives and served until 1990.

Grillades

4 pounds beef/veal rounds, ½ inch thick	2 cups chopped tomatoes
½ cup bacon drippings, divided	½ teaspoon tarragon (optional)
½ cup flour, divided	⅔ teaspoon thyme
1 cup chopped onions	1 cup water
2 cups chopped green onions	1 cup red wine
¾ cup chopped celery	3 teaspoons salt
1½ cups chopped green bell pepper	½ teaspoon black pepper
2 cloves garlic, minced	2 bay leaves
	½ teaspoon Tabasco
	2 tablespoons Worcestershire
	3 tablespoons chopped parsley

Remove fat from meat. Cut meat into serving-size pieces. Pound to ¼-inch thickness. In a Dutch oven, brown meat well in 4 tablespoons bacon grease. As meat browns, remove to warm plate. To Dutch oven, add 4 tablespoons bacon grease and flour. Stir and cook to make a dark brown roux. Add onions, green onions, celery, green pepper, and garlic, and sauté until limp. Add tomatoes, tarragon, and thyme, and cook for 3 minutes. Add water and wine. Stir well for several minutes; return meat; add salt, pepper, bay leaves, Tabasco, and Worcestershire. Lower heat, stir, and continue cooking. If veal rounds are used, simmer covered approximately one hour. If beef rounds are used, simmer covered approximately 2 hours. Remove bay leaves. Stir in parsley; cool; let grillades sit several hours or overnight in refrigerator.

More liquid may be added. Grillades should be very tender. Heat and serve over grits or rice.

The Plantation Cookbook (Louisiana)

The origin of grillades (pronounced GREE-yahds) has been the subject of many arguments in Louisiana Bayou Country. Like many other great dishes from New Orleans, it comes from meager times, when a piece of meat needed to be stretched to feed a whole family. Today, grillades and grits are a Louisiana tradition and can be found even on the finest tables of New Orleans.

Chicken Fried Steak and Cream Gravy

2 pounds boneless round steak	½ teaspoon garlic salt
1 cup all-purpose flour	2 eggs
1 teaspoon salt	¼ cup milk
1 teaspoon pepper	Vegetable oil

Trim excess fat from steak; pound steak to ¼-inch thickness, using a meat mallet. Cut into serving-size pieces. Combine flour, salt, pepper, and garlic salt. Combine eggs and milk; beat well. Dredge steak in flour mixture, dip in egg mixture, then dredge in flour mixture again. Lightly pound steak. Heat 1 inch of oil in a skillet to 375°. Fry steak in hot oil until browned, turning steak once. Drain steak on paper towels. Reserve ¼ cup pan drippings for gravy. Serve steak with Cream Gravy. Yields 6–8 servings.

CREAM GRAVY:

¼ cup all-purpose flour	½ teaspoon salt
¼ cup pan drippings	¼ teaspoon pepper
2–3 cups milk	

Add flour to pan drippings; cook over medium heat until bubbly, stirring constantly. Gradually add milk; cook until thickened and bubbly, stirring constantly. Stir in salt and pepper.

Golden Moments (Mississippi)

Pepper Steak

1 pound round steak	1 medium onion, sliced
2 teaspoons plus 1 tablespoon cornstarch, divided	1 or 2 green peppers, sliced
2 or 3 tablespoons soy sauce, divided	¼ cup water
	1 (4-ounce) can sliced mushrooms
2 teaspoons cooking oil	

Slice steak in thin strips. If steak is partially frozen, it is easier to cut (freeze about one hour). Marinate in 2 teaspoons cornstarch and a little soy sauce for about 20 minutes. Stir-fry in oil until pink is gone. Add onion and pepper slices. Sauté about 3 minutes. Add one cup water and soy sauce to taste. Turn down heat and simmer, covered, for approximately 30 minutes. You may simmer longer and add water if dinner is delayed. Just before serving, add about one tablespoon cornstarch dissolved in water. Add mushrooms. Serve hot over rice.

Variation: Other vegetables can be added such as one can sliced water chestnuts, or 2 cups bamboo shoots, or one cup celery sliced into thin strips.

Feeding His Flock (Mississippi)

Swiss Steak

2 pounds round steak, cut into serving pieces	1 cup chopped onion
Salt and cayenne pepper to taste	½ cup chopped bell peppers
	½ cup chopped celery
¼ cup flour	2 cups water
4 tablespoons shortening	1 (16-ounce) can whole tomatoes
1 bay leaf	1 cup chopped mushrooms
	3 small chopped carrots

Season meat well using salt and pepper. Dust in flour. In a heavy iron skillet, brown meat on all sides in oil until done. Remove and set aside. Add all seasonings. Sauté until done (approximately 5 minutes). Add water. Bring to a rapid boil, reducing heat to simmer. Add meat, and all the vegetables. Cover and cook over medium heat approximately 2 hours.

Editor's Extra: Good to serve over rice.

The Encyclopedia of Cajun and Creole Cuisine (Louisiana)

Spicy Meat Loaf

1 pound ground beef
8 ounces lean hot sausage
½ large onion, minced
1 rib celery, chopped
1 egg, beaten
1 teaspoon MSG (optional)
¼ teaspoon garlic salt

½ teaspoon salt
½ teaspoon pepper
6 ounces chili sauce
¼ cup milk
1 cup herb-seasoned stuffing
  mix
Tomato Sauce

Combine ground beef, sausage, onion, celery, egg, MSG, garlic salt, salt, pepper, chili sauce, milk, and stuffing mix in a large bowl; mix well using your hands. Shape into a loaf. Press into greased 5x9-inch loaf pan. Bake at 350° for 1 hour. Remove from oven and pour off excess grease. Spread Tomato Sauce over top. Bake 15 minutes or until cooked through. Makes 8 servings.

TOMATO SAUCE:

1 (16-ounce) can chopped
  tomatoes
1 (6-ounce) can tomato paste

2 tablespoons minced onion
2 teaspoons oregano

Combine tomatoes, tomato paste, onion, and oregano in a bowl and mix well. Yields about 3 cups.

Savor the Spirit (Alabama)

Helen Keller was born June 27, 1880, in Tuscumbia, Alabama. She lost her sight and hearing at nineteen months old. With the help of Anne Sullivan, better known as the Miracle Worker, Helen grew up to become a famous speaker who helped to set up the American Foundation for the Blind. The first U.S. circulating coin to feature braille, the Alabama quarter features an image of Helen Keller with her name in English, as well as in a reduced-size version of braille. In 1954, Helen Keller's birthplace "Ivy Green" was placed on the National Register of Historic Places. Here you can see and touch the actual well-pump where Anne Sullivan reach into the dark, silent world of Helen's mind and opened the window of communication.

Meatloaf Stuffed Tomato

3 teaspoons minced garlic
½ cup diced red onions
½ cup diced white onions
2 tablespoons oil
2½ pounds ground beef
  tenderloin
¾ cup toasted bread crumbs

1 cup shredded Parmesan
  cheese, divided
Salt and pepper to taste
6 large tomatoes (cored and
  insides removed)
½ cup Maytag blue cheese
  (crumbled)

Sauté vegetables in oil. Add meat and bread crumbs and brown to medium. Once cooked, add ½ the Parmesan cheese and blend until melted. Season with salt and pepper. Cool in large container covered with perforated plastic wrap to allow steam to escape. When cool, add blue cheese. Place 3-ounce portion into tomato. Bake at 350° for 10 minutes. Garnish with remaining Parmesan and top with Brown Gravy. Yields 6 servings.

BROWN GRAVY:
¾ cup ketchup
½ cup red wine

4 teaspoons Worcestershire

Combine ingredients in saucepan and heat over medium heat. Serve over baked tomatoes.

Recipe from Julep Restaurant and Bar, Jackson
Fine Dining Mississippi Style (Mississippi)

Meatballs in Brown Gravy

Meatballs and gravy may be served over steaming rice, but it is best over spaghetti, topped with Parmesan cheese. Petit pois add a nice finishing touch as a side dish. This freezes well and leftovers make delicious po-boys!

MEATBALLS:

2½–3 pounds ground beef
1 pound lean ground pork
3 teaspoons salt
½ teaspoon red pepper
½ teaspoon black pepper

1 tablespoon ketchup
⅓ cup finely chopped onion
2 slices broken white bread,
  soaked in ⅔ cup milk
⅓ cup oatmeal

To make meatballs, place all ingredients in a large bowl and mix together well. Form balls of desired size, about 3 dozen. Roll lightly in flour. Cover bottom of large skillet with vegetable oil, heat to medium, and brown meatballs on all sides. Remove from skillet, and drain on paper towels.

BROWN GRAVY:

½ cup oil
¾ cup flour
1 large onion, finely chopped
½ green pepper, finely chopped

2 cloves garlic, finely chopped
5–6 cups hot water
1 (14½-ounce) can beef broth
  (optional)

To prepare gravy, make a roux with oil and flour. When roux becomes a dark brown, add onion, pepper, and garlic. Sauté until tender, then add hot water and beef broth. Allow this mixture to boil 15–20 minutes, stirring occasionally.

Add meatballs and reduce heat to medium. Cover and cook 1 hour. Add water, if needed, to thin gravy to desired consistency, stirring occasionally. Serves 14–16.

Louisiana LEGACY (Louisiana)

Spaghetti Sauce

SAUCE:

2 large onions, chopped fine
3 pounds ground steak*
Oil
6 (6-ounce) cans thick tomato
  paste
6–8 cans water
6 cloves garlic, chopped fine

6 pieces celery, chopped fine
2 tablespoons salt
2 tablespoons sugar
3 tablespoons chili powder
2 bay leaves
1 teaspoon leaf oregano
Red and black pepper

Brown onions and meat in oil; add remaining ingredients. Cover and cook slowly 4 hours.

Note: If making meatballs, use half the meat in sauce and half in meatballs. Serves 12.

MEATBALLS FOR SPAGHETTI:

1½ pounds ground steak
  (from above)
5 slices bread, crustless,
  moistened
2 cloves garlic, chopped fine
2 teaspoons salt

1 tablespoon grated Parmesan
  cheese
1 small onion, chopped
1 teaspoon chili powder
4 eggs

Put meat in bowl; add crumbled bread and other ingredients. Add eggs and mix thoroughly. Roll into balls and chill. Fry in oil until brown; cool. Put in sauce and cook slowly for about an hour. Makes 24 meatballs.

Editor's Extra: Meatballs may be baked in 375° oven for 15 minutes before adding to sauce.

Gourmet of the Delta (Mississippi)

The Pascagoula River, also known as Singing River, makes a strange singing sound resembling a swarm of bees in flight. Scientists have said the sound could be made by fish, or sand scraping the hard bottom of the river, or natural gas escaping from a sand bed—but the cause has never been proven. Legend has it that the tribe of Pascagoula Indians, realizing they could not win a battle with the Biloxi tribe, walked singing into the river to their deaths . . . their voices can still be heard.

Red-Neck Spaghetti Sauce

2 ounces olive oil
2 onions, chopped
2 pounds ground beef
1 tablespoon minced garlic
½ cup diced celery
1 tablespoon parsley flakes
½ cup chopped mushrooms
2 tablespoons sugar
½ teaspoon black pepper
½ teaspoon salt
1 teaspoon Italian seasoning
½ teaspoon marjoram
4 cups tomato sauce
2 cups stewed tomatoes
2 ounces red wine
8 ounces water
2 ounces grated Cheddar cheese

Put olive oil, onions, and beef in a large heavy pot. Cook over medium heat until beef is brown. Add remaining ingredients and simmer for at least 4 hours—the longer the better. (You may have to add a little more water after a few hours.) Serve over cooked, drained spaghetti. Serves 12–15.

Temptations (Mississippi)

Beef Stroganoff

3 tablespoons flour
1½ teaspoons salt
¼ teaspoon pepper
1 pound beef tenderloin,
  ¼ inch thick
1 clove garlic, halved
¼ cup butter or margarine
½ cup minced onion
¼ cup water
1 (10¾-ounce) can cream of
  chicken soup, undiluted
1 pound sliced mushrooms
1 cup commercial sour cream
Snipped parsley, chives, or dill

Combine flour, salt and pepper. Trim fat from meat. Rub both sides of meat with garlic. With rim of saucer, pound flour mixture into both sides of meat. Cut meat into 1- or 1½-inch strips. In hot butter in Dutch oven or deep skillet, brown meat strips, turning them often. Add onion; sauté until golden. Add water; stir to dissolve brown bits in bottom of Dutch oven. Add soup and mushrooms; cook uncovered over low heat, stirring occasionally, until mixture is thick and meat is fork-tender, about 20 minutes. Just before serving, stir in sour cream; heat but do not boil. Sprinkle with parsley. Serve with hot fluffy rice or wild rice, boiled noodles, or mashed potatoes. Makes 4–6 servings.

Hospitality Heirlooms (Mississippi)

Firecracker Casserole

2 pounds ground beef
1 medium onion, chopped
1 (15-ounce) can black beans,
   rinsed, drained
1–2 tablespoons chili powder
2–3 teaspoons ground cumin
½ teaspoon salt
4 (7-inch) flour tortillas

1 (10¾-ounce) can condensed
   cream of mushroom soup,
   undiluted
1 (10-ounce) can diced tomatoes
   and green chiles, undrained
1 cup (4 ounces) shredded
   Cheddar cheese

In a skillet, cook beef and onion until meat is no longer pink;
drain. Add beans, chili powder, cumin, and salt. Transfer to a
greased 9x13-inch baking dish. Arrange tortillas over the top.
Combine soup and tomatoes; pour over tortillas. Sprinkle with
cheese. Bake uncovered at 350° for 25–30 minutes, or until heated thoroughly. Serves 8.

Picnic in the Park (Mississippi)

Easy Chop Suey

2 pounds ground beef
1 cup chopped onion
1 cup chopped celery
½ cup chopped bell pepper
1 cup rice, uncooked
1 (10¾-ounce) can cream of
   mushroom soup
1 (10¾-ounce) can cream of
   chicken soup
¼ cup soy sauce

1 tablespoon pepper
1 (15-ounce) can bean sprouts
   (save liquid)
1 (4-ounce) can mushrooms
   (save liquid)
1 (8-ounce) can water chestnuts,
   drained, sliced
1½ cups liquid (water plus
   saved juices)
1 can Chow Mein noodles

Brown beef in skillet. Add onion, celery, and bell pepper; sauté
until tender. Drain excess fat. Add rice, undiluted soups, and
other ingredients except noodles. Mix well. Place in 3-quart
casserole (or 2 [2-quart] casseroles and freeze one). Bake at 350°
for 45 minutes. Top with noodles and return to oven until noodles are toasted.

Sumpthn' Yummy (Alabama)

Mock Filet

1 pound ground beef
1 cup cracker crumbs
1 egg, beaten
⅓ cup ketchup
¼ cup lemon juice
1 cup grated Cheddar cheese

¼ cup chopped green bell
  pepper
2 tablespoons chopped onion
Salt and pepper to taste
Bacon slices

Combine all ingredients except bacon. Preheat oven to 400°. Make into patties and wrap ½ slice of bacon around each patty. Bake 15–20 minutes.

The Mississippi Cookbook (Mississippi)

Tommy's Beef Jerky

Perfect for boy scout trips as well as divine with a drink.

Round steak or flank steak
  (7 pounds will net about
   3 pounds jerky)
Lemon pepper
Seasoned salt

Garlic salt
Soy sauce
Juice of 2 lemons
Worcestershire

Have butcher slice meat thin with the grain, into strips. If you choose to slice it yourself, it is easier to do if meat is slightly frozen. Be sure to trim off all fat.

Season both sides of meat and marinate in soy sauce, Worcestershire, and lemon juice about 6 hours or overnight in refrigerator.

When ready to bake, place strips on a rack with a drip pan underneath. Cook at 200° for about 6 hours. The meat will be dark and very dry in appearance.

This meat will keep safely for a long time, however, it is so good you'll have trouble keeping it at all.

Pineapple Gold (Mississippi)

Natchitoches Meat Pies

Be sure to make the roux. It makes all the difference in this recipe.

FILLING:

2 tablespoons flour	½ pound ground beef
1 tablespoon oil	½ pound ground pork
2 large onions, chopped	3 tablespoons chopped parsley
6 green onions, chopped	Salt and pepper to taste

Make a roux with flour and oil. Add all the other ingredients; salt and pepper to taste and cook thoroughly. Cool in refrigerator before making pies.

PASTRY:

½ cup Crisco, melted	2 eggs, beaten
2 teaspoons baking powder	Milk to make stiff dough
1½ teaspoons salt	4 cups all-purpose flour

Mix all ingredients in a large bowl, adding enough flour to make the dough stiff. Turn out on floured surface. Roll and cut out circles the size of a saucer. Place chilled meat on half the circle; fold over, dampen edges, and crimp with a fork. Fry pies in deep vegetable shortening until golden brown, turning once.

Recipes from Bayou Pierre Country (Louisiana)

Reuben Pie

1 egg, beaten	1 (8-ounce) can sauerkraut,
⅓ cup evaporated milk	drained, snipped
¾ cup rye bread crumbs	12 ounces corned beef, chopped
¼ cup chopped onion	(1½ cups thinly sliced)
¼ teaspoon salt	Pie pastry for 1 deep-dish pie
Dash of pepper	crust
½ teaspoon prepared mustard	6 ounces Swiss cheese, grated
½ ground chuck, browned	

In mixing bowl, combine first 7 ingredients. Add chuck, sauerkraut, and corned beef. Mix well. Place half of meat mixture into pastry shell and sprinkle with half of cheese. Cover with remaining meat mixture. Top with cheese and bake at 400° for 25–30 minutes. Serves 6.

Southern Sideboards (Mississippi)

Farmhouse BBQ Muffins

1 (10-count) can buttermilk
  biscuits
1 pound ground beef
½ cup ketchup

3 tablespoons brown sugar
½ teaspoon chili powder
1 cup shredded cheese

Press each biscuit into bottom of greased muffin pan. Brown beef and drain. In bowl, mix ketchup, brown sugar, and chili powder; stir until smooth. Add meat and mix well. Divide mix into biscuit cups. Sprinkle with cheese. Bake at 375° for 18–20 minutes.

Picnic in the Park (Mississippi)

Sticky Bones

1 cup vinegar
½ cup ketchup
½ cup honey
2 tablespoons Worcestershire
1 teaspoon salt

1 teaspoon ground mustard
1 teaspoon paprika
1 clove garlic, minced
¼ teaspoon pepper
4 pounds bone-in beef short ribs

In a saucepan, combine vinegar, ketchup, honey, Worcestershire, salt, mustard, paprika, garlic, and pepper. Bring to a boil. Reduce heat; cover and simmer for 15 minutes. Set aside one cup for basting. Place ribs in a greased roasting pan; pour remaining marinade over ribs. Cover and refrigerate for at least 2 hours.

  Drain and discard marinade. Bake, uncovered, at 325° for one hour or until meat is tender, basting frequently with reserved marinade. Makes 4 servings.

Simply Southern (Mississippi)

Pork Rub

1 tablespoon finely ground
  lemon peel
1 tablespoon garlic powder
1 tablespoon onion salt
1 tablespoon chili powder

1 tablespoon paprika
½ tablespoon each: white, red,
  and black pepper
2 tablespoons salt
3 tablespoons dark brown sugar

Mix all ingredients together, removing all the lumps. Store in tight container.

From the Firehouse to Your House (Mississippi)

Sam's Ole Time BBQ Sauce

4 tablespoons shortening
1 cup chopped onion
4 tablespoons vinegar
4 tablespoons brown sugar
½ cup lemon juice
6 tablespoons Worcestershire
2 cups water

2 tablespoons liquid smoke
2 tablespoons salt
¼ tablespoon cayenne pepper
  (for medium, ½ tablespoon;
  for hot, 1 tablespoon)
2 cups ketchup

Heat shortening. Stir in onion and brown. Pour off drippings. Add remaining ingredients, and cook over low heat for 25 minutes or until thick.

Great American Recipes from Southern 'n' Cajun Cook'n'
(Mississippi)

Pork Tenderloin with Mustard Sauce

2 pounds whole pork
  tenderloin (1–1½ inches
  in diameter)
1 clove garlic, cut in half

1½ teaspoons salt
1 cup red wine
½ teaspoon onion salt
½ teaspoon Beau Monde

Thoroughly rub tenderloin with cut garlic. Sprinkle with salt, and bake in a shallow baking pan about 1¼ hours (until tender) at 325°. Combine wine, onion salt, and Beau Monde, and simmer 1 minute.

MUSTARD SAUCE:
1 cup mayonnaise
1 tablespoon honey
1 tablespoon finely chopped
  fresh parsley

2 teaspoons prepared mustard
1 teaspoon curry powder
½ teaspoon paprika

Combine all ingredients. Slice tenderloin, pour hot wine sauce over slices, and serve Mustard Sauce in a separate dish. Serves 4–6.

Bravo! Applaudable Recipes (Alabama)

Grilled Pork Loin with Honey Sauce

¾ cup margarine
1 cup honey
1 cup Worcestershire
½ cup Italian dressing
¼ cup lemon juice
3 tablespoons mustard
2 tablespoons brown sugar

2 teaspoons garlic salt
1½ teaspoons celery salt
1½ teaspoons onion powder
1 teaspoon pepper
1 teaspoon liquid smoke
1 (3- to 4-pound) split pork loin

Melt margarine in saucepan. Add remaining ingredients, except loin, to make sauce. Bring to a boil. Reduce heat and simmer 2 minutes.

Place loin on grill over medium-high heat. Sear both sides. Baste thoroughly with sauce. Turn and baste every 15 minutes until cooked, approximately 2½ hours. (Thicker cuts will require longer cooking time.) Serves 8.

Dinner on the Ground (Louisiana)

Marinated Pork Tenders on the Grill

½ cup soy sauce
½ cup dry sherry
2 cloves garlic, minced
1 tablespoon dry mustard

1 teaspoon thyme
1 teaspoon ginger
5 pounds pork tenders

About 24 hours ahead, mix together all marinade ingredients. Put tenders in refrigerator overnight, shifting the meat in the marinade from time to time.

When the fire is ready, remove meat from marinade. Cook on grill for about an hour, depending on size of tenders. Base with marinade while cooking. Serves 12.

One of a Kind (Alabama)

Alabama is home to Dreamland Bar-B-Q Ribs, which serves what many people consider some of the best ribs in the world. In the original restaurant in Tuscaloosa, there are no side dishes . . . only ribs, bread, and sauce. The original restaurant was started by John "Big Daddy" Bishop (whose pipe-smoking likeness you see on their logo) in 1958, and was little more than a shack built around an outdoor-style pit barbecue.

Mandarin Pork Chops

4 (4-ounce) center-cut pork
  chops
1 tablespoon vegetable oil
½ cup orange juice
¼ cup water
3 tablespoons brown sugar
2 tablespoons lemon juice

1 tablespoon cornstarch
2 teaspoons chicken bouillon
  granules
1 (11-ounce) can Mandarin
  oranges, drained
1 medium green bell pepper,
  sliced

Brown pork chops on both sides in oil in a skillet. Remove from skillet and set aside. Add orange juice, water, brown sugar, lemon juice, cornstarch, and bouillon to skillet. Cook until thickened, stirring constantly. Add pork chops. Simmer, covered, for 20 minutes or until pork chops are tender and cooked through. Add oranges and bell pepper. Cook until heated through. Yields 4 servings.

Calling All Cooks, Four (Alabama)

Pork Chops with Apples, Onions, and Raisins

4 pork chops, center cut
  (1½ inches thick)
Salt and pepper to taste
1 tablespoon cooking oil
1 large yellow onion, sliced

¼ cup raisins
1 large sweet apple, cut in
  wedges
1 ounce port wine
⅓ stick butter

Use a 10- or 12-inch skillet that can be covered. Season chops with salt and pepper. Oil skillet and brown chops well on both sides. Place sliced onion over chops, and cover skillet. Cook slowly for 15 minutes. Remove cover. Place pork chops over the onions. Sprinkle raisins around pan bottom. Place wedged apple around chops, add wine, cover and simmer 15 minutes. Turn apple wedges during cooking to assure even cooking. Remove skillet top and simmer an additional 5 minutes to thicken sauce. Serve chops with sauce, and apples, onions, and raisins garnish. Serves 4.

Paul Naquin's French Collection II: Meats & Poultry (Louisiana)

Pork Chop Casserole

6 pork chops, boneless,
  trimmed
Seasoned salt
1 (10¾-ounce) can cream of
  celery soup
½ cup milk
½ cup sour cream
¼ teaspoon black pepper
1 (24-ounce) package hash
  brown potatoes, thawed
1 cup shredded Cheddar cheese,
  divided
1 (3½-ounce) can French-fried
  onions, divided

Brown pork chops in lightly greased skillet. Sprinkle with seasoned salt, and set aside. Combine soup, milk, sour cream, pepper, and ½ teaspoon seasoned salt. Stir in potatoes, ½ cup
cheese, and ½ can onions. Spoon mixture into a 9x13-inch glass
baking dish. Arrange pork chops over potatoes. Bake, covered, in
a preheated 350° oven for 40 minutes. Top with remaining cheese
and onions. Bake uncovered for 5 minutes longer. Yields 8–10
servings.

With Special Distinction (Mississippi)

Pork Chops in Mushroom Gravy

2 (1-inch-thick) loin pork chops
2 tablespoons all-purpose flour
1 teaspoon paprika
Salt and pepper to taste
1 tablespoon oil
1 small onion, minced
½ green bell pepper, minced
6–8 mushrooms, chopped
1 cup milk
Juice of ½ lemon

Remove excess fat from edge of chops. Combine flour, paprika,
salt and pepper; dredge chops in mixture. Set aside remaining
flour mixture. Brown chops in oil and remove to shallow casserole. Add onion, green pepper, and mushrooms to skillet; sauté
until soft. Add reserved flour mixture; cook, stirring, 3 minutes.
Blend in milk and cook until thickened, stirring constantly. Stir in
lemon juice. Pour sauce over chops; cover and bake at 350° for 1
hour. Remove cover and bake 10 more minutes. Yields 2 servings.

Bell's Best 2 (Mississippi)

Baked Liver and Onions
(with Bacon)

6 slices bacon, divided
2 large onions
¼ stick butter or margarine
½ cup dry red wine
¼ cup chopped parsley
1 bay leaf, crumbled

1 teaspoon thyme
6 slices beef liver
1 teaspoon salt
Freshly ground black pepper
½ cup water
½ cup flour

Place 3 slices bacon on bottom of baking dish. Cut onions into ½-inch slices, and arrange in baking dish on top of bacon. Add 3 slices bacon on top of onions and dot with butter. Add wine, parsley, bay leaf, thyme, salt, pepper, and ½ cup water. Cover and bake in preheated oven (350°) for 30 minutes.

Coat liver with flour; place on top of bacon and onion slices, then cover and bake 30 minutes. Baste 2 or 3 times. Remove cover and bake 10 minutes. Serves 6. Try it!

Tony Chachere's Cajun Country Cookbook (Louisiana)

Rack of Lamb

Be sure your butcher trims between the bones. This is called "Frenching" the lamb.

1½ cups packed fresh parsley
(leaves and stems)
6 tablespoons chopped fresh
rosemary
6 tablespoons grated Parmesan
cheese

3 garlic cloves
9 tablespoons olive oil
Salt and pepper to taste
1 (4½- to 5-pound) rack of
lamb, at room temperature

Combine parsley, rosemary, cheese, and garlic in a food processor and process until it reaches coarse paste consistency. Add olive oil in a fine stream, processing constantly. Season the pesto with salt and pepper.

Place lamb on a rimmed baking sheet. Sprinkle with salt and pepper. Spread the pesto evenly over the rounded side of the lamb, using all of the pesto. Roast on center oven rack at 450° for 10 minutes. Reduce oven temperature to 400°. Roast 15 minutes longer for medium-rare, or to the desired degree of doneness. Cut the lamb between the bones into chops. Divide chops among 6 dinner plates. Garnish with fresh rosemary sprigs. Yields 6 servings.

Southern Scrumptious Entertains (Alabama)

POULTRY

Avery Island is the home of Tabasco sauce, abundant wildlife, and a jungle garden and bird sanctuary. Its "Bird City" is home to thousands of Snowy Egrets.

Smothered Chicken

1 (3-pound) fryer
Salt and pepper to taste
½ cup vegetable oil
½ cup flour
1 cup chopped onions
1 cup chopped celery
3 cloves garlic, chopped
½ cup chopped green onions
(reserve tops to garnish)
1 small bell pepper, chopped
1 cup chopped mushrooms
1 quart water

Cut fryer into serving pieces and season with salt and pepper; set aside. In a heavy pot, make roux using oil and flour. Cook until brown. Add all seasonings except mushrooms. Sauté until done (15 minutes). Add chicken and stir well. Cook approximately 20 minutes. Add water, mushrooms and green onion tops. Cover and let simmer for approximately 1 hour. Season to taste.

The Encyclopedia of Cajun and Creole Cuisine (Louisiana)

Mississippi Fried Chicken

6 chicken breast halves
Salt and pepper to taste
1 cup all-purpose flour
½ teaspoon salt
½ teaspoon black pepper
1 teaspoon baking powder
Cooking oil

In colander, rinse chicken breasts. Salt and pepper. Let stand to drain. In plastic sack, combine flour, salt, pepper, and baking powder. Shake chicken in this mixture until well coated. Put chicken in refrigerator for ½–6 hours.

Put 1 inch cooking oil in large skillet. Heat to medium high. Place chicken pieces in skillet. When they are hot and cooking well, turn heat to medium low. Cook 7–10 minutes on each side or until well browned. Serves 6.

Best of Bayou Cuisine (Mississippi)

The Best Fried Chicken

5–6 pieces of chicken	**Buttermilk**
1 teaspoon salt	**2–3 cups self-rising flour**

When you buy fresh chicken to fry, I recommend immediately skinning and rinsing it well. Place the chicken in an airtight container with water, some ice, and salt. (The amount of salt depends on the amount of chicken. For 5–6 pieces, 1 teaspoon of salt dissolved in water is enough.) When we prepare our chicken this way at the Irondale Cafe, we never add extra salt. Store the chicken in the refrigerator for up to 2 days; drain water, and pour buttermilk over chicken. Return it to the refrigerator until you are ready to fry it.

Sift flour into a large mixing bowl; set aside. Remove cleaned and skinned chicken from refrigerator. Remove from buttermilk and place on platter; let excess buttermilk drain off. Place drained chicken into flour, turning to coat well, patting it on if necessary.

Heat oil in frying pan or fryer to approximately 350°. Place pieces of chicken in pan (place chicken breasts with the thick side down, bone turned toward center of pan). You may have to turn the heat down some, but remember that the cold chicken will cool the oil, and if the oil is not hot enough, the chicken will absorb the oil and be soggy.

Fry at medium-high heat approximately 7 minutes; turn chicken over; brown other side for 6–7 minutes. Be sure chicken is well done. Fry dark meat as long as white meat because of the larger bones in the leg and thigh.

Note: You may cover the chicken and let it steam for a few minutes, but for crispier chicken, leave it uncovered.

Irondale Cafe Original WhistleStop Cookbook (Alabama)

The Irondale Cafe in Irondale, Alabama, is the setting for the novel *Fried Green Tomatoes at the Whistle Stop Cafe* by Alabama native Fannie Flagg. The first edition was published in 1987. It is the story is of an unfulfilled housewife who befriends an elderly woman in a nursing home. The older woman tells her life story in the now-abandoned town of Whistle Stop, Alabama, and helps the younger woman to cope with her own life. In January 1992, the movie *Fried Green Tomatoes* hit the big screen.

In 1972, the McMichael family bought the Irondale Cafe from Ms. Flagg's great Aunt Bess. The little cafe has grown from a seating capacity of 32 seats in 1972 to 260 seats in 2005. Everyone who comes to the cafe for the first time wants to know all about Miss Bess and the restaurant, and almost all the customers, new and old, order fried green tomatoes. The Irondale Cafe fries 60–70 pounds of fried green tomatoes every weekday . . . and more than that on Sundays!

Spicy Fried Chicken

3 pounds chicken parts, or 1
  (2½-pound) fryer, cut up
½ cup all-purpose flour
1 teaspoon salt or garlic salt
1 teaspoon dry mustard
1 teaspoon chili powder
1 teaspoon paprika
½ teaspoon cayenne pepper
¼ teaspoon freshly ground
  pepper
Corn oil

Dry chicken pieces on paper towels. Combine flour and seasoning in paper bag. Place chicken pieces a few at a time in bag, twist
end, and shake vigorously to coat chicken well. Heat 1½ inches
corn oil in deep skillet until temperature reaches 365°. Lower
chicken into hot oil and cook 8–10 minutes to a side or until gold-
en brown. Lift out and drain well on paper towels. Serves 3–4.

Loaves and Fishes (Alabama)

Baked Chicken Breasts

½ cup grated Parmesan
  cheese
2 cups seasoned bread
  crumbs
3 tablespoons sesame seeds
3–4 chicken breasts
½ cup butter, melted

Mix first three above ingredients. Dip pieces of chicken breasts
into melted butter and then into crumb mixture. (Can freeze or
refrigerate until ready to cook.) Bring to room temperature to
cook. Place in shallow pan, dot with butter, and bake 1 hour at
350°. Serve with Cumberland Sauce.

CUMBERLAND SAUCE:
1 cup red currant jelly
1 (6-ounce) can frozen orange
  juice
4 tablespoons dry sherry
1 teaspoon dry mustard
¼ teaspoon ginger
¼ teaspoon hot pepper sauce

Combine and simmer until smooth.

More Fiddling with Food (Alabama)

Poppy Seed Chicken

2 pounds chicken breasts,
  cooked, boned and cubed
1 (8-ounce) carton sour cream
1 (10¾-ounce) can cream of
  chicken soup

1 stack Ritz Crackers
1 tablespoon poppy seeds
1 stick margarine, melted

Place chicken in casserole dish. Mix sour cream and soup. Pour over chicken. Mix cracker crumbs, melted margarine, and poppy seeds. Sprinkle over top. Bake 30 minutes at 350°.

Treasured Favorites (Alabama)

Chicken Parmesan

1½ cups Italian bread crumbs
  (or homemade)
½ cup grated Parmesan
  cheese

1 tablespoon salt
1 teaspoon pepper
6 chicken breast halves
1½–2 sticks butter, melted

Combine crumbs, cheese, salt, and pepper. Dip breasts in melted butter, then in crumb mixture, being careful to coat breasts evenly.

Place breasts skin side up in a buttered baking dish and bake in a 350° oven for 35–40 minutes. Do not turn chicken.

Recipe may be prepared the day before and refrigerated, then baked. Also freezes well both before and after baking. To reheat after thawed, heat in a 325° oven.

Pineapple Gold (Mississippi)

What does the word Mississippi mean? The name roughly translated from Native American folklore means "Father of Waters." The translation comes from the Chippewa words "mici zibi" meaning "great river" or "gathering in of all the waters," and the Algonquin word "Messipi," meaning "big river."

Italian Chicken Delight

6 boned and skinned breast
  halves
1 egg, beaten
¾ cup Italian bread crumbs
½ cup oil
1 (15-ounce) can tomato sauce

Salt and pepper to taste
1 tablespoon butter
1 tablespoon basil
Generous amount garlic powder
¾ cup grated Parmesan cheese
Mozzarella cheese

Dip chicken breasts halves into beaten egg, coating well. Roll breasts in bread crumbs. Brown in oil. Drain chicken and place in casserole dish in single layer.

To oil in skillet, add tomato sauce, salt, pepper, butter, basil, and garlic powder. Simmer and pour over chicken. Sprinkle with Parmesan cheese. Seal top with foil. Bake at 350° for 30 minutes. Uncover and top with triangles of mozzarella cheese. Bake 10 more minutes. Serves 4–6.

Bouquet Garni (Mississippi)

Creamy Chicken Enchiladas

4 skinless, boneless chicken
  breast halves
1 tablespoon butter
2 tablespoons chopped onion
2 tablespoons chopped green
  chiles
1 (3-ounce) package cream
  cheese, diced

10 corn tortillas
1 cup grated Cheddar cheese
1 cup grated Monterey Jack
  cheese with jalapeño peppers
1 cup salsa
1 cup whipping cream

Cook chicken (poach or grill) until done, and cube. In a saucepan, melt butter. Add onion and sautè until translucent. Add green chiles and cream cheese; stir constantly until blended. Remove from heat; stir in chicken. Soften tortillas according to package directions. Place 3 tablespoons chicken in center of each tortilla. Top evenly with cheeses and salsa. Roll up tortillas and place, seam-side-down in a greased 2-quart casserole dish. Pour whipping cream over enchiladas. Top with any remaining cheese. Bake at 350° for 25 minutes or until hot and bubbly. Serves 4–6.

Food for Thought (Alabama)

Southern Pecan Chicken

Can substitute fish for the chicken for an equally good variation.

6–8 boneless chicken breasts
Salt and pepper to taste
2 eggs
2 teaspoons Creole mustard
½ cup finely chopped pecans

1 cup plain bread crumbs
¼ cup butter or margarine,
 divided
¼ cup vegetable oil, divided

Lay chicken breasts out on wax paper. Season with salt and pepper. In a small bowl, beat eggs with mustard. In another bowl, combine pecans and bread crumbs. Dip chicken in egg mixture, then coat with bread crumb mixture.

Preheat oven to 350°. In a large skillet over medium-high heat, melt 2 tablespoons butter and 2 tablespoons oil. Sauté half the chicken until golden brown on each side. Place in an ovenproof dish. Wipe out skillet, pouring off any drippings (so second batch will have a clean, fresh look after browning). Sauté the rest of the chicken in remaining 2 tablespoons of butter and oil. Place in oven and bake 15 minutes.

SAUCE:
¼ cup butter
½ cup coarsely chopped pecans

1 teaspoon lemon juice

Melt butter in a small saucepan over low heat. Stir in pecans and lemon juice. Serve over chicken. Serves 6–8.

Kay Ewing's Cooking School Cookbook (Louisiana)

Grilled Chicken

1 chicken (fryer)
¼ cup butter
1 cup Worcestershire
3 tablespoons lemon juice

½ teaspoon garlic salt
½ teaspoon onion powder
½ teaspoon celery salt
¼ teaspoon pepper

Cut chicken in half. Place on hot grill and sear. Turn and sear other side. Melt butter in pan. Add all ingredients and stir until mixture boils. Baste chicken halves and turn. Continue basting and turning every 5–10 minutes until cooked. Grill approximately 40 minutes. Serves 4.

Big Mama's Old Black Pot Recipes (Louisiana)

Baked Chicken Breasts

6 chicken breast halves,
   skinned and boned
1 cup dairy sour cream
2 tablespoons lemon juice
2 teaspoons Worcestershire
½ teaspoon celery salt

1 teaspoon paprika
¼ teaspoon garlic powder
1½ teaspoons salt
¼ teaspoon red pepper
1 cup seasoned bread crumbs
¼ cup margarine

Rinse and dry 6 chicken breast halves with paper towels. In a 2-quart dish, combine sour cream, lemon juice, Worcestershire, celery salt, paprika, garlic powder, salt and pepper. Add chicken to sour cream mixture, coating each piece well. Let stand, covered, in refrigerator overnight or at least eight hours.

Carefully remove coated chicken from sour cream mixture. Roll in crumbs, coating evenly. Arrange single layer in an 8-inch square shallow baking dish. Micromelt margarine in a 1-cup glass measuring cup on HIGH (100%) 1 minute and drizzle over chicken. Microwave on HIGH (100%) 10 minutes or until chicken is tender. Yields 4–6 servings.

Tout de Suite à la Microwave II (Louisiana)

Honey Mustard Chicken

1 (20-ounce) can pineapple
   slices
4 boneless, skinless chicken
   breast halves
Salt and pepper to taste
2 cloves garlic, pressed

1 teaspoon thyme
2 tablespoons vegetable oil
1 tablespoon cornstarch
¼ cup honey
¼ cup Dijon mustard

Drain pineapple; reserve juice. Sprinkle chicken with salt and pepper. Rub with garlic and thyme. Brown in hot oil. Combine 2 tablespoons reserved juice with cornstarch; set aside. Combine honey and mustard; stir in skillet with remaining juice. Spoon sauce over chicken. Cover and simmer for 15 minutes. Stir cornstarch mixture into pan juice. Add pineapple. Cook, stirring, until sauce boils and thickens. Serves 4.

Munchin' with the Methodists (Mississippi)

Mississippi State Chicken-On-A-Stick

4 boneless, skinless chicken
  breasts
Salt to taste
2 medium onions
1 large bell pepper
24 dill pickles (chips)
1 (15-ounce) can whole potatoes
2 eggs, beaten
¼ cup buttermilk
1 cup flour
1 teaspoon paprika
Red pepper to taste

Cut chicken breasts into bite-size cubes, and salt to taste. Quarter onions. Chop pepper into bite-size pieces. Place chicken, onions, bell pepper, dill pickles, and potatoes on wooden skewers. (Use proportions that suit your family—some like more vegetables, and some like loads of chicken!)

Combine eggs and milk in a plate. Combine flour, paprika, and red pepper in a plate. Dredge skewer of chicken and vegetables in flour. Then, drench in egg-milk mixture. Dredge in flour again. Fry skewer in deep, hot fat until golden brown.

Variation: For more heat, place some hot sauce in egg-milk mixture and increase red pepper in flour. Also, add some whole jalapeño peppers for a real spice!

Offerings for Your Plate (Mississippi)

Chicken, Mushroom, and Artichoke Bake

4–6 boneless chicken breast
  halves
Salt, pepper, and paprika
  to taste
½ cup butter
½–1 pound mushrooms, sliced
2 tablespoons flour
1 (10-ounce) can condensed
  chicken broth
½ cup sherry
1 (14-ounce) can artichoke
  hearts, drained

Season chicken with salt, pepper, and paprika. In large skillet, melt butter and sauté chicken until lightly browned. Remove to baking dish. In same skillet, sauté mushrooms; add flour and mix well. Stir in broth and sherry. Season with salt and pepper. Simmer 5–10 minutes and pour over chicken breasts. Bake at 375° for 1 hour. Top with artichoke hearts and cook 20–30 minutes. Makes 4 servings.

Celebrations on the Bayou (Louisiana)

Chicken and Artichoke Casserole

1 (3-pound) fryer, and 2 or 3
  extra breast halves
1 cup butter
½ cup all-purpose flour
3½ cups milk
3 ounces Gruyére or Swiss
  cheese
⅛ pound rat cheese (mellow
  Cheddar), grated

1 tablespoon Ac'cent
2 cloves garlic, pressed
½ tablespoon red pepper (or
  less)
2 large cans button mushrooms,
  drained
2 large cans artichoke hearts,
  drained

Boil chicken in seasoned water. Remove skin and bones and cut meat into large pieces. Set aside. Melt butter, and stir in flour until blended. Slowly add milk and stir until the sauce is smooth. Add cheese, seasonings, and remaining ingredients. Put combined mixture in a casserole dish and bake 30 minutes at 350°. Serves 10.

Variation: This is good served with buttered noodles. Lobster, crab, or shrimp may be substituted.

One of a Kind (Alabama)

Quick Chicken and Broccoli Crêpes

1 (10-ounce) package frozen,
  chopped broccoli
1 (10¾-ounce) can cream of
  chicken soup
½ teaspoon Worcestershire
⅓ plus ¼ cup grated
  Parmesan cheese, divided

2 cups cooked, chopped chicken
9–10 crêpes
⅓ cup mayonnaise
1 tablespoon milk

Cook broccoli according to package directions; drain thoroughly. Combine with soup, Worcestershire, ⅓ cup cheese, and chicken. Fill crêpes with chicken mixture; roll up and place in shallow baking pan. Combine mayonnaise with milk; spread over crêpes. Sprinkle with remaining ¼ cup cheese. Broil until bubbly. Yields 9–10 crêpes.

Festival Cookbook (Mississippi)

Chicken Sauce Piquante

4–6 pounds chicken, cut in
  pieces
1 cup oil
2 cups chopped onions
1 cup chopped celery
1 cup chopped green bell
  pepper
1 (16-ounce) can whole
  tomatoes

1 (16-ounce) can tomato juice
5 cups water
1 (4-ounce) can mushrooms
1 teaspoon sugar
4 cloves garlic, chopped fine
Salt, black pepper, and cayenne
  pepper
½ cup chopped green onions
  and parsley

Season chicken and fry in oil in heavy, covered iron pot. Stirring occasionally, cook about ½ hour or until chicken becomes tender. Take chicken out of pot and set aside. Add onions, celery, and bell pepper to oil and cook slowly until onions are wilted. Add whole tomatoes, tomato juice, and water. Cook over medium heat until oil floats above tomatoes, or about 25 minutes.

Add chicken, mushrooms, sugar, and chopped garlic. Season to taste with salt, black pepper, and cayenne, leaning heavily on the cayenne to give the sting (which is piquante). Cook for 20 minutes. Add green onions and parsley. Serve over steamed rice. Serves 8.

Secrets of The Original Don's Seafood & Steakhouse (Louisiana)

Chicken à la King

4 tablespoons butter
1 cup sliced mushrooms
1 bell pepper, chopped
2 tablespoons flour
1 cup chicken broth
2 cups chopped cooked chicken

2 eggs
1 cup sour cream
1 cup chopped pimentos
2 tablespoons sherry
Salt and pepper to taste

Melt butter in skillet. Add mushrooms and bell pepper. Stir. Add 2 tablespoons flour, and mix thoroughly. Add chicken broth and chicken. Cook on low heat 10 minutes. Beat eggs and add sour cream and add to mixture. Add pimentos. Heat (do not boil). Add salt and pepper and sherry. Serve in pastry or on rice. Serves 6 or 7.

Heavenly Hostess (Alabama)

Chicken Pie-Pinwheel Crust

1 (3½- to 4-pound) hen
1 tablespoon salt
2 cups water
3 tablespoons flour

1½ cups milk
1½ cups chicken broth
1 tablespoon lemon juice

Boil hen in salted water until done. Remove from bones. Place chicken in a 3-quart casserole dish. Make a sauce by blending flour, milk, and broth. Cook slowly until thick. Add lemon juice and pour over chicken in casserole. Set aside while you make Crust.

CRUST:

3 tablespoons shortening
1½ cups all-purpose flour
3 tablespoons baking powder
½ teaspoon salt

½ cup milk
3 pimentos, chopped
¾ cup grated Cheddar cheese

Cut shortening into flour to which baking powder and salt has been added. Add milk. Form a ball and chill 30 minutes. Roll out ¼-inch thick. Spread pimento and grated cheese over pastry and roll up, starting at the short end. Slice. Place slices over chicken mixture and bake at 400° for 40 minutes, or until brown.

Dixie Dining (Mississippi)

Deep-Dish Chicken Pie

PASTRY:

1¼ cups flour
¼ teaspoon salt
¼ cup butter, cut in pieces
2 tablespoons shortening, cut
  in pieces

1 egg
2 tablespoons cold water,
  divided

Sift flour and salt into bowl. Add butter and shortening; mix until crumbly. Separate egg, saving white. Beat yolk with 1 tablespoon cold water and pour liquid into flour. Stir with wooden spoon until mixture begins to form a ball. Cover with wax paper and refrigerate.

FILLING:

¼ cup butter
1 small onion, chopped
¼ cup finely chopped celery
3 tablespoons flour
2 cups chicken broth
6 cups cubed cooked chicken

½ cup fresh or frozen peas
¼ pound mushrooms,
  quartered
2 small carrots, peeled and
  sliced
Salt and pepper to taste

In saucepan over medium heat, melt butter, add onion and celery, and cook until soft. Stir in flour; cook until thickened. Gradually stir in broth, stirring constantly, until mixture bubbles and thickens. Mix in chicken, peas, mushrooms, and carrots. Season to taste. Set aside to cool.

   Preheat oven to 425°. Roll out cold Pastry on floured surface into a 12-inch circle. Mix egg white with 1 tablespoon cold water; brush on pastry (reserve some for top.) Pour cooled chicken mixture into a straight-sided, 9-inch baking dish 2 inches deep. Place Pastry, glazed side down, over filling. Trim edges and cut slits in crust to allow steam to escape. Brush top with reserved egg wash. Bake until Pastry is golden brown, 30–40 minutes.

Heart & Soul Cookbook (Alabama)

Chicken Biscuit Pot Pie

1⅔ cups frozen mixed
vegetables, thawed
1½ cups cooked chicken,
cubed
1 (10¾-ounce) can condensed
cream of chicken soup,
undiluted

¼ teaspoon dried thyme
1 cup biscuit mix
½ cup milk
1 egg

In bowl, combine vegetables, chicken, soup, and thyme. Pour into an ungreased, deep-dish, 9-inch pie plate. Combine biscuit mix, milk, and egg. Pour over chicken mixture. Bake at 400° for 25–30 minutes or until golden brown. Yields 6 servings.

Iuka Masonic Lodge Cookbook (Mississippi)

Chicken Crescents

5 tablespoons melted butter,
divided
1 (3-ounce) package cream
cheese, softened
2 cups chopped cooked
chicken or turkey

1 tablespoon finely chopped
onion
¼ cup chopped pimiento
1 (8-ounce) can crescent rolls

Mix 3 tablespoons melted butter and cream cheese. Add chicken, onion, and pimiento. Separate rolls into 4 rectangles. Seal perforations. Place chicken mixture in center and pull up 4 corners. Seal edges. Drizzle remaining 2 tablespoons butter over rolls. Bake at 350° for 30 minutes.

Recipe by Wesley Walls, Pontotoc County, San Francisco 49'er
Mississippi Stars Cookbook (Mississippi)

Chicken and Dumplings

CHICKEN AND STOCK:

1 frying chicken, cut into pieces (or equivalent breasts and thighs)
2 quarts (or more) water to cover chicken
2 ribs celery, cut into large pieces

1 onion, quartered
3 sprigs fresh parsley
Salt and black pepper to taste
Canned chicken broth as needed
½ cup sweet milk
¼ stick butter, cut into small pieces

Place all ingredients, except canned broth, in a large stockpot and bring to a boil. Reduce heat and simmer until chicken is very tender (about one hour). Allow to cool.

Remove meat from bones and discard bones. Cut deboned chicken into medium-size pieces; wrap tightly in plastic wrap, and refrigerate overnight. Strain the stock and discard vegetables. If stock does not come to 1¾ quarts, add enough canned broth to make that amount. Refrigerate stock overnight.

DUMPLINGS:

Fat from chicken broth
Vegetable shortening as needed

3 cups all-purpose flour
¾ teaspoon salt
Ice water

Skim the solidified chicken fat from the refrigerated stock and reserve. If fat does not come to ⅓ cup, add enough vegetable shortening to make that amount. Separate fat into small pieces and place in a mixing bowl. With your hands, briefly mix fat with flour and salt until fat is the size of peas. Add ice water one tablespoon at a time, stirring gently with your hands until mixture holds together and is the consistency of flaky pie crust dough.

On a lightly floured surface with a rolling pin, roll dough as thin as possible without breaking it. Cut dough into rectangles about 1 x 2 inches.

Place cooked, chopped chicken into strained, de-fatted stock and bring to a gentle simmer (not a boil). Drop Dumplings into simmering broth and cook about 30 minutes or until liquid begins to thicken. Turn off heat. When liquid stops simmering, add sweet milk and butter. Stir very gently until butter dissolves. Serves 6–8.

The Southern Cook's Handbook (Mississippi)

Easy Chicken and Dumplings

4 chicken breasts, boiled (or
  equivalent canned chicken)
4 cups chicken broth
1 (10¾-ounce) can cream of
  mushroom soup
1 (10¾-ounce) can cream of
  chicken soup

12 flour tortillas, cut into 1-inch
  strips
All-purpose flour
Salt and pepper to taste
½ cup milk
¼ stick margarine

Save broth from boiling chicken and add canned chicken broth as needed to make 4 cups. Cut chicken into bite-size pieces and return to broth. Add both soups and bring to a boil. Add strips of tortillas which have been dusted with flour. Add salt and pepper to taste. Cover and cook for 12–15 minutes, stirring occasionally. Add milk and margarine just before removing from heat. Stir well and serve while hot. Yields 8 servings.

With Special Distinction (Mississippi)

Five Mississippians have made unforgettable marks in the world of football:
• Archie Manning (Drew) was one of the most exciting college football players in history. He holds a SEC-record 540 yards of total offense in a prime-time TV loss (33-32) to Alabama in 1969. He was drafted No. 2 overall by the New Orleans Saints in 1971 and had a 14-year NFL career.
• Jerry Rice (Crawford) is the greatest pass receiver in football history. He is the leading touchdown scorer in NFL history (194) and holds 13 other NFL records. He holds 11 Super Bowl records and has caught a record 33 passes for 589 yards and eight touchdowns in four Super Bowl appearances.
• Walter Payton's (Columbia) accomplishments on and off the field help put Mississippi on the map. Known as "Sweetness," Payton's NFL career spanned 13 years. His 16,726 rushing yards rank second on the NFL's all-time list. Payton had 10 seasons with 1,000 or more yards, and led the league in rushing four times. His career rushing attempts (3,838) and most games rushing for 100 yards or more (77) are among the NFL's best.
• Brett Favre (Kiln) is as gutsy as they come. He makes things happen, and with the game on the line, you want him at quarterback. Favre is the only three-time MVP in NFL history. His NFL records include: most career touchdown passes (442), most career passing yards (61,655), most career pass completions (5,377), most career pass attempts (8,758), most career interceptions thrown (288), most consecutive starts among NFL quarterbacks (253; 275 total starts including playoffs), and most career victories as a starting quarterback (160).
• Steve McNair (Mount Olive) was exciting in high school, amazing in college, and dangerous in the NFL. He owns the Alcorn State record book, throwing eight touchdown passes in one game. McNair finished his college career with an NCAA record 16,823 total yards, a record for all divisions, and the NCAA I-AA record with 14,496 passing yards. He led the NFL's Tennessee Titans to the Super Bowl in 2000 and had them within one game of the Super Bowl in 2003. —*Van Dyess*, Clarion-Ledger

Baked Turkey

1 (10- to 12-pound) turkey
Salt and pepper to taste
Butter
1 Rome apple, quartered

1 onion, quartered
3 stalks celery, cut in quarters
1 pint water

Preheat oven to 500°. Clean turkey; salt and pepper to taste; butter inside and out. Place apple and onion quarters and celery stalks inside turkey. Place turkey in baking pan with lid. Pour water in pan; put lid on tightly. Bake turkey in 500° oven for 1 hour. Turn stove off, and DO NOT OPEN OVEN DOOR TILL THE NEXT MORNING (8–10 hours).

Heart & Soul Cookbook (Alabama)

Tony's Deep-Fried Turkey

The most-requested recipe by far!

1 tablespoon Worcestershire
2 tablespoons Creole mustard
3 (2-ounce) bottles garlic juice
3 (2-ounce) bottles onion juice
1 (3-ounce) bottle hot pepper
  sauce
¼ cup Tony's Creole
  Seasoning

1 cup water
1 (approximately 14-pound)
  turkey
Additional mustard and Tony's
  for rubbing turkey

Mix all ingredients except turkey in blender 2 days before cooking. Pour into a jar and refrigerate. You can keep this marinade in the refrigerator for months. Use at Thanksgiving then again at Christmas.

Inject turkey with a syringe using the blended mixture. Rub turkey with additional mustard, and season generously with Tony's Creole Seasoning. When ready to cook, heat 5 gallons of peanut oil to 350°; carefully submerge turkey and let fry for 4 minutes per pound of turkey. Yields 15 servings.

Tony Chachere's Second Helping (Louisiana)

Traditional Southern Cornbread Dressing

This makes a very tasty moist dressing to serve with turkey.

6 cups cornbread crumbs
2 cups biscuit crumbs
½ teaspoon salt
½ teaspoon pepper
1½ tablespoons rubbed sage
½ cup butter or margarine

1 medium onion, finely chopped
2 cups chopped celery
½ cup water
2 cups broth
½ cup vegetable oil
3 eggs, slightly beaten

Combine cornbread crumbs and biscuit crumbs in large bowl. Sprinkle seasonings over crumbs; set aside. Combine margarine, onion, celery, and water in saucepan. Cook over medium heat until margarine is melted. Add onion mixture, broth, and oil to crumbs; stir well, mashing crumbs. Add eggs; stir until blended. Pour mixture into baking dish or pan; bake at 350° about 35–40 minutes or until golden brown. Yields 15 servings.

Irondale Cafe Original WhistleStop Cookbook (Alabama)

Dressing for a Crowd

1 large onion, chopped
1 cup chopped celery
1 stick margarine, melted
6 cups crumbled cornbread
4 cups white bread crumbs

1 tablespoon black pepper
Sage to taste
4 eggs, beaten
Chicken broth (about 1 quart)

Sauté onion and celery in margarine. Add to crumbs in large pan. Add remaining ingredients. Dressing should be thin enough to pour into a buttered casserole dish or large baking pan. Bake at 450° until center is bubbly, about 30 minutes.

Bountiful Blessings–Dumas (Mississippi)

GAME

On the summit of Red Mountain, overlooking downtown Birmingham, Alabama, weighing approximately 126,000 pounds, stands a 56-foot statue of Vulcan, the Roman god of fire. Built in 1904, he is the world's largest cast metal statue, and the largest statue ever made in the United States.

Smothered Doves and Mushrooms

8 doves
Salt, pepper, and cayenne
  pepper
½ cup bacon drippings
2 medium onions
1 pound small-to-medium
  fresh mushrooms

1 teaspoon finely chopped garlic
½ stick butter
1 tablespoon flour
1 cup milk
2 ounces port wine
2 tablespoons chopped green
  onion tops

Sprinkle inside and out of doves with salt and pepper, and lightly sprinkle inside of doves with cayenne (red) pepper. Heat bacon drippings, and brown the doves on all sides. Place doves in casserole dish that can be covered. Retain bacon drippings. Slice onions ½-inch thick, separate rings, then brown in drippings. Remove onion and place over doves in casserole. Spread mushrooms over onions and doves. Spread chopped garlic over all.

Add butter to drippings and heat. Add flour and cook on medium-high fire, stirring constantly until flour browns lightly. Lower fire and slowly add milk, stirring constantly to mix evenly. Add port wine, mix well, and pour this mixture into casserole of doves. Sprinkle lightly with salt and pepper. Sprinkle green onion tops over all. Cover dish and place in a 300° oven one hour. Serves 4.

Paul Naquin's French Collection III: Louisiana Wild Game
(Louisiana)

PHOTO COURTESY OF FLORENCE/LAUDERDALE TOURISM

W. C. Handy has been called the Father of the Blues, having single-handedly introduced this new style of music to the world. In his hometown of Florence, Alabama, the log cabin where he was born has been restored and turned into a museum that houses mementos from his life. The city of Florence holds an annual music festival in his honor.

Smothered Quail

Salt and pepper
12 quail (allow 2 per person)
¼ cup vegetable oil
10 tablespoons unsalted butter, divided
¾ cup plus 5 tablespoons all-purpose flour, divided
1 teaspoon paprika
1 teaspoon black pepper
½ teaspoon dried marjoram
½ teaspoon grated nutmeg
½ teaspoon dried thyme
½ teaspoon dried sage
½ cup finely chopped onion
½ cup finely chopped celery
½ cup finely chopped carrots
5 cups hot chicken stock
⅓ cup dry red wine

Salt and pepper birds inside and out. Set aside. Heat oil and 2 tablespoons butter in a large skillet over medium heat. Mix ¾ cup flour with remaining dry ingredients, and dredge quail. Shake off excess. Place quail in skillet and fry evenly. Cook for 20 minutes, until quail are golden brown with darker flecks. Remove to a warm plate. Discard oil.

In a large Dutch oven, melt the remaining 8 tablespoons butter over medium heat. Add vegetables. Sauté for 5 minutes, until vegetables are wilted. Sprinkle remaining 5 tablespoons flour over all and cook about 15 minutes, until flour turns reddish brown, turning and stirring all the while. Do not let flour burn.

When flour is dark, gradually whisk in hot stock until smooth. Add wine and simmer over low heat for 5 minutes. Add quail and cover. Cook over very low heat for 1½–2 hours, until birds are tender, but not yet falling apart. Add more liquid if necessary.

Note: This recipe also works well for smothered chicken, dove, or ducks.

The Southern Cook's Handbook (Mississippi)

Grilled Duck Breasts

You've never tasted better!

8 tablespoons butter
1 tablespoon Worcestershire
1 garlic clove, finely minced
¾ cup thinly sliced fresh
  mushrooms

6 duck breasts, removed from
  bone, skinned
Salt, freshly ground black
  pepper, and cayenne pepper
6 strips bacon

Melt butter in a saucepan and add Worcestershire, garlic, and mushrooms; cook until mushrooms become slightly soft. Remove from heat. Light a fire in the barbecue pit and allow coals to get glowing red hot. While you're waiting, rub duck breasts well with salt, black pepper, and cayenne. Carefully wrap each breast with a strip of bacon, securing it with toothpicks. Let stand at room temperature. (You might want to take this time to fix a green salad with creamy spicy dressing and some wild rice cooked with a handful of chopped roasted pecans.)

When coals are ready, grill breasts quickly, 3–4 minutes on each side if you like them juicy and with a little red in the meat; longer if you prefer you meat well done. Baste with butter sauce. To serve, place breasts on toasted slices of bread, and pour remaining butter and mushroom sauce over each breast. Serves 2.

Who's Your Mama, Are You Catholic, and Can You Make a Roux?
(Louisiana)

Established in 1821, the Academy of the Sacred Heart in Grand Coteau, Louisiana, is the second oldest institution of learning west of the Mississippi. It is the oldest, continually running member of the Network of Sacred Heart Schools in the world. It is also the oldest independent school in the Acadiana region. In its gracious oak alley setting, the all-girls Academy has remained in continuous operation through fire, epidemics, and war.

Although thousands of Federal troops were encamped in the fields surrounding the Academy during the Civil War, the school was not touched. Union General Nathaniel Banks had a daughter in a school in New York run by the Religious of the Sacred Heart, and he was asked to look after the Grand Coteau sisters and their students.

On campus is a small chapel honoring St. John Berchmans, a Jesuit who appeared to a novice, Mary Wilson, in an apparition and cured her of a fatal illness in 1866. This miracle eventually led to the canonization of John Berchmans. It is the only shrine at the exact location of a confirmed miracle in the United States.

Mississippi Delta Duck

4 duck breasts
8 slices bacon
1 onion, sliced, separated into rings, divided
1 lemon

Pepper to taste
1 cup soy sauce
½ cup Worcestershire
Lemon pepper
Salt to taste

Fillet meat from bone, making 8 duck breast halves. Wrap each half with a slice of bacon; secure with a toothpick. Layer bottom of a covered container with ½ the onion rings; place duck breasts on top. Squeeze lemon over duck; season with pepper. Combine soy sauce and Worcestershire; pour over duck. Sprinkle generously with lemon pepper. Top with remaining onion rings. Marinate 6 hours; turn duck after 3 hours. Cook in a water smoker with the top on for 20 minutes; turn and cook 25 additional minutes. Add salt to taste when cooked. Serves 4.

Taste of the South (Mississippi)

Turtle Sauce Piquant

20 pounds turtle meat
5 pounds onions, finely chopped
2 bunches shallots, finely chopped
4 bell peppers, finely chopped
⅓ bunch celery, finely chopped
1 bunch garlic, finely chopped
1 small bunch parsley, finely chopped
2 (8-ounce) cans mushrooms, drained

4 (10¾-ounce) cans cream of mushroom soup
6 serving spoons flour
1 pint cooking oil
2 (10-ounce) cans Ro-Tel tomatoes and peppers
Salt and pepper to taste
⅓ small bottle Lea & Perrins Worcestershire
3 tablespoons French mustard

Brown turtle meat; add onions, shallots, peppers, celery, garlic, parsley, mushrooms, and mushroom soup. Cook until onions and seasonings cook to juice. Brown flour and cooking oil until dark brown, then add with tomatoes and let simmer. Let cook 4–5 hours. Add salt and pepper to taste. Add Lea & Perrins and mustard about 20 minutes before serving. Serve with rice. Serves 50.

The Encyclopedia of Cajun and Creole Cuisine (Louisiana)

Alligator Creole

This is a recipe from my first volume on Louisiana seafood for Shrimp Creole that has been altered only by substituting alligator meat for the shrimp. The alligator meat is boiled prior to using in the Creole sauce so as to make it tender and also to flavor the meat. Boil the alligator meat the same way you would boil shrimp, your favorite way, or by using the boiled shrimp recipe in my book.

1 cup olive oil
¾ cup flour
2 cloves garlic, chopped
2 cups chopped yellow onions
1 cup chopped celery
½ cup chopped bell pepper
4 ripe medium tomatoes
2 (6-ounce) cans tomato paste
1 (12-ounce) can tomato sauce

3 cups water
2 teaspoons salt
¼ cup chopped green onion
4 tablespoons chopped fresh
   parsley
4 pounds alligator meat (whole
   chops, steaks, or diced meat)
¼ teaspoon black pepper
¼ teaspoon cayenne pepper

In a large heavy skillet, heat olive oil. Add flour and make a brown roux by constantly stirring flour and oil until flour turns to color of brown paper bag. Add garlic, onions, celery, and bell pepper, and cook until soft. Add tomatoes, tomato paste, and tomato sauce. Blend. Add 3 cups water. Mix and simmer 30 minutes. Add alligator meat and remaining ingredients. Mix well and cook slowly for 1 hour. Serve over hot rice. Serves 8–10.

Editor's Extra: May substitute shrimp for alligator.

Paul Naquin's French Collection III: Louisiana Wild Game
(Louisiana)

Ro-Tel Roast

1 deer roast
2 tablespoons cooking oil
1 (10-ounce) can Ro-Tel
  tomatoes
2 (1-ounce) envelopes onion
  soup mix
1 cup water
1 onion, chopped
1 green pepper, chopped
2 cloves garlic, minced

Brown roast on both sides in oil in large saucepan with lid. Add
Ro-Tel tomatoes, onion soup mix and water. Cover and cook on
medium heat. Keep liquid in saucepan at all times; add water a
little at a time as needed. Cook about 3 hours. Add onion, green
pepper, and garlic. Cook until meat falls apart.

This can be cooked in a pressure cooker to decrease cooking
time. Great over rice or on po-boy buns.

Going Wild in Mississippi (Mississippi)

Venison Pepper Steak

2 pounds venison steak
Dash of garlic salt
Dash of powdered ginger
½ cup butter
½ cup soy sauce
1 cup beef bouillon
3 green bell peppers, sliced
6 scallions, sliced (including
  tops)
Salt and pepper to taste
4 tablespoons cornstarch
½ cup water or white wine

Remove all tendons and slice steak in thin strips (easier to cut if
slightly frozen). Season with garlic salt and ginger; cook over
medium heat in butter until well browned. Add soy sauce and
bouillon; cover and simmer until tender. Add peppers and scallions; cook a few minutes more. Season. Add cornstarch mixed
with water or wine and stir on low heat until sauce is clear and
thickened. Serve with rice or Chinese noodles.

Madison County Cookery (Mississippi)

Chunky Venison Chili
with Dumplings

2 cups venison, cut into
½-inch cubes
1 cup water
1 (15-ounce) can tomato sauce
1 (1¾-ounce) package chili
seasoning mix
1 (15-ounce) can black beans,
undrained
1 (8-ounce) can kidney beans,
undrained

1 (8-ounce) can whole-kernel
corn, undrained
Quick Dumplings
Tabasco to taste
Salt and pepper to taste
½ cup shredded Cheddar
cheese

Mix venison, water, tomato sauce, and seasoning mix in a 4-quart Dutch oven. Heat to boiling; reduce heat. Cover and simmer 10 minutes, stirring constantly. Stir in beans and corn. Prepare Quick Dumplings. Heat chili to boiling; reduce heat to low. Drop 12 spoonfuls dumplings into the hot chili. Cook uncovered 10 minutes. Cover and cook 10 minutes longer. Season to taste. Sprinkle with cheese. Cover and cook about 3 minutes or until cheese is melted. Serves 6.

QUICK DUMPLINGS:
1½ cups Bisquick
½ cup yellow cornmeal

⅔ cup whole milk
½ teaspoon sugar

Mix all ingredients until soft dough forms. Roll out and cut into 1x2-inch rectangles.

The Complete Venison Cookbook (Mississippi)

SEAFOOD

MISSISSIPPI DEVELOPMENT AUTHORITY, DIVISION OF TOURISM

In 2003, there were approximately 400 catfish farms in Mississippi. Nationally, there are nearly 1,200 catfish farms, but because Mississippi farms are larger, the state maintains more than half of the nearly 190,000 water-surface acres of catfish farming in America.

Shrimp Scampi

½ cup butter
3 cloves garlic, crushed
2 tablespoons olive oil
24 large or jumbo shrimp,
  peeled and deveined
2 tablespoons chopped parsley

2 tablespoons dry white wine
1 tablespoon lemon juice
1 tablespoon Worcestershire for
  chicken (green label)
Salt and pepper to taste

Heat butter, garlic, and olive oil in large skillet. Add shrimp and sauté on both sides until done (about 5 minutes). Pour pan drippings into small saucepan. Add remaining ingredients. Cook over high heat for one minute. Pour sauce over shrimp and serve with rice to absorb the juice. Serves 4–6.

Capitol Cooking (Alabama)

Shrimp Creole

4 tablespoons butter
1 tablespoon oil
1 cup chopped onions
1 cup chopped celery
1 cup chopped bell pepper
6 cloves garlic, chopped
½ cup chopped green onions
6 tablespoons flour

1 (16-ounce) can tomato sauce
½ cup hot water
½ teaspoon sugar
Juice of 1 lemon
4 bay leaves
Salt and cayenne pepper to taste
3 pounds peeled, deveined
  medium shrimp

In a heavy pot, melt butter. Add oil. Sauté all seasonings until done (approximately 5 minutes). Add flour and blend well. Add tomato sauce, hot water, and sugar. Cook over medium heat approximately 30 minutes. Season to taste. Add shrimp; cook 30 minutes longer. Remove bay leaf.

The Encyclopedia of Cajun and Creole Cuisine (Louisiana)

Alabama's Bayou La Batre is known as the Seafood Capital of the South. To commemorate the fishing industry, the nationally known Blessing of the Fleet is held there each May. Bayou La Batre was made famous by the movie *Forrest Gump* and the fictionalized Bubba Gump Shrimp Company.

Shrimp Boats

4 individual loaves French
  bread
16 large shrimp (about 1
  pound), peeled, deveined
¼ cup vegetable oil

1 clove garlic, minced
Dash bottled hot pepper sauce
1 cup shredded lettuce
Guacamole

Cut thin slice from top of each individual bread loaf; hollow out loaves leaving ½-inch shell. Thread shrimp on metal skewers. Combine oil, garlic, and hot pepper sauce in small bowl; brush on shrimp. Cook on preheated gas grill using medium setting, 5–10 minutes, or until shrimp turn pink and are tender. Fill loaves with lettuce and Guacamole; top with shrimp. Makes 4 servings.

GUACAMOLE:
1 avocado, peeled, seeded,
  coarsely mashed
½ cup mayonnaise or salad
  dressing
1 tablespoon sliced green
  onion and top

½ cup chopped tomato
2 tablespoons minced cilantro or
  parsley
2 teaspoons lemon juice
Dash of salt

Combine all ingredients. Makes about 1¼ cups.

A Taste of the South (Alabama)

Bob's Barbecued Shrimp

5 pounds medium to large
  shrimp, headless
½ pound butter
½ pound margarine
½ teaspoon rosemary
3 ounces Worcestershire

2½ tablespoons black pepper
2 tablespoons salt
2 lemons, sliced thin
2 cloves garlic, minced
½ tablespoon Tabasco
1 ounce soy sauce

Wash shrimp and place in a large baking dish. Combine remaining ingredients; bring to a boil. Pour over shrimp. Bake at 400° for 20 minutes. Serve hot with plenty of garlic bread.

Hallmark's Collection of Home Tested Recipes (Alabama)

Shrimp with Eggplant Casserole

1 large eggplant
16 ounces raw shrimp
1 cup chopped onion
1 cup chopped green bell
  pepper
1 cup chopped celery
1 clove garlic, minced
½ teaspoon black pepper

1 (10¾-ounce) can Campbell's
  Healthy Request cream of
  mushroom soup
4 ounces light Cheddar cheese,
  shredded
½ cup dry seasoned bread
  crumbs, divided

Puncture eggplant several times and cook on HIGH in microwave 30 minutes. Set aside to cool. When cool, pull skin off and chop. Sauté shrimp, onion, bell pepper, celery, and garlic in cooking spray until shrimp turn pink. Add pepper, soup, and cheese; heat and set aside. Mix with ¼ cup seasoned bread crumbs and chopped eggplant. Top with remaining bread crumbs and spray with cooking spray. Bake at 350° for 25 minutes. Yields 8 servings.

Gone with the Fat (Louisiana)

Fried Shrimp

1 cup all-purpose flour
½ teaspoon sugar
½ teaspoon salt
1 cup ice water (leave 1 or
  2 cubes in)

1 egg, slightly beaten
2 tablespoons oil
2 pounds fresh, frozen shrimp,
  peeled, leave tails intact

Combine ingredients, except shrimp; stir until smooth, then set in refrigerator or freezer to chill.

Butterfly shrimp by cutting lengthwise to tail. Dry shrimp, dip into batter, and fry in deep hot fat (350°–400°) till floating and golden brown, 3–5 minutes. Serve immediately.

Note: Also good for frying soft- and hard-shelled crabs, eggplants, onions, etc.

Cajun Cooking (Louisiana)

Pascagoula Shrimp Boil

3 ounces prepared shrimp boil
1 small onion, sliced
1 lemon, sliced
1 clove garlic, sliced

1 gallon water
½ cup salt
5 pounds shrimp, fresh or
  frozen

Tie shrimp boil, onion, lemon, and garlic in a piece of cheesecloth. Place water in large container. Add salt and bag of seasonings. Cover and bring to boiling point over a hot fire. Add shrimp and return to boiling point. Cover and cook 5 minutes or until shrimp are tender. Drain.

Note: If shrimp is to be used for salad or cocktails, cook as above, remove from water, peel, devein, and chill.

PEPPY SEAFOOD SAUCE:

½ cup chili sauce
½ cup ketchup
3 tablespoons freshly squeezed
  lemon juice
1 tablespoon horseradish
1 tablespoon mayonnaise or
  salad dressing

1 teaspoon Worcestershire
½ teaspoon grated onion
¼ teaspoon salt
3 drops Tabasco
Dash of pepper

Mix ingredients well. Serve with shrimp.

Dixie Dining (Mississippi)

Seafood Cocktail Sauce

⅔ cup ketchup
3 tablespoons chili sauce
2 tablespoons horseradish

3 tablespoons fresh lemon juice
Hot pepper sauce to taste

Mix all ingredients well; refrigerate until ready to serve. Serve with any fried or boiled seafood.

Cajun Cooking (Louisiana)

Cajun Peppered Shrimp & Grits

A delightful combination of flavors straight from the South! Try serving this impressive dish for brunch.

GRITS:

6 cups water	1 (6-ounce) roll garlic cheese
2 teaspoons salt	1 cup grated Cheddar cheese
1½ cup quick grits	1 teaspoon Worcestershire
2 tablespoons butter	

Preheat oven to 350°. Grease a large saucepan with cooking spray, add water, and bring to a boil over high heat. Stir in salt and grits. Lower heat and cook, stirring occasionally, until water is absorbed and grits thicken. Add butter, cheeses, and Worcestershire. Cook until cheese melts. Pour in a greased casserole dish and bake for 20 minutes to set.

SHRIMP:

½ cup butter or margarine	½ teaspoon salt
¼ cup olive oil	1 teaspoon pepper
3 pounds medium shrimp, peeled	¼ teaspoon cayenne pepper
1 cup chopped green onions	½ teaspoon paprika
1 cup sliced mushrooms	¼ teaspoon basil, thyme, and oregano
½ cup chopped parsley	1 tablespoon lemon juice

In a large saucepan, melt butter and oil over medium heat. Add shrimp and sauté just until pink. Stir in all other ingredients and seasonings. Simmer about 10 minutes. Mixture will be very saucy.

Serve a scoop of grits surrounded with shrimp and sauce. Serve with hot French bread for dipping. Serves 8.

Editor's Extra: If you can't find a roll of garlic cheese, substitute 6 ounces Velveeta and ½ teaspoon garlic powder.

Kay Ewing's Cooking School Cookbook (Louisiana)

The Acadians were French-speaking refugees from Nova Scotia (Acadia) who came to south Louisiana in 1763. Their name was soon shortened to "Cajuns." Farmers by tradition, they settled along the dense swamps and bayous, and by the Gulf where they harvested shrimp, crabs, crawfish, and oysters. They built boats out of cypress trees—pirogues—and trapped for furs. Many Cajuns speak a dialect of North American French. In recent decades Cajun cuisine, noted for its use of spicy seasonings, and zydeco music have become popular among non-Cajuns.

Rémoulade Sauce

½ cup tarragon vinegar
4 tablespoons Creole mustard
1 teaspoon horseradish
2 hard-boiled egg yolks,
  chopped fine
4 tablespoons mayonnaise
3 green onions and tops,
  chopped fine

1 large rib celery, chopped fine
3 teaspoons paprika
Dash of thyme
Dash of garlic salt
Dash of Worcestershire
Salt and cayenne pepper to taste
½ cup olive oil

In a bowl, whisk together all ingredients except olive oil. Whisk in olive oil a little at a time. Taste for salt and pepper. Chill well. If serving shrimp remoulade, go ahead and add cooked, peeled shrimp before chilling.

Cooking on the Coast (Mississippi)

Christopher's Favorite Shrimp, Crab, and Cheese Casserole

A delightful luncheon or brunch dish when accompanied by fresh asparagus and fresh seasonal fruit.

8–9 slices white bread,
  trimmed, cubed
2 pounds fresh, small or
  medium shrimp, cooked,
  peeled
2 pounds fresh crabmeat,
  drained, well picked
¾–1 pound sharp Cheddar
  cheese, grated

½ cup butter
2½ cups milk (or cream)
4 eggs, beaten
¾ teaspoon Colman's Dry
  Mustard
Salt to taste
Cayenne pepper to taste
Dash of Tabasco

Arrange bread, shrimp, crab, and cheese in layers in a 3-quart casserole. Pour melted butter over these layers. Mix milk (or cream), eggs, dry mustard, salt, cayenne pepper, and Tabasco. Pour this mixture slowly over layers. Lightly cover. Refrigerate 4 hours or overnight.

Bake, lightly covered with foil tent, at 350° for 1 hour or until bubbly. Remove foil and brown top by placing under broiler. Serves 6–8.

Variation: May sprinkle top with bread crumbs before placing under broiler.

A Samford Celebration Cookbook (Alabama)

Crabmeat Caroline

2 tablespoons butter
2 tablespoons flour
¼ cup minced green onions
¼ cup minced green pepper
1 clove garlic, minced
⅙ teaspoon rosemary
1 tomato, peeled and chopped
¼ cup dry white wine
1 cup heavy cream

1 teaspoon salt
¼ teaspoon Tabasco
⅓ cup grated Gruyère cheese
⅙ teaspoon dry mustard
1 pound lump crabmeat
3 tablespoons grated mozzarella cheese
3 tablespoons grated Parmesan cheese

Preheat oven to 350°. In a large skillet, melt butter and gradually blend in flour. Cook 2 minutes, stirring constantly. Add onions, green pepper, garlic, rosemary, and tomato; sauté 2–3 minutes. Add wine and continue cooking until vegetables are tender. Lower heat, and gradually add cream, salt, and Tabasco. Blend well. Remove from heat and stir in Gruyère cheese and mustard. Gently fold crabmeat into sauce and spoon into individual buttered ramekins. Combine cheeses and sprinkle on top. Bake 10–15 minutes, until browned and bubbly. Serves 4.

Jambalaya (Louisiana)

Crabmeat Imperial

1 green bell pepper, finely diced
2 pimentos, finely diced
1 tablespoon Dijon mustard
1 tablespoon salt
2 teaspoons white pepper

2 eggs, slightly beaten
1 cup mayonnaise
3 pounds lump crabmeat
1 tablespoon mayonnaise, for topping
Paprika, for topping

In a large mixing bowl, combine pepper, pimentos, mustard, salt, white pepper, eggs, and mayonnaise. Mix well. Add crabmeat and stir carefully so lumps are not broken. Place in well-greased 2-quart casserole. Top lightly with mayonnaise and sprinkle with paprika. Bake at 350° about 30 minutes. Serves 8–10.

Bravo! Applaudable Recipes (Alabama)

Almond Topped Crab Quiche

Pastry for 9-inch pie shell
1 cup shredded Swiss cheese
½ pound fresh crabmeat
2 green onions, sliced
3 eggs
1 cup half-and-half

½ teaspoon salt
½ teaspoon grated lemon rind
Dash of dry mustard
Dash of pepper
¼ cup sliced almonds

Line a 9-inch quiche dish with pastry. Trim excess from edges. Bake at 400° for 3 minutes; remove from oven, and gently prick with fork. Bake 5 minutes longer. Cool on rack.

Sprinkle cheese in pastry shell. Remove cartilage from crabmeat; place on top of cheese. Sprinkle with green onions. Beat eggs until foamy; stir in half-and-half, salt, lemon rind, dry mustard, and pepper. Pour into pastry shell. Sprinkle with almonds. Bake at 325° for 1 hour. Let stand 10 minutes before serving.

Hospitality Heirlooms (Mississippi)

Crabmeat au Gratin

½ cup finely chopped celery
1 cup chopped onion
1 stick butter
½ cup flour
1 (14-ounce) can evaporated
  milk

2 egg yolks
1 teaspoon salt
¼ teaspoon red pepper
Black pepper to taste
8 ounces grated Cheddar cheese
1 pound lump crabmeat

Sauté celery and onion in butter until soft. Add flour to this mixture. Add milk gradually, stirring constantly. Add egg yolks, salt, red and black pepper. Cook for 10 minutes. Put crabmeat in a bowl and pour sauce over the crabmeat. Blend well and place in a lightly greased casserole and sprinkle with grated cheese. Bake at 375°, until browned, approximately 15 minutes. Serves 4–6.

Paul Naquin's French Collection I: Louisiana Seafood
(Louisiana)

Crawfish Étouffée

1 bunch green onions, chopped
1 green bell pepper, chopped
4 tablespoons butter
1 (10-ounce) can Ro-Tel
  tomatoes
1 (8-ounce) can tomato sauce
1 (10¾-ounce) can cream of
  mushroom soup
1 pound crawfish tails

Sauté green onions and bell pepper in butter until wilted. Add Ro-Tel tomatoes, tomato sauce, and mushroom soup. Over low heat, bring to a boil; add crawfish and let cook until thick. Serve over rice.

In the Pink (Louisiana)

Crawfish Étouffée à la Arceneaux

½ cup margarine
1½ cups finely chopped onion
¾ cup finely chopped green
  bell pepper
1 clove garlic, minced, or ¼
  teaspoon garlic powder
2 tablespoons flour
2 heaping tablespoons undiluted
  cream of celery soup
1 (10-ounce) can Ro-Tel
  tomatoes and green chiles,
  puréed with liquid
1 cup beer
2 teaspoons salt
1 teaspoon cayenne pepper
1 pound peeled crawfish

Micromelt margarine in a 3-quart glass dish on HIGH (100%) 1 minute. Add onion, bell pepper, and garlic. Sauté on HIGH (100%) 6 minutes or until tender.

Add flour and celery soup. Stir in puréed Ro-Tel, beer, salt, and pepper. Microwave on HIGH (100%) 6 minutes.

Add crawfish. Cover. Microwave on HIGH (100%) 4 minutes. Serve étouffée over rice. Yields 4 servings.

Tout de Suite à la Microwave II (Louisiana)

Spicy Fried Crawfish Tails

6 tablespoons flour
2 teaspoons salt
1 teaspoon black pepper
2 tablespoons liquid crab boil
2 eggs, beaten

2 tablespoons milk
2 pounds crawfish tails
½ teaspoon salt
½ teaspoon Cayenne pepper
1 quart oil

Preheat oven to 250°. In bowl, mix flour, salt, pepper, crab boil, and eggs. Add milk, a teaspoon at a time, until batter is thick. Season crawfish with salt and Cayenne. Add to batter and let stand at least an hour.

In Dutch oven, heat oil until a wooden kitchen match floating on top ignites. Drop crawfish into hot oil, a handful at a time, making sure to separate them as they cook. Fry until golden brown, about 1 minute. Drain on a platter lined with paper towels, and keep warm in oven. When all crawfish have been fried, serve immediately. Serves 6.

Jambalaya (Louisiana)

Crawfish Dog

3 tablespoons shortening
3 tablespoons flour
1 medium onion, chopped
½ pound crawfish tails,
    peeled, ground

½ cup crawfish fat
¼ cup water
1 teaspoon red pepper
2 teaspoon salt

Make roux with shortening and flour; cook until light brown. Add onion; cook until done. Add crawfish and fat, water, and seasonings. Cook 20 minutes and serve on open-face hot dog bun.

Cajun Cooking (Louisiana)

Chretien Point Plantation just north of Lafayette, Louisiana, was built in 1831. The 12-room mansion features a magnificent staircase that was reproduced for Tara in the movie *Gone With the Wind.* Legend has it that a thieving pirate was shot on his way up that staircase, and that his ghost climbs it still.

Oyster Stew

6 green onions (scallions),
  chopped fine
1 rib celery, chopped fine
1 stick butter or margarine
2 tablespoons flour
2–3 dozen small oysters
  with liquid

1 quart milk
Salt and pepper to taste
Worcestershire
Slices of toast bread, cut into
  croutons
2 sprigs parsley, minced

Sauté chopped vegetables in margarine and flour. Drain oysters and add liquid to vegetables. Add preheated milk, then oysters, and simmer until oysters are plump and edges begin to turn. Add salt, pepper, and Worcestershire to taste. Serve with croutons. Sprinkle with parsley. Serves 4.

Louisiana's Original Creole Seafood Recipes (Louisiana)

Oysters Oregano

¼ cup butter
1 large onion, chopped
½ teaspoon thyme
¾ teaspoon oregano
3 cloves garlic, finely chopped
2 tablespoons chopped parsley

¼ teaspoon red pepper
Salt and pepper to taste
4 dozen oysters with liquor
1 cup Italian-style bread crumbs
½–¾ cup Parmesan cheese

In a skillet melt the butter. Add the onion, and sauté until limp. Add all of the seasonings and mix well. Add the oysters and when the edges curl, add the oyster liquor. Fold in the bread crumbs. Transfer the mixture to a buttered casserole. Sprinkle the dish heavily with Parmesan cheese. Bake at 350° for 15–20 minutes. Serves 4.

La Bonne Cuisine (Louisiana)

Rockefeller Sauce

3 (10-ounce) bags fresh spinach
1 bunch green onions
Leaves from ½ bunch celery
1 whole bulb garlic, peeled and
  separated
1 bunch fresh parsley
4 cups water
1 cup grated Parmesan cheese
1 cup bread crumbs
1 pound butter, melted
1 jigger Pernod (anise liqueur)

In a large pot, boil spinach, onions, celery leaves, garlic, and parsley in water 20 minutes. Drain and chop in a food processor. Return to pot and add cheese, bread crumbs, and melted butter. Mix. Add Pernod and stir. Serve over oysters. Freezes well. For 5 dozen oysters.

Jambalaya (Louisiana)

Catfish Cakes

Catfish are plentiful in this part of the country. Crabs are not; hence, this cotton country version of the crab cake. Serve as an entreé, or serve one or two on some curly lettuce leaves for a hearty first course.

1½ pounds catfish fillets
1 large potato, peeled
2 eggs, beaten
1 large onion, finely chopped
1–2 tablespoons chopped
  fresh parsley
2–3 drops hot pepper sauce
1 clove garlic, minced
1 teaspoon salt
½ teaspoon pepper
½ teaspoon dried basil
2 cups finely crushed butter-
  flavor crackers
Vegetable oil
Tartar sauce (optional)

Poach or bake the fish; drain well. Cover and chill thoroughly. Boil or bake potato; mash well. Flake fish into a large bowl. Add potato, eggs, onion, parsley, hot pepper sauce, garlic, salt, pepper, and basil; mix well. Shape mixture into 8 patties. Coat with cracker crumbs. Heat a small amount of oil in a large skillet; add the patties. Cook until evenly browned and heated through. Serve with tartar sauce, if desired. Yields 8 servings.

Southern Settings (Alabama)

Oven Baked Catfish

6 catfish fillets, each about 6
  ounces
½ teaspoon Creole seasoning
1 (8-ounce) carton sour cream
1 cup mayonnaise

1 (1-ounce) package ranch-style
  dry salad dressing mix
1 (2.8-ounce) can French fried
  onion rings

Preheat oven to 350°. Put fillets in shallow bowl and sprinkle evenly with Creole seasoning. Set aside. In a small bowl, combine sour cream, mayonnaise, and salad dressing mix. Blend well. Pour mixture into shallow bowl. Process onion rings in blender or food processor until finely crushed. Put into another shallow bowl. Dip fillets first in sour cream mixture, then in crushed onion rings and coat evenly. Put fish in an ungreased shallow baking pan. Bake uncovered until fish flakes easily when tested with a fork, about 20 minutes. Makes 6 servings.

Cajun Cooking for Beginners (Louisiana)

PHOTO COURTESY OF COOPWOOD COMMUNICATIONS

The Delta Blues Museum, housed in the former Yazoo and Mississippi River Valley Railroad Depot in Clarksdale, exhibits photos, instruments, and local artifacts relating to the history and significance of the Delta Blues.

Blackened Catfish

½ teaspoon sage
½ teaspoon garlic powder
½ teaspoon cumin
¼ teaspoon cayenne
¼ teaspoon onion powder
1 teaspoon paprika

½ teaspoon sugar
½ teaspoon salt
4 (4-ounce) catfish fillets
Nonstick cooking spray
1 teaspoon olive oil
Lemon slices and chutney

Place all herbs and spices in a zip-loc bag and shake until well blended. Rinse fillets and pat dry. Place fillets, one at a time, in bag and coat thoroughly. Spray nonstick skillet with cooking spray and add 1 teaspoon olive oil. Cook catfish fillets 4–5 minutes per side on medium-high flame until blackened. Serve with lemon slices and chutney.

Incredible Edibles: A Gardener's Cookbook (Alabama)

Mississippi Catfish Fillets

¾ cup yellow cornmeal
¼ cup self-rising flour
½ teaspoon salt
½ teaspoon black pepper

1 teaspoon garlic salt
½ teaspoon cayenne red pepper
2 pounds catfish fillets
Oil for frying

Mix meal, flour, salt, pepper, garlic salt, and cayenne. Roll fish in mixture until coated good. Have oil hot, about 400°. Add fish in single layer. Fry until golden brown, to your desire. Drain on paper towels or brown bag. Serve hot. Also good cold or warmed in microwave.

Recipe by Blanch Baker, Pontotoc County artist
Mississippi Stars Cookbook (Mississippi)

The Blues originated in the rural Mississippi Delta region at the beginning of the 20th century. Famous Mississippi Blues artists include Robert Johnson, B.B. King, John Lee Hooker, Son House, Willie Dixon, Howlin' Wolf, "Honeyboy" Edwards, and Muddy Waters among many others. The University of Mississippi Blues Archive in Oxford houses one of the largest collections of blues recordings, publications, and memorabilia in the world.

·Spicy Catfish Amandine

¼ cup butter, melted
3 tablespoons lemon juice
6 (6-ounce) catfish fillets

1½ teaspoons Creole
  seasoning
½ cup sliced almonds

Combine butter and lemon juice; dip each fillet in butter mixture; arrange in 9x13-inch baking dish. Sprinkle fish with Creole seasoning and almonds. Bake at 375° for 25–30 minutes or until fish flakes easily when tested with fork. Serves 4–6.

Grits 'n Greens and Mississippi Things (Mississippi)

Steamed Redfish with Creole Sauce

1 (4- to 5-pound) redfish,
  cleaned
1 (14.5-ounce) can stewed
  tomatoes or equivalent of
  fresh stewed tomatoes
2 tablespoons chopped onion
½ teaspoon salt

Salt and pepper to season
½ cup water
4 tablespoons chopped green
  pepper
6 stuffed olives, chopped
2 tablespoons butter or
  margarine

Wash redfish and dry thoroughly. Sprinkle with salt and pepper and tie in cheesecloth; steam 45 minutes to 1 hour depending upon the size of the fish. Remove cheesecloth, place fish in center of hot platter, and pour Creole sauce over it.

Steaming can be accomplished by placing fish in a deep pan and adding a rack. Place fish on pan rack so that it does not touch water. Cover dish. Cook either in oven (medium heat) or on top of stove, being careful to observe throughout the cooking process that water is still in pan for steaming.

For Creole sauce, put tomatoes in blender and purée. Remove and put in heavy skillet. Add remaining ingredients. Simmer over low heat for 1 hour. Add small amounts of water if it dries out. Serve over redfish.

Louisiana Keepsake (Louisiana)

Trout Amandine

¼ cup reduced-calorie
　margarine
1 tablespoon chopped onion
1 tablespoon plus 2 teaspoons
　lemon juice, divided
¼ cup almonds, toasted lightly

1 tablespoon chopped parsley
4 (4-ounce) rainbow trout fillets
¼ teaspoon salt
⅛ teaspoon pepper
⅛ teaspoon ground red pepper

Combine margarine, chopped onion, and 1 tablespoon lemon juice in a saucepan. Cook over medium heat 5 minutes. Stir in almonds and parsley. Set aside and keep warm. Line 7x11x1½-inch baking dish with foil. Place fillets in dish and sprinkle with salt, peppers, and 2 teaspoons lemon juice. Broil 5½ inches from heat with door partially opened for 8 minutes, or until fish is flaky. Transfer to platter; top with almond/butter mixture. Yields 4 servings.

Field O' Dreams Farm Cookbook II (Alabama)

Tommy's Terrific Trout

This is one terrific recipe! The fillets are cooked in a garlic-butter Worcestershire mixture. Do not overcook fillets. If your fillets are thin, adjust cooking time. The fish, a crisp green salad, and hot French bread are all you need for a perfect meal.

6 trout fillets
Salt, black peppers and
　cayenne pepper to taste
6 tablespoons butter or
　margarine
2 cloves garlic, minced

1½ tablespoons
　Worcestershire
½ cup Italian bread crumbs
1 lemon, sliced for garnish
⅓ cup white wine

Season fish with salt and peppers. Melt butter in a 9x13-inch baking dish. Add garlic and Worcestershire to butter. Coat both sides of fish with butter mixture, and place fillets in dish. Bake in 400° oven 20 minutes, depending on size of fillets. Pull out dish on oven rack and sprinkle crumbs over fish. Garnish with lemon slices. Add wine to pan juices. Turn oven to broil. Return fish to oven. Broil until surface is brown and crispy, watching closely. Serve piping hot. Serves 3–6, depending on size of fillets.

Extra! Extra! Read All About It! (Louisiana)

Stuffed Flounder

2 eggs
2 cups cooked shrimp or
  crabmeat
1 cup cream
2 tablespoons butter
½ cup sliced mushrooms

2 teaspoons chopped chives
1 tablespoon flour
4 tablespoons sherry
4 (¾-pound) flounders
Additional butter

Mix eggs, shrimp, and cream. Melt butter; add mushrooms and chives, and sauté until soft; add flour and cook until bubbly. Add shrimp mixture and sherry, and cook until thick. Slit flounder along backbone and cut flesh of fish away from bone, but leave intact. Spoon as much stuffing into slit as possible. Top with butter and bake in 300° oven until done, about 30 minutes.

If you want to use fewer flounders, the stuffing may be made as directed, and the remainder can be stored in the refrigerator for use at a later date.

The Pick of the Crop (Mississippi)

CAKES

Mardi Gras is music, parades, excitement . . . and one big holiday in New Orleans, Louisiana! Parade riders wear elaborate costumes and throw beads from beautifully decorated floats. The party begins on the Twelfth Night Feast of the Epiphany, and ends on "Fat Tuesday," the day before Ash Wednesday.

Lemon Ice Box Cake

Delicious and beautiful.

FILLING:

2 (14-ounce) cans sweetened   ⅔ cup fresh lemon juice
condensed milk

Preheat oven to 350°. In a bowl, combine Filling ingredients. Place in refrigerator to thicken while preparing Cake.

CAKE:

1 (18¼-ounce) box yellow cake   ⅓ cup vegetable oil
   mix   ⅓ cup sugar
1 (8-ounce) carton sour cream   ⅓ cup water
4 eggs   1 teaspoon vanilla

Combine all Cake ingredients. Pour into 4 greased and floured 8-inch round cake pans. Bake 20–22 minutes. Let cool. Set aside ¾ cup Filling mixture. Spread cake layers with remaining Filling mixture.

ICING:

¾ cup Filling mixture   1 (8-ounce) carton frozen
                                    nondairy whipped topping,
                                    thawed

Combine reserved Filling mixture and whipped topping. Use wooden skewers, if necessary, to secure cake layers while icing. Keep cake refrigerated. Makes 12 servings.

Prime Meridian (Mississippi)

Meridian
Mississippi

Jimmie Rodgers has long been recognized as "The Father of Country Music," and was the first name placed in the Country Music Hall of Fame in Nashville, Tennessee, in 1961. Although his career spanned a brief six years, he made over 100 recordings. (Rodgers died of tuberculosis at the height of his fame.) Rodgers combined popular tunes with rural instrumentation, and punctuated his best-known songs with an original "blue yodel" that has since been widely imitated. In the midst of the Great Depression, each Rodgers release sold nearly a million copies. The Jimmie Rodgers Museum is located in his hometown of Meridian, Mississippi.

Lemon Apricot Cake

3 eggs
⅓ cup canola oil
1 (10-ounce) can apricot nectar

1 (18¼-ounce) package yellow
cake mix (pudding in mix)

Heat oven to 350°. Combine all ingredients in large bowl and beat at medium speed for 2 minutes. Bake in greased and floured 10-inch tube pan for 40–45 minutes. Cool right side up 20–25 minutes before removing from pan. Spread Icing while still warm.

ICING:
¼ cup butter or margarine,
   softened
2½ cups sifted confectioners'
   sugar

¼ cup lemon juice
⅛ teaspoon grated lemon rind
   (optional)

Blend until smooth and spread over cooled cake.

L'Heritage Du Bayou Lafourche (Louisiana)

Hummingbird Cake

3 cups all-purpose flour
2 cups sugar
1 teaspoon salt
1 teaspoon baking soda
1 teaspoon cinnamon
3 eggs, beaten

1½ cups oil
1½ teaspoons vanilla
1 (8-ounce) can crushed
   pineapple, drained
2 cups chopped bananas
1 cup chopped nuts

Mix by hand. Combine dry ingredients; add eggs and oil. Stir until well mixed. Add vanilla, pineapple, bananas, and nuts. Spoon batter into large greased and floured sheet pan. Bake at 350° for 40–45 minutes.

ICING:
1 box confectioners' sugar
½ cup margarine
1 (8-ounce) package cream
   cheese

1 teaspoon vanilla
1 cup chopped nuts

Combine first 4 ingredients. Sprinkle with chopped nuts on top of Icing.

Calling All Cooks (Alabama)

Fresh Strawberry Cake

1 (18¼-ounce) box yellow
 cake mix
1 (8-ounce) package cream
 cheese, softened
½ cup powdered sugar

½ cup sugar
1 (16-ounce) carton Cool Whip
2 cartons fresh strawberries,
 sliced thin
1 jar strawberry glaze

Bake cake according to package directions for 2 cake pans; allow
to cool. Cut the layers with a piece of thread to make 4 layers.
Mix cream cheese and sugars together. Fold in Cool Whip. In
another bowl, mix strawberries and glaze together. Start with one
layer of cake; spread with a layer of cream cheese mixture, then a
layer of strawberry glaze mixture. Repeat with each layer. Keep
in refrigerator.

Recipes & Remembrances (Alabama)

Strawberry Cream Cake

Light and refreshing.

1 angel food cake, baked
 according to directions
1 (8-ounce) package cream ,
 cheese softened
1 (14-ounce) can sweetened
 condensed milk

⅓ cup lemon juice
1 teaspoon almond extract
2 cups sliced strawberries
1 (8-ounce) carton Cool Whip or
 whipped cream
Additional strawberries

Bake cake and cool completely. Cut a 1-inch slice from top of
cake and set aside. Cut one inch from center hole and outer edge
and remove center of cake, pulling with fingers. Leave 1 inch at
bottom.

   Beat cream cheese; add condensed milk, lemon juice, and
almond extract. Fold in cake pieces and strawberries. Spoon into
center of cake. Top with reserved top slice. Chill 8 hours or
overnight. Frost with Cool Whip and additional strawberries.

Note: Can use fat-free cream cheese and fat-free sweetened condensed
milk for a very low-fat dessert. It is just as delicious. May use store-
bought angel food cake.

Shared Treasures (Louisiana)

Fresh Apple Cake

3 cups all-purpose flour
½ teaspoon salt
1½ teaspoons baking soda
2 teaspoons nutmeg
2 tablespoons cinnamon
2 cups sugar

2 eggs
1½ cups oil
2 teaspoons vanilla
3 cups chopped, peeled apples
1 cup chopped pecans

Sift flour, salt, baking soda, and spices in bowl. Mix in sugar. Make a hole and put eggs and oil in; mix. Add vanilla, apples, and nuts. Blend well. Bake in greased, floured Bundt or tube pan at 300° for 1 hour and 15 minutes. Serve with Hot Buttered Rum Sauce.

HOT BUTTERED RUM SAUCE:

1 cup sugar
½ cup butter or margarine

1 cup light cream
1 teaspoon rum extract

Combine sugar, butter, and cream in saucepan. Mix well. Heat over low heat, stirring occasionally until hot. Stir in rum flavoring. Serve over Apple Cake.

L'Heritage Du Bayou Lafourche (Louisiana)

Upside-Down Apple Cake

4 or 5 tart cooking apples
Lemon juice
2 tablespoons butter
1 cup packed light brown
  sugar, sifted
1 egg

1 cup sugar
1 cup whipping cream
1 teaspoon vanilla extract
2 cups all-purpose flour
2 teaspoons baking powder
Confectioners' sugar

Peel apples and remove cores. Slice apples paper thin, then sprinkle lightly with lemon juice to keep from discoloring. Place butter in 9-inch-round, shallow baking dish. Place in preheated 325° oven until melted, then remove from oven. Do not turn off heat. Sprinkle brown sugar over butter. Overlap apple slices in baking dish, working from center to edges, until bottom is covered.

Place egg in medium-size mixing bowl and beat well with electric mixer. Gradually add sugar and beat until mixed. Mix cream and vanilla. Sift flour with baking powder, then add to egg mixture alternately with cream mixture, beating well after each addition. Pour over apples. Bake about 35 minutes or until cake tester inserted comes out clean. Let cool 10 minutes, then turn onto rack and cool. Place on cake plate and cut into servings. Sprinkle with confectioners' sugar. Yields 8 servings.

Dining Under the Magnolia (Alabama)

© LIBRARY OF CONGRESS

Rosa Louise Parks (February 4, 1913–October 24, 2005) was an African American seamstress and civil rights activist whom the U.S. Congress later called "Mother of the Modern Day Civil Rights Movement." On December 1, 1955, in Montgomery, Alabama, Parks refused to give up her seat on a city bus to a white man. This act of courage sparked the 381-day Montgomery Bus Boycott led by Dr. Martin Luther King, Jr. Finally, the ruling came in November 1956 from the Supreme Court that segregation on transportation was unconstitutional.

Fig Cake

2 cups all-purpose flour
2 cups sugar
⅔ cup cooking oil
4 eggs, beaten
1 teaspoon vanilla

2 cups mashed figs
2 teaspoons cinnamon
½ teaspoon baking soda
1 cup chopped pecans

Mix all ingredients together and place in greased 11x15-inch pan. Bake at 350° for 25–30 minutes.

Family Favorites (Louisiana)

Jan's Fig Cake

This cake will stay moist for a week or as long as it lasts.

2 cups all-purpose flour
1 teaspoon cinnamon
1 teaspoon cloves
1 teaspoon nutmeg
1 teaspoon salt
1 teaspoon baking soda
1½ cups sugar

1 cup oil
3 eggs
1 cup buttermilk
1 cup fig preserves
1 cup chopped pecans
1 teaspoon vanilla

Grease and flour a tube or sheet cake pan. Preheat oven to 350°. Mix flour, cinnamon, cloves, nutmeg, salt, baking soda, and sugar in large mixing bowl. Add oil; beat well. Alternately add eggs, one at a time, and buttermilk, ⅓ cup at a time, beating after each addition. Add chopped fig preserves (juice and all), pecans, and vanilla. Mix well. Bake for one hour or until done. Make Sauce and pour over hot cake. Let cool in the pan. Does not have to be refrigerated.

SAUCE:
1 tablespoon white corn syrup
½ teaspoon baking soda
1 cup sugar

½ stick butter or margarine
½ cup buttermilk
1 teaspoon vanilla

Mix together all ingredients in saucepan. Boil 3 minutes, stirring constantly; pour hot Sauce over cake immediately. Let cool in pan; cover with lid.

Lake Guntersville Bed & Breakfast Cookbook (Alabama)

Watermelon Cake

*Make several cakes when you have a watermelon. Freeze on a cardboard base;
cover well with several layers of plastic wrap and then wrap in foil.*

1 (18¼-ounce) box white or
  yellow cake mix
1 tablespoon flour
1 (3-ounce) package
  watermelon Jell-O

¾ cup oil
4 eggs
1 cup watermelon pieces

Preheat oven to 325°. Mix cake mix, flour, Jell-O, oil, and eggs.
Add watermelon; beat, leaving a few little bits of watermelon
showing in batter. Pour batter into greased and floured Bundt
pan. Bake 45 minutes to 1 hour, until toothpick inserted comes
out clean. Invert onto wire rack; cool completely before frosting.

FROSTING:
⅓ stick margarine, softened
1 (1-pound) box powdered
  sugar

¼ cup watermelon pieces
  or a little more

Beat margarine and powdered sugar together, adding watermelon
a little at a time to keep the Frosting rather thick so it will spread
over the cake without running down. Adjust thickness with more
powdered sugar or watermelon.

Sharing Our Best (Alabama)

Mary McDonald's Sour Cream Coconut Cake

1 (18¼-ounce) package butter
  yellow cake mix
1½ cups sugar
2 (8-ounce) cartons sour cream

2 (6-ounce) packages frozen
  coconut, thawed
1 (8-ounce) carton whipped
  topping, thawed

Prepare and bake cake mix in 2 layers. Cool; split both layers. Combine sugar, sour cream, and coconut; chill 30 minutes or so. (Reserve 1 cup sour cream mixture for frosting.) Spread cream mixture between layers. Combine reserved mixture with whipped topping, and ice cake. Refrigerate 3 days before serving. Cover cake well with heavy-duty foil.

Hospitality Heirlooms (Mississippi)

Caramel-Nut Pound Cake

1 cup butter
½ cup shortening
1 cup sugar
1 (1-pound) box brown sugar
5 large eggs
3 cups sifted, all-purpose flour

½ teaspoon salt
½ teaspoon baking powder
1 (5-ounce) can evaporated milk
½ cup water
1 tablespoon vanilla
1 cup chopped nuts

Preheat oven to 325°. Cream butter and shortening until fluffy. Add sugar and brown sugar one cup at a time. Add eggs one at a time. Sift flour, salt, and baking powder together. Add to creamed mixture alternately with evaporated milk and water. Add vanilla and nuts. Pour into greased and floured tube pan. Bake 1½ hours. Cake may be frosted or served plain.

FROSTING:

¼ cup butter or margarine,
  softened
2 cups sifted confectioners'
  sugar

1 cup chopped, butter-roasted
  pecans
1 teaspoon vanilla
¼–½ cup milk

Cream butter and confectioners' sugar; add pecans. Add vanilla and enough milk for consistency desired. Spread over warm cake. Serves 16.

Sterling Service (Alabama)

Wash Day Cake

1 (18¼-ounce) box yellow
  cake mix
1 cup coconut
1 cup chopped pecans
1 stick butter, melted

3 eggs, divided
1 (8-ounce) package cream
  cheese, softened
1 (1-pound) box confectioners'
  sugar

Mix cake mix, coconut, pecans, butter, and 1 egg. Pour into a greased 9x13-inch pan. Mix cream cheese, 2 eggs, and sugar; place on top of cake mixture. Bake at 350° for 45 minutes.

Favorite Recipes (Alabama)

Sour Cream Pound Cake

This has a crusty top.

3 cups all-purpose flour
¼ teaspoon baking soda
2 sticks butter, softened
3 cups sugar

6 eggs
1 cup sour cream
1 teaspoon vanilla

Sift flour and measure; resift twice with soda. Set aside. Cream butter and add sugar slowly, beating constantly to cream well. Add eggs, one at a time, beating after each addition. Stir in sour cream. Add flour mixture, ½ cup at a time, beating well. Stir in vanilla and turn batter into well-greased and floured 10-inch tube pan. Bake at 325° about 1½ hours or until cake is done. Place pan on rack to cool 5 minutes. Loosen cake around edge of pan and edge of tube with dull side of knife. Press toward pan rather than toward cake. This protects crust. Turn cake onto rack to cool completely. Serve plain.

Note: One teaspoon lemon extract or ½ teaspoon almond flavoring may be used instead of vanilla.

Bell's Best (Mississippi)

Pecan Pie Cake

3 eggs, divided
1 (18¼-ounce) box yellow
  cake mix
½ cup butter, softened
1 (1-pound) box powdered
  sugar

1 (8-ounce) package cream
  cheese, softened
1 teaspoon vanilla
1 cup (or more) coarsely
  chopped pecans

Mix 1 egg, cake mix, and butter together. Pat in bottom of a greased, 9x13-inch baking pan. Mix 2 eggs, powdered sugar, cream cheese, vanilla, and pecans together, and cover the cake mixture completely. Bake 1 hour and 15 minutes at 350°. Cut into squares. Serve hot or cold.

Note: Keep a check on the color. When it starts turning brown, it is done.

From the Firehouse to Your House (Mississippi)

Toasted Butter Pecan Cake

1⅓ cups chopped pecans
1½ cups butter, divided
3 cups all-purpose flour
2 teaspoons baking powder
1 teaspoon salt

2 cups sugar
4 eggs
1 cup milk
2 teaspoons vanilla

Toast pecans in ¼ cup butter on baking sheet at 350° (about 7–10 minutes; be careful not to burn). Sift flour, baking powder, and salt. Cream remaining butter, gradually adding sugar. Cream well. Blend in eggs, beating after each addition. Add dry ingredients with milk, vanilla, and pecans. Bake in 3 pans at 350° for 20 minutes, or until tests done.

FROSTING:
¼ cup butter, softened
¼ cup cream cheese, softened
1 (1-pound) box powdered
  sugar

1 teaspoon vanilla
4–6 teaspoons whipping cream
⅔ cup chopped pecans

Combine all ingredients, and spread on cooled cake layers and top.

Hope in the Kitchen (Mississippi)

Hot Fudge Sundae Cake

1 cup Gold Medal flour	1 teaspoon vanilla extract
¾ cup sugar	1 cup chopped nuts
2 tablespoons cocoa	1 cup brown sugar
2 teaspoons baking powder	¼ cup packed cocoa
¼ teaspoon salt	1¾ cups hottest tap water
½ teaspoon milk	Favorite ice cream
2 tablespoons vegetable oil	

Heat oven to 350°. In ungreased 9x9-inch pan, stir together flour, sugar, 2 tablespoons cocoa, baking powder, and salt. Mix in milk, oil, and vanilla with fork until smooth. Stir in nuts. Spread evenly in pan. Sprinkle with brown sugar and ¼ cup cocoa. Pour hot water over batter. Bake 40 minutes. Let stand 15 minutes, then cut into squares. Invert onto dish. Spoon over ice cream with sauce that is formed on bottom of cake pan. Serves 8.

The Best of South Louisiana Cooking (Louisiana)

Butterfingers Cake

1 (18¼-ounce) yellow cake mix	8 (2.1-ounce) Butterfinger candy bars, crushed, divided
1 (14-ounce) can condensed milk	1 (16-ounce) container Cool Whip
1 (12-ounce) jar caramel topping	

Bake cake in a 9x13-inch pan according to directions on box. Mix condensed milk and caramel topping. While cake is still hot, poke holes in top and pour caramel mixture over cake so that the liquid seeps through the holes. Sprinkle crumbs from 6 of the candy bars on top, and let cool. Cover with plastic wrap and refrigerate until cold. Frost with Cool Whip. Sprinkle remaining candy crumbs on top.

Treasured Favorites (Alabama)

Heavenly Hash Cake

1 cup sugar
8 tablespoons margarine
2 eggs
¾ cup self-rising flour
1 cup chopped pecans

1 teaspoon vanilla
3 tablespoons cocoa
1½ cups miniature
  marshmallows

Cream sugar and margarine. Add eggs and other ingredients except marshmallows. Bake in buttered 9x9x2-inch pan, at 350° for 30–35 minutes. Test with toothpick. While cake bakes, make Icing.

ICING:
2 tablespoons cocoa
2 tablespoons margarine
½ box powdered sugar

2–4 tablespoons evaporated
  milk (icing will be thin)

Remove cake from oven and while cake is hot, pour marshmallows over cake to cover. When completely cooled, put icing on cake in pan. Cut in 36 squares (1½ inches each).

Recipes and Reminiscences of New Orleans I (Louisiana)

Chocolate Éclair Cake

1 (1-pound) box graham
  crackers
2 (3-ounce) packages French
  vanilla instant pudding

3½ cups milk
1 (8-ounce) container frozen
  whipped topping, thawed

Butter bottom of 9x13-inch cake pan. Line with whole graham crackers. Mix pudding and milk. Beat at medium speed for 2 minutes. Blend in whipped topping. Pour ½ pudding mixture over crackers. Place second layer of crackers over pudding. Pour remaining pudding mixture over top, and cover with graham crackers. Refrigerate 2 hours, then frost.

FROSTING:
2 squares unsweetened
  chocolate
2 teaspoons white Karo syrup
2 teaspoons vanilla

3 teaspoons butter, softened
½ cup confectioners' sugar
3 tablespoons milk

Melt chocolate in microwave for 1½ minutes or until melted. Add rest of ingredients and beat until smooth. Spread on cake. Refrigerate at least 24 hours.

Let's Get Together (Mississippi)

Chocolate Cookie Sheet Cake

The cinnamon makes the difference!

2 cups all-purpose flour	3 tablespoons cocoa
2 cups sugar	2 eggs
½ teaspoon salt	1 teaspoon baking soda
1 teaspoon cinnamon	½ cup buttermilk
1 cup margarine	1 teaspoon vanilla
1 cup water	

Sift flour, measure, and resift with sugar, salt, and cinnamon. Bring margarine, water, and cocoa to a boil. Pour over flour and sugar mixture. Mix well. Mix eggs, soda, buttermilk, and vanilla. Add to above mixture. Mix well. Bake in greased and floured 10x15-inch pan for 20 minutes at 350°, or a 9x13-inch pan about 40 minutes.

ICING:

½ cup margarine	1 box confectioners' sugar
2 tablespoons cocoa	½ cup chopped pecans
6 tablespoons milk	1 teaspoon vanilla

Start cooking Icing the last 5 minutes cake is baking. Mix margarine, cocoa, and milk in saucepan over low heat. Remove and add sugar, nuts, and vanilla. Frost cake while hot. Makes 36 squares.

Cotton Country Cooking (Alabama)

Turtle Cake

1 (18¼-ounce) box chocolate
  cake mix
1 (14-ounce) package caramels

1 (6-ounce) can evaporated milk
1 cup chocolate chips
1 cup chopped pecans

Preheat oven to 350°. Grease and flour the bottom of a 9x13-inch baking pan. Mix cake according to directions on box. Spread ½ of prepared cake batter into pan and bake for 20 minutes. In a saucepan, melt caramels and milk together. Pour caramel mixture over hot cake; sprinkle chocolate chips and pecans over. Spoon remaining cake batter over top and continue baking 25 minutes.

Festival Cookbook (Mississippi)

Luscious Chocolate Cake

3 (1-ounce) squares
  unsweetened chocolate
1 stick butter, softened (no
  substitute)
1½ cups firmly packed brown
  sugar
3 eggs

½ teaspoon salt
2 teaspoons baking soda
2¼ cups cake flour, sifted
½ cup buttermilk
2 teaspoons vanilla
1 cup boiling water

Preheat oven to 375°. Grease 2 round cake pans and line with wax paper. Melt chocolate. Cream butter and sugar, then add eggs and melted chocolate. Stir in salt and baking soda. Alternately add flour and buttermilk, vanilla, and then boiling water. Bake for 45 minutes or until cake tester comes out clean. Check after 30 minutes.

FROSTING:

2 cups whipping cream
3 tablespoons cocoa

½ teaspoon vanilla
Chocolate shaving for garnish

Mix ingredients together and chill for at least 2 hours. Whip cream mixture and frost cool cake. Top with chocolate shavings and store in refrigerator.

Magic (Alabama)

Mrs. Burton's Neshoba County Red Mud Cake

1 pound butter, softened
1 (16-ounce) box confectioners' sugar
3 cups plain flour
¼ cup granulated sugar
½ teaspoon baking powder

7 large eggs, room temperature
1 tablespoon milk
½ tablespoon vanilla
5 drops red food coloring
7 drops yellow food coloring

Grease and flour tube pan. Using large mixing bowl, cream butter and confectioners' sugar together until light and fluffy. Mix flour with granulated sugar and baking powder. With mixer, gradually add flour mixture to butter mixture alternately with eggs, one at a time. Add 1 tablespoon milk, beating 4–5 minutes. Add vanilla and food colorings. Bake in 250° oven for 2½ hours. Turn out of pan and cool slightly before glazing.

GLAZE:

4 tablespoons butter
1½ cups sifted confectioners' sugar
3 tablespoons hot water

2 drops red food coloring
3 drops yellow food coloring
1 teaspoon vanilla

Melt butter; remove from heat. Stir in sugar and water. Add food colorings and vanilla. Mix well. Add more water, if needed. Spread on slightly cooled cake.

Why Gather in the Kitchen? (Mississippi)

Coca Cola Cake

2 cups unsifted all-purpose
  flour
2 cups sugar
2 sticks margarine
2 tablespoons cocoa
1 cup Coca Cola

½ cup buttermilk
2 eggs, unbeaten
1 teaspoon baking soda
1 teaspoon vanilla
1½ cups miniature
  marshmallows

Combine sugar and flour in a bowl. Heat margarine, cocoa, and Coca Cola to boiling; pour over sugar and flour mixture. Mix well then add buttermilk, eggs, soda, and vanilla. Mix well and add marshmallows to top. Bake in greased 9x13x2-inch pan for 35 minutes at 350°.

ICING:

1 stick margarine
2 tablespoons cocoa
6 tablespoons Coca Cola

1 pound powdered sugar
1 cup chopped nuts

Combine butter, cocoa, and Coca Cola, and bring to a boil. Pour over powdered sugar. After beating well, add pecans and pour over hot cake.

More Fiddling with Food (Alabama)

Mississippi's original soft drink, Barq's Root Beer, was invented in 1898 by Edward Barq, Sr., in Biloxi (pronounced Bah LUX see). The building in Biloxi where the drink was first made and bottled still stands. Barq's brand of root beer was notable for being the first major North American root beer to contain caffeine. A Mississippi Gulf Coast favorite, the number of franchise bottlers grew to over 200 by 1950. Barq's was acquired by the Coca Cola Bottling Company in 1995 and is now sold throughout the United States.

Italian Cream Cake

½ cup shortening
1 stick butter, softened
2 cups sugar
5 eggs, separated
2 cups flour
½ teaspoon salt

1 teaspoon baking soda
1 cup buttermilk
2 cups shredded coconut
1 cup chopped pecans
1 teaspoon vanilla

Cream shortening, butter, and sugar. Add egg yolks one at a time. Mix dry ingredients and add alternately with buttermilk. Stir in coconut and pecans. Add beaten egg whites and vanilla. Bake in 3 greased, 9-inch pans at 350° for 35–40 minutes or until done.

CREAM CHEESE FROSTING:

1 cup butter, softened
2 (8-ounce) packages cream
cheese, softened
2 (16-ounce) packages
powdered sugar

2 teaspoons vanilla
1 cup chopped pecans

Mix butter and cream cheese until creamy. Add sugar gradually. Add vanilla. Fold in pecans. Frost layers, top, and sides of cooled cake.

Bountiful Blessings–DeKalb (Mississippi)

Covering thirteen acres, the Louisiana Superdome, often referred to as simply the Superdome, is a large, multipurpose sports and exhibition facility in New Orleans. Bonds were passed for construction of the Superdome on November 8, 1966, seven days after NFL Commissioner Pete Rozelle awarded New Orleans the 25th professional football franchise. It is the current home of the NFL's New Orleans Saints. Designed in 1967 by the New Orleans modernist architectural firm of Curtis and Davis, it did not open until August 1975, due to political delays. The Superdome was the largest fixed domed structure in the world at the time, but has since been surpassed by the Georgia Dome in Atlanta in 1992 and by London's Millennium Dome in 1999.

More Super Bowls have been played at the Louisiana Superdome than at any other sports facility: 1978, 1981, 1986, 1990, 1997, and 2002. The Superdome has a listed maximum football seating capacity of 72,003 (expanded), a maximum basketball seating capacity of 55,675, and a maximum baseball capacity of 63,525; however, published attendance figures from events such as the Sugar Bowl football game have exceeded 79,000. A 1980s Rolling Stones concert attracted over 87,500 spectators.

Carrot Cake

2 cups all-purpose flour	1 teaspoon salt
2 cups sugar	1 cup oil
2 teaspoons baking soda	4 eggs
1½ teaspoons cinnamon	3 cups grated carrots

Preheat oven to 350°. Sift dry ingredients together, and add oil and eggs. Blend well. Add carrots and mix about 2 minutes. Pour into 2 (9-inch) greased pans and bake about 25–30 minutes. Frost when cool.

ICING:

1 (1-pound) box confectioners' sugar, sifted	1 stick margarine, softened
	1 teaspoon vanilla
1 (8-ounce) package cream cheese, softened	1 cup chopped pecans

Blend sugar, cream cheese, and margarine until smooth. Add vanilla and pecans. Frost cooled cake.

Bouquet Garni (Mississippi)

Eggnog Cakes

¾ cup butter, softened	3 teaspoons baking powder
1¼ cups sugar	¼ teaspoon salt
8 egg yolks	¾ cup milk
2½ cups sifted flour	1 teaspoon vanilla

Cream butter and sugar well. Add egg yolks and blend well. Sift dry ingredients 3 times; add to sugar mixture. Alternate with milk and vanilla. Beat until smooth. Pour into 3 square pans lined with wax paper. Bake 20 minutes at 350°. After cake cools, cut into small squares.

WHISKEY SAUCE:

1 stick butter, softened	1 cup bourbon
1 (1-pound) box sifted confectioners' sugar	½ cup chopped nuts
	½ box vanilla wafers, crushed

Cream butter and sugar. Mix well and add whiskey and nuts. Dip squares of cakes on all sides with whiskey mix and roll in crumb mixture. Store in air-tight container. Improves with age. Do not taste for 3 days. Freezes well.

The Pick of the Crop (Mississippi)

Amaretto Cake

1 cup butter, softened
2½ cups sugar
6 eggs
1 cup sour cream
1 teaspoon vanilla
1 teaspoon orange extract

1 teaspoon lemon extract
2 teaspoons almond extract
¼ teaspoon baking soda
½ teaspoon salt
3 cups sifted cake flour
½ cup Amaretto de Saronno

Preheat oven to 325°. Have all ingredients at room temperature. Beat butter and sugar until creamy. Add eggs one at a time, beating well after each egg has been added. Add sour cream, beat, then add extracts, baking soda, and salt. Gradually beat in flour that has been sifted 3 times and then measured. Add amaretto and beat well. Pour into large greased Bundt cake pan. Bake 1 hour and 15 minutes, or until done. Turn out on wire rack and cool.

GLAZE FOR CAKE:

1 (8-ounce) jar orange
  marmalade
½ jar (about 4 ounces)
  apricot preserves

¼ cup Amaretto de Saronno
1 cup chopped toasted almonds

Heat marmalade, preserves, and amaretto until melted. Drizzle on cooled cake, then sprinkle with almonds.

Giant Houseparty Cookbook (Mississippi)

Elvis Presley Cake

1 (18¼-ounce) box yellow
   cake mix
1 (3-ounce) box vanilla
   pudding (not instant)
4 eggs

½ cup oil
1 cup milk
1 (16-ounce) can crushed
   pineapple, undrained
1 cup sugar

Mix cake mix, pudding, eggs, oil, and milk. Beat until smooth. Bake in greased, 9x13-inch pan in 350° preheated oven for 1 hour (or until center springs back). While cake is baking, boil pineapple and sugar on top of stove until sugar has melted. While cake is still hot, punch holes in cake and pour hot pineapple over cake. Let cool. (More pineapple may be added, if desired.)

FROSTING:

1 (8-ounce) package cream
   cheese, softened
1 stick butter or margarine,
   softened

3 cups confectioners' sugar
½ cup chopped pecans
   (optional)

Beat cream cheese and butter until smooth. Add confectioners' sugar gradually and beat until creamy. Add pecans, if desired, and mix well. Frost cake.

Cooking with Gilmore (Mississippi)

Elvis Aaron Presley, in the humblest of circumstances, was born to Vernon and Gladys Presley in a two-room house in Tupelo, Mississippi, on January 8, 1935. His twin brother Jessie Garon was stillborn, leaving Elvis to grow up as an only child. He and his parents moved to Memphis, Tennessee, in 1948, and Elvis graduated from high school there in 1953.

In 1954, he began his singing career with the legendary Sun Records label in Memphis. By 1956, he was an international sensation. With a sound and style that uniquely combined his diverse musical influences and blurred and challenged the social and racial barriers of the time, he ushered in a whole new era of American music and popular culture.

Elvis starred in 33 successful films. Globally he has sold over one billion records, more than any other artist. Among his many awards and accolades were 14 Grammy nominations (three wins), and the Grammy Lifetime Achievement Award, which he received at the age of 36.

Known the world over by his first name, he is regarded as one of the most important figures of 20th century popular culture. Elvis died at his Memphis home, Graceland, on August 16, 1977. A cultural icon, he is commonly referred as the "The King of Rock 'n' Roll," or "The King."

Praline Cheesecake

GRAHAM CRACKER CRUST:

1 cup graham cracker crumbs	**¼ cup sugar**
¼ cup butter, melted	**¾ cup ground pecans**

Lightly grease the sides of springform pan. Mix all ingredients together and press in the bottom of springform pan: bake at 375° for 8–10 minutes.

2 cups sugar	**2 teaspoons vanilla**
¼ cup water	**6 eggs, room temperature**
2 cups light cream	**⅓ cup Kahlúa liqueur**
2 pounds cream cheese, room	
temperature	

In a saucepan, heat the sugar and ¼ cup water, and cook over medium heat until sugar has turned golden brown and has liquefied. Pour in the cream, and cook until the sugar has dissolved. Set this aside and let cool. In a large bowl, cream the cream cheese until fluffy. Mix in the vanilla and eggs, 1 at a time, until well blended. Add the cooled praline mixture and mix well. Stir in the Kahlúa and pour the batter in a springform pan lined with Graham Cracker Crust. Bake at 400° for 15 minutes, then at 300° for 1 hour. Turn off the oven, crack the door, and leave in the oven for 30 minutes. Refrigerate for at least 4 hours before removing from pan.

La Bonne Louisiane (Louisiana)

There are many variations on the story of how the praline came to be, but most of them revolve around the manor house of the 17th-century French diplomat Cesar du Plessis Praslin—a name that later morphed into the term for the candy. A chef in the kitchen there developed a technique for coating almonds in cooked sugar which, competing stories hold, were used by his courtly employer either as a digestive aid or as gifts to the ladies he visited. These early confections traveled with Frenchmen to their new colony on the banks of the Mississippi, a land where both sugar cane and nuts were cultivated in abundance. In local kitchens, Louisiana pecans were substituted for the more exotic almonds, cream was added, giving the candy more body, and a southern tradition was born. The local and proper pronunciation is "PRAH-leen," while the nut most commonly used in it is pronounced "pih-KAHN."

Irish Cream Cheesecake

This will be a WOW!!! dessert at your next party.

CRUST:

2 cups Oreo cookie crumbs
¼ cup sugar

6 tablespoons butter, melted
1 cup semisweet chocolate chips

Preheat oven to 350°. Combine Oreo crumbs and sugar in bowl; add melted margarine. Mix well, and press into bottom of a 9-inch springform pan. Bake 7–10 minutes.

FILLING:

4 (8-ounce) packages cream
   cheese, softened
1⅔ cups sugar

5 eggs
1½ cups Irish cream liqueur
1 tablespoon vanilla

Beat cream cheese until smooth; add sugar and eggs, beating until fluffy. Add liqueur and vanilla; mix well. Sprinkle chocolate chips over crust. Spoon Filling over chips. Bake for 1 hour and 20 minutes, or until center is set. Cool completely in pan.

TOPPING:

1 cup whipping cream
2 tablespoons sugar

½ cup semisweet chocolate
   chips, melted

Beat cream and sugar in a large, chilled bowl until stiff. Continue to beat while adding melted chocolate. Spread mixture over cheesecake.

CHOCOLATE CURLS:

2 cups semisweet chocolate chips

Melt chocolate in a small saucepan over low heat. Pour onto a baking sheet. Let stand at room temperature until set, but not firm. To make curls, pull a thin knife or cheese plane across surface of chocolate (curls will break if chocolate is too firm). Remelt and cool as necessary to form desired number of curls. Arrange on cake. Refrigerate until ready to serve. Serves 16 or more.

A Pinch of Rose & A Cup of Charm (Mississippi)

Cheesecake

1 (6-ounce) box zwieback or
  graham crackers, crushed
1¼ cups sugar, divided
½ teaspoon cinnamon
¼ cup butter, melted
4 eggs, separated

1 cup sour cream
1 teaspoon vanilla extract
2 tablespoons flour
¼ teaspoon salt
1 pound cream cheese, softened

Combine crackers, ¼ cup sugar, cinnamon, and butter; press into bottom of a 9-inch springform pan. Bake at 350° for 10 minutes and let cool. Beat egg whites until stiff with ¼ cup sugar. Set aside. Without washing the beater, beat egg yolks until thick. Add sour cream and vanilla. Beat in remaining ¾ cup sugar, flour, salt, and cream cheese. Mix well and then fold in egg whites. Pour into springform pan. Bake at 350° for 50–55 minutes. Cool and chill. Top with Strawberry-Raspberry Glaze, if desired, or for an easy topping, use 1 can cherry or blueberry pie filling. Yields 12–15 servings.

STRAWBERRY-RASPBERRY GLAZE: (OPTIONAL)

2 pints strawberries
1 (12-ounce) jar red raspberry
  jelly

1 tablespoon cornstarch
¼ cup Cointreau
¼ cup water

Wash and hull berries and let dry completely. Combine a little jelly with cornstarch in saucepan and mix well. Add remaining jelly, Cointreau, and water and cook over medium heat, stirring frequently, until thickened and clear, 5–10 minutes. Cool to luke-warm, stirring occasionally. Arrange berries pointed end up all over top of cake. Spoon glaze over berries, allowing some to drip down sides of cake. Return to refrigerator until glaze is set.

Vintage Vicksburg (Mississippi)

COOKIES and CANDIES

Dr. Martin Luther King, Jr. served as pastor at Dexter Avenue Baptist Church in Montgomery, Alabama, from 1954–1959. In 1964, King received the Nobel Peace Prize for his work to end segregation and racial discrimination through non-violent means. Martin Luther King, Jr. Day was established as a national holiday in the United States in 1986.

Potato Chip Shortbread Cookies

These buttery cookies are delicious!

4 sticks butter (no substitute)
1 cup sugar
1 teaspoon vanilla

3½ cups all-purpose flour
1 cup chopped pecans
2 cups crushed potato chips

Preheat oven to 350°. Cream butter and sugar. Add vanilla and gradually add flour. Stir in nuts and potato chips. Drop by teaspoonfuls onto greased cookie sheet. Bake for 15 minutes. Yields 5 dozen.

Magic (Alabama)

Sand Tarts

2 sticks butter, softened
4 tablespoons sugar
2½ cups all-purpose flour

1 teaspoon vanilla
1 cup chopped pecans
Powdered sugar

Cream butter and add sugar slowly. Then add flour while still stirring. Add vanilla and pecans. Shape into crescents on a large cookie sheet. Bake in a slow oven until light brown (250° for about 45 minutes). After cookies cool, roll in powdered sugar.

The Gulf Gourmet (Mississippi)

Authentic Southern Soft Teacakes

These are soft, just like Granny used to make.

1 cup shortening
1¾ cups sugar
2 eggs
½ cup milk

½ teaspoon vanilla extract
¼ teaspoon almond extract
3 cups self-rising flour

In a mixing bowl, cream together shortening and sugar; beat in eggs; add milk and extracts; stir in flour. Drop by tablespoonfuls about 2½ inches apart onto greased cookie sheets. Bake 15–20 minutes at 350°. Makes about 3 dozen.

Family Traditions (Louisiana)

White Chocolate and Macadamia Cookies

1 stick butter, softened
4 ounces cream cheese, softened
½ teaspoon brown sugar
½ cup sugar
1 egg
2 teaspoons vanilla
2 cups flour
1 teaspoon baking soda
1 cup white chocolate morsels
½ cup macadamia nuts

Cream butter, cream cheese, and sugars. Add egg and vanilla. Add dry ingredients, and mix on low speed just until combined. Do not over mix. Bake at 300° for 18–20 minutes.

Breaking Bread Together (Mississippi)

Judy's Chocolate Crinkle Cookies

They look so pretty and taste like brownies.

½ cup vegetable oil
4 ounces unsweetened chocolate, melted
2 cups granulated sugar
4 eggs
2 teaspoons vanilla
2 cups unsifted all-purpose flour
2 teaspoons baking powder
½ teaspoon salt
1 cup confectioners' sugar

Mix oil, chocolate, and granulated sugar. Blend in 1 egg at a time till well mixed. Add vanilla; stir in flour, baking powder, and salt; chill overnight.

Preheat oven to 350°. Drop dough by teaspoon into confectioners' sugar—don't attempt to shape yet. Coat lightly with confectioners' sugar—this makes it crinkle. Pick up, roll into a ball, and roll again in confectioners' sugar. Place 2 inches apart on greased baking sheets. Bake 10–12 minutes. Do not overcook. They will be a little soft to the touch. Makes about 4 dozen small cookies.

Hors D'Oeuvres Everybody Loves (Mississippi)

Chocolate Chubbies

6 ounces semisweet chocolate,
   cut into small pieces
2 ounces unsweetened
   chocolate, cut into small
   pieces
5 tablespoons unsalted butter
3 eggs
1 cup (scant) sugar

¼ cup flour
½ teaspoon (scant) baking
   powder
Pinch of salt
8 ounces semisweet chocolate
   chips
8 ounces broken-up pecans
8 ounces broken-up walnuts

Combine semisweet and unsweetened chocolate pieces with butter in a double boiler. Cook over hot water until chocolate is melted, stirring frequently. Remove from heat and let stand to cool slightly. Beat eggs and sugar in a bowl until smooth. Add cooled chocolate mixture, beating constantly.

Sift flour, baking powder, and salt together into a bowl. Add to the chocolate mixture, stirring until moistened. Fold in chocolate chips, pecans, and walnuts. Drop batter by tablespoonfuls onto 2 greased cookie sheets, leaving 2 inches between cookies. Bake at 325° for 15–20 minutes or until lightly browned. Yields 3 dozen large cookies.

Southern Scrumptious: How to Cater Your Own Party (Alabama)

E-Z Peanut Butter Cookies

1 cup creamy peanut butter
1 egg, slightly beaten

1 cup granulated sugar
1 teaspoon vanilla extract

Heat oven to 325°. Mix all ingredients thoroughly. Drop by teaspoonfuls onto baking sheet and press with fork. Bake approximately 10 minutes. Cool before removing from baking sheet. Makes 2–3 dozen cookies.

The Five Star Family Book of Recipes (Alabama)

Butter Pecan Turtle Cookies

2 cups all-purpose flour
1 cup firmly packed brown
  sugar
½ cup butter, softened
1 cup whole or chopped pecans

⅔ cup butter
½ cup firmly packed brown
  sugar
1 cup chocolate chips

Preheat oven to 350°. In a 3-quart bowl, combine flour, 1 cup brown sugar, and ½ cup softened butter. Mix at medium speed, scraping sides of bowl often for 2–3 minutes or until well-mixed and particles are fine. Pat firmly into an ungreased 9x13x2-inch pan. Sprinkle pecans evenly over unbaked crust and press in lightly.

In a heavy 1-quart saucepan, combine ⅔ cup butter and ½ cup brown sugar. Cook over medium heat, stirring constantly, until entire surface of mixture begins to boil. Boil 1 minute, stirring constantly.

Pour caramel mixture over pecans and crust. Bake near the center of the oven for 18–22 minutes, or until entire caramel layer is bubbly and crust is light golden brown. Remove from oven, and immediately sprinkle with chocolate chips. Allow chips to melt slightly (1–2 minutes), then swirl chips as they melt. Leave some whole for a marbled effect, and do not spread. Cool completely, and cut into desired size. Makes about 75 bite-size squares.

Le Bon Temps (Louisiana)

Hiram King "Hank" Williams was born in 1923, in the small town of Mount Olive, about eight miles southwest of Georgiana, Alabama. Williams had eleven number-one hits in his short career, as well as many other Top 10 hits. He has become an icon of country music and one of the most influential musicians and songwriters of the 20th century. A leading pioneer of the honky tonk style, his songbook is one of the backbones of country music, and several of his songs are pop standards as well. His songs have been covered in a range of pop, gospel, blues, and rock styles. Williams' death at the age of twenty-nine helped fuel his legend. His son (Randall) Hank Williams, Jr., nicknamed "Bocephus," his daughter Jett Williams, and his grandchildren (Shelton) Hank Williams III, Holly Williams, and Hilary Williams are also professional singers. The Official Hank Williams Museum is in Montgomery, where Hank lived from 1937–1953. The Hank Williams, Sr. Boyhood Home & Museum in Georgianna houses a large collection of Hank Williams, Sr. memorabilia, including recordings, posters, and sheet music.

Giant Cookie Pizza

Great for birthday parties.

½ cup (1 stick) margarine, softened
½ cup firmly packed brown sugar
1 egg
½ teaspoon vanilla extract
1 cup all-purpose flour
¾ cup old-fashioned oats
½ teaspoon baking soda
¼ teaspoon salt

1 cup semisweet chocolate chips
1 cup prepared chocolate frosting
⅔ cup M&Ms Chocolate Candies
3 ounces white chocolate bark, grated
½ cup chopped gumdrops
1 piece strawberry fruit roll-ups

Cream margarine and brown sugar in a bowl with an electric mixer. Beat in egg and vanilla, mixing well. Combine flour, oats, baking soda, and salt in a bowl. Add flour mixture to the creamed mixture. Stir in chocolate chips. Spread cookie mixture on a greased 12-inch baking sheet and bake at 350° for 14–16 minutes or until golden brown.

Cool cookie completely on a wire rack. Spread frosting over cookie with a knife. Sprinkle cookies with M&M's, grated white chocolate, and gumdrops. Cut strawberry fruit roll-ups into circles for the "pepperoni" look and arrange them on cookie pizza. Cut into wedges. Yields 10—12 servings.

Calling All Kids (Alabama)

PHOTO COURTESY OF ALABAMA TOURISM

Tuskegee University was established in 1880 by an act of the Alabama State Legislature. The school's first president, Dr. Booker T. Washington, officially opened the Normal School for Colored Teachers on July 4, 1881, and served until his death in 1915. Dedicated in 1922, the Booker T. Washington Monument, called "Lifting the Veil," stands at the center of campus.

Colossal Cookies

½ cup margarine, softened
1½ cups white sugar
1½ cups brown sugar
4 eggs
1 teaspoon vanilla

2 cups chunky peanut butter
6 cups uncooked oats
2½ teaspoons baking soda
1 (12-ounce) package chocolate
   chips

In large bowl, beat together butter and sugars. Blend in eggs and vanilla. Add peanut butter. Mix well. Stir in oats, soda, and chocolate chips. Drop by teaspoons onto greased (if uncoated) cookie sheets (or roll into balls). Flatten with fork. Bake at 350° for 10–12 minutes. Makes a bunch.

Note: There is no flour in this recipe. It works better if you make the batter up and let it sit a while before you start to drop it onto the cookie sheets. The oats form a gluten that helps hold the cookie together better.

Sofilthy's Vittles Cookbook (Mississippi)

Coconut Cookies

When you taste this cookie, you will know the difference real butter makes! There is really no substitute!

2 sticks butter, softened
½ cup sugar
2 cups all-purpose flour
1 teaspoon vanilla

1 (3-ounce) can Baker's Angel
   Flake Coconut
Confectioners' sugar

Cream butter and sugar thoroughly. Add flour, vanilla, and coconut. Roll by hand into small balls. Put on a cookie sheet about an inch apart. Flatten these balls with a fork that has been dipped in cold water. Bake at 350° for 20–25 minutes. Cool cookies and dust with confectioners' sugar. These are very simple to make but very, very good and pretty on your cookie tray.

Cooking & Gardening with Dianne (Louisiana)

Chocolate Almondines

1 (18¼-ounce) box devil's
  food cake mix
1 stick (½ cup) margarine,
  softened
1½ teaspoons almond
  flavoring, divided
3 eggs

1 (8-ounce) package cream
  cheese, softened
1 (1-pound) box confectioners'
  sugar
¼ cup cocoa
1 (4-ounce) package sliced
  almonds

Butter and flour (or use Baker's Joy) a 9x13 or 11x14-inch pan.
Thoroughly mix together the cake mix, margarine, 1 teaspoon
almond flavoring, and 1 egg. Press into prepared pan. Mix
together remaining eggs and almond flavoring, cream cheese,
sugar, and cocoa. Pour over first mixture. Sprinkle top with
sliced almonds. Bake at 350° for 40–50 minutes.

Favorite Flavors of First (Alabama)

Chess Squares

1 (18¼-ounce) box yellow
  cake mix with pudding
1 stick butter, softened
½ cup chopped pecans
1 (8-ounce) package cream
  cheese, softened

1 (1-pound) box confectioners'
  sugar
2 eggs
½ teaspoon vanilla

Preheat oven to 350°. Cream butter and cake mix by hand. Press
mixture into 9x13-inch pan. Sprinkle with pecans. Mix remaining ingredients with electric mixer until smooth. Pour this mixture over cake mixture. Bake for 40 minutes or until top is gold-
en brown. Let cool and cut into squares. Best if made a day
ahead, and can be frozen. Yields 2 dozen cookies.

Magic (Alabama)

Butterscotch Squares

½ cup butter or margarine
3 cups light brown sugar
3 eggs
2 cups flour (if eggs are large,
   may need 2 tablespoons more)

¼ teaspoon salt
3 teaspoons baking powder
2 teaspoons vanilla
1 cup chopped nuts

Melt butter slowly over low heat in a skillet. Add sugar. Let cool. Beat eggs together and add to mixture. Sift dry ingredients together and add to mixture. Add vanilla and nuts. Put in a greased 8x13-inch pan. Bake at 325° for 35 minutes. Leave in pan to cool, then cut. Makes 16–20 squares.

Southern Generations (Mississippi)

Shortbread Toffee Squares

1 stick butter, softened, divided
6 tablespoons sugar, divided
1 cup self-rising flour
1 (14-ounce) can sweetened
   condensed milk

¼ cup chopped pecans
½ teaspoon vanilla
4 ounces German sweet
   chocolate, melted in
   1 tablespoon water

Cream ½ stick butter with 4 tablespoons sugar. Blend in flour. Spread onto greased 8-inch square pan, and bake at 350° for 20 minutes. In saucepan, mix together remaining ½ stick butter, 2 tablespoons sugar, condensed milk, and pecans and cook, stirring until mixture leaves sides of pan. Add vanilla. Pour over shortbread. Cool. Spread melted chocolate over toffee. Cool. Cut into squares. Makes about 12.

The Twelve Days of Christmas Cookbook (Mississippi)

Brownies in a Jar

⅔ teaspoon salt
½ plus ⅛ cup flour
⅓ cup cocoa
½ cup flour
⅔ cup firmly packed brown
  sugar

⅔ cup sugar
½ cup semisweet chocolate
  chips
½ cup pecans (optional)

Layer in order given in clean quart jar; salt, ½ plus ⅛ cup flour, cocoa, ½ cup flour, brown sugar, sugar, chocolate chips, and pecans. Seal jar with lid.

Decorate jar with fabric and/or ribbon. Attach a tag to the jar with these instructions: Combine contents of this jar with 1 teaspoon vanilla, ⅔ cup vegetable oil, and 3 eggs. Pour batter into a greased pan. Bake at 350° for 32–37 minutes.

Calling All Kids (Alabama)

Chocolate Syrupy Brownies

1 cup walnuts, divided
1 cup sifted flour
¼ teaspoon baking powder
½ cup butter or margarine,
  softened

¾ cup brown sugar
1 large egg
1 teaspoon vanilla
1 (5½-ounce) can chocolate
  syrup

Chop ¾ cup walnuts coarsely and the remainder fine for tops of brownies. Sift flour with baking powder. Combine butter, sugar, egg, and vanilla; beat well. Stir in chocolate syrup, then flour mixture. Add coarsely chopped nuts. Turn into greased, 8-inch-square baking pan. Spread level. Sprinkle with finer walnuts. Bake at 350° for about 50 minutes. Cool. Cut in squares.

Devine Dishes (Mississippi)

Butter Crème Brownies

1 square semisweet chocolate	½ cup sugar
¼ cup butter	¼ cup flour
1 egg	¼ cup finely chopped pecans

Melt chocolate and butter together over hot water and cool slightly. Beat egg until frothy. Stir into chocolate mixture. Add sugar. Blend well. Add flour and nuts and stir until well blended. Pour into 8x8-inch pan. Bake 13–15 minutes at 350°. Cool and cover with Butter Crème Filling. Yields 2 dozen.

BUTTER CRÈME FILLING:

1 cup powdered sugar	1 tablespoon heavy cream or
2 tablespoons butter, softened	evaporated milk
¼ teaspoon vanilla extract	

Cream together and spread over brownie layer. Put pan in refrigerator for 10 minutes. Remove and spread with Glaze.

GLAZE:

2 tablespoons butter	2 squares semisweet chocolate

Melt butter and chocolate together. Spread gently over filled brownie layer being careful not to disturb filling. Chill in refrigerator until Glaze sets. Cut into small finger strips. Can be frozen.

Note: Food coloring can be added to crème filling for different holidays and occasions.

Vintage Vicksburg (Mississippi)

Chocolate Cream Cheese Brownies

1 (4-ounce) package German
  sweet chocolate
3 tablespoons butter or
  margarine
2 eggs
¾ cup sugar

½ cup all-purpose flour
½ teaspoon baking powder
¼ teaspoon salt
1 teaspoon vanilla extract
¼ teaspoon almond extract
½ cup chopped nuts

In a saucepan, melt chocolate and butter over low heat, stirring frequently. Set aside. In a bowl, beat eggs. Gradually add sugar, beating until thick. Combine flour, baking powder, and salt. Add to egg mixture. Stir in melted chocolate, extracts, and nuts. Pour half of batter into greased, 8-inch-square baking pan; set aside.

FILLING:

2 tablespoons butter or
  margarine, softened
1 (3-ounce) package cream
  cheese, softened

¼ cup sugar
1 egg
1 tablespoon all-purpose flour
½ teaspoon vanilla

Beat butter and cream cheese in mixing bowl until light. Gradually add sugar, beating until fluffy. Blend in egg, flour, and vanilla; mix well. Spread over batter in pan. Dollop remaining batter on top. With a knife, cut through the batter to create a marbled effect. Bake at 350° for 35–40 minutes or until brownies test done. Cool and store in refrigerator. Yields 2 dozen.

Cooking with Friends (Mississippi)

Marshmallow Brownies

CAKE:

2 sticks butter, softened
4 eggs
2 cups sugar
2 teaspoons vanilla
4 tablespoons cocoa

1½ cups all-purpose flour
1 cup chopped pecans
1 (7-ounce) jar marshmallow
  crème

Mix butter, eggs, sugar, and vanilla; cream well. Sift cocoa and flour together; add pecans; mix well. Pour into a well-greased 9x13-inch pan and bake at 350° for 25–30 minutes. Remove from oven and immediately spread marshmallow crème on top. Set aside and prepare Topping.

TOPPING:

½ cup butter, softened
3 tablespoons cocoa
1 teaspoon vanilla

2 cups powdered sugar
4 tablespoons evaporated milk

Combine all ingredients and mix well. Spread over marshmallow crème. Swirl. Set in refrigerator until cool; remove and cut as desired.

Shared Treasures (Louisiana)

Knock You Nakeds

Quite simply divine!

1 (18¼-ounce) package
  German chocolate cake mix
1 cup chopped nuts
⅓ plus ½ cup evaporated
  milk, divided

¾ cup butter, melted
60 pieces caramel candy
½ cup evaporated milk
1 cup chocolate chips

Combine cake mix, nuts, ⅓ cup milk, and butter; mix well. Press half of mixture into bottom of a greased 9x13-inch glass baking dish; bake at 350° for 8–12 minutes, till baked. Melt caramel candy in top of double boiler with remaining ½ cup milk. When caramel mixture is well mixed, pour over baked mixture. Cover with chocolate chips, and pour rest of dough on top of chips. Bake 18 minutes at 350°. Cool before slicing. Yields 18–20 squares.

Great Flavors of Mississippi (Mississippi)

Chocolate Sin

1 stick margarine, softened	1 cup powdered sugar
1 cup all-purpose flour	1 (16-ounce) carton whipped
½ cup finely chopped pecans,	topping, divided
divided	3 cups milk
1 (8-ounce) package cream	2 (3-ounce) packages instant
cheese, softened	chocolate pudding

Mix margarine, flour, and most of the pecans, and pat into a 9x13-inch glass baking dish. Bake 15 minutes and cool. Mix cream cheese, sugar, and 1 cup topping. Spread this carefully over first layer. Mix milk into pudding and beat for 2 minutes. Spread this over second layer. Spread remaining topping on top, and sprinkle with remaining chopped pecans. Refrigerate. When ready to serve, cut into squares and stand aside!

Cajun Men Cook (Louisiana)

Santa Claus Whiskers

1 cup margarine, softened	¾ cup chopped red and green
1 cup sugar	candied cherries
2 tablespoons milk	½ cup chopped pecans
1 teaspoon almond flavoring	¾ cup shredded coconut
2½ cups all-purpose flour	

Cream margarine and sugar, then blend in milk and almond flavoring. Stir in flour, cherries, and nuts. Dough will be stiff. Divide into 2 parts and form into 2 logs about the size of slice-and-bake cookies. Roll dough in coconut, then cover logs with plastic wrap; chill overnight. Logs may be frozen for one month until ready to bake. Slice and bake at 375° for 12 minutes or until edges are brown. Makes 5 dozen cookies.

Cooking with Gilmore (Mississippi)

 In 1836, Alabama was the first state in the United States to declare Christmas a legal holiday.

Martha's Toffee Candy

This candy makes a great gift in a Christmas tin.

1 (12-ounce) package milk chocolate chips, divided	2 sticks butter
	1 cup sugar
2 cups sliced roasted almonds, divided	3 tablespoons water

Place ½ of the chips and almonds in a coated 9x13-inch baking dish. Combine butter, sugar, and water in a saucepan; cook to the hard-crack stage, 300° on a candy thermometer. Pour over chips and almonds. Add remaining chips and almonds; smoothing out the chocolate chips. Allow to harden and break into pieces.

Alabama, Rich in Flavor (Alabama)

Toffee Pecan Bites

Graham crackers	1 cup light brown sugar
2 sticks margarine	1 cup finely chopped pecans

Fill large cookie sheet with crackers laid with sides touching. (Don't break crackers while placing in pan, because this will cause the syrup to run down in the pan and off the cookie.) Bring margarine and brown sugar to a boil. Boil for 5 minutes, stirring constantly. Remove from heat. Add chopped nuts. Pour this mixture over graham crackers that have been placed flat on a large cookie sheet. Bake at 325° for exactly 10 minutes. When completely cool, break into bites.

Mississippi Stars Cookbook (Mississippi)

Mama's Pralines

3 cups sugar	½ stick butter
1 cup buttermilk	1 teaspoon vanilla
1 teaspoon baking soda	3 cups pecans

Put all ingredients except vanilla and pecans into a big boiler and boil until mixture turns brown and forms soft ball in cold water. Add one teaspoon vanilla and beat a little (till slightly creamy). Stir in pecans and drop on wax paper.

A Cook's Tour of Shreveport (Louisiana)

Microwave Pecan Pralines

½ pint whipping cream   2 tablespoons margarine
1 pound light brown sugar   2 cups pecans

Microwave whipping cream and brown sugar in large microwave-safe bowl 13 minutes on HIGH. Then add margarine and pecans. Stir until not shiny. Drop on foil. Makes about 24 pralines.

Easy Hospitality (Mississippi)

Orange Pecan Pralines

Make plenty of these beauties; they go fast!

3 cups sugar   1 teaspoon vanilla
⅔ cup milk   1 tablespoon butter
⅓ cup evaporated milk   1 cup chopped pecans
Grated rind of 1 orange   2 drops yellow food coloring
Dash of salt   2 drops red food coloring

Combine sugar, milk, orange rind and salt in a large saucepan. Bring to a boil and cook over medium heat, stirring occasionally until soft-ball stage (235°). Remove from heat. Add vanilla, butter, pecans, and food coloring. Beat until mixture has thickened. Drop by spoonfuls onto wax paper. Yields 3 dozen pralines.

Louisiana LEGACY (Louisiana)

Pecan Rolls

1 (7-ounce) jar marshmallow   1 (14-ounce) package assorted
   crème   vanilla and chocolate caramels
1 (1-pound) package powdered   1–2 tablespoons water
   sugar   1–1½ cups chopped pecans
1 teaspoon vanilla

Combine marshmallow crème, sugar, and vanilla, mixing well with hands. Shape mixture into 5 (4x1-inch) rolls. Mixture will be very dry. Chill for 2–3 hours. Peel caramels and combine with water in a microwave-safe dish. Microwave for 4 minutes on HIGH until smooth, stirring after 2 minutes. Dip rolls in melted caramel then roll each in chopped pecans. Chill one hour; cut in slices to serve.

Field O' Dreams Farm Cookbook (Alabama)

Orange-Coconut Balls

More flavorful when made at least one day before serving.

1 (6-ounce) can frozen orange
  juice
1 (16-ounce) box vanilla
  wafers, crushed
1 stick margarine
1 (16-ounce) box confectioners'
  sugar
½–1 cup chopped nuts
1 (7-ounce) can shredded
  coconut

Mix first 5 ingredients thoroughly. Form into small balls and roll in coconut. Makes 100.

When Dinnerbells Ring (Alabama)

Chocolate Orange Truffles

¼ cup (½ stick) butter,
  cut into small pieces
⅓ cup whipping cream
7 ounces semisweet chocolate,
  chopped
1 egg yolk
1 teaspoon grated orange zest
2 tablespoons Grand Marnier
  (optional)
Baking cocoa or finely chopped
  pecans

Combine butter and cream in a small saucepan. Cook over low heat until butter melts and cream bubbles around edge, stirring occasionally. Remove from heat. Add chocolate. Stir until smooth. Stir in egg yolk. Add orange zest and Grand Marnier; mix well. Chill until firm. Roll into 1-inch balls. Roll in baking cocoa or chopped pecans to coat.

May microwave butter, cream, and chocolate in a microwave-safe dish on MEDIUM until melted. Stir until smooth. Proceed as above. Yields 4–6 servings.

Southern Scrumptious Entertains (Alabama)

Bourbon Balls

2 tablespoons cocoa
1 cup powdered sugar
¼ cup bourbon whiskey
2 tablespoons light corn syrup

2½ cups crushed vanilla wafers
1 cup chopped pecans
Additional powdered sugar to
  coat

Sift together cocoa and sugar. Combine and stir in whiskey and corn syrup. Add and mix thoroughly the vanilla wafers and pecans. Roll mixture into small balls and dredge in powdered sugar.

Fannye Mae's Home Made Candy (Mississippi)

Peanut Butter Turtles

1 pound semisweet chocolate
  morsels
1 pound light caramels

½ pound peanut butter morsels
1 (1-pound) package pecan
  halves, divided

Melt chocolate morsels. In a separate pan, slowly melt caramels; when partially melted, add peanut butter morsels. Mix thoroughly. Add ¾ of pecans to caramel/peanut butter mixture. Alternate drops of chocolate, then caramel mixture, then chocolate; top with pecan half. Works best if dropped onto wax paper.

Hearthside at Christmas (Alabama)

Approximately 40% of the total peanuts produced in the United States are grown within a 100-mile radius of Dothan, Alabama. The National Peanut Festival takes place there every November. A giant, gold peanut sculpture at the Visitor Information Center helps to proclaim Dothan as Peanut Capital of the World.

Crazy Cocoa Krisps

20 ounces almond bark   **2 cups dry roasted peanuts**
2 cups Cocoa Krispies

Place almond bark in microwave dish and cook one minute on high. Stir and heat at 30 second intervals until melted, stirring at each interval. Stir in cereal and peanuts. Spread on wax paper on jellyroll pan or cookie sheet and allow to cool. Break into pieces and store in airtight container. May be dropped by teaspoon instead. Yields 36 pieces.

Great Performances (Mississippi)

Heavenly Hash

12 marshmallows   **1 pound milk chocolate**
1 cup chopped nuts

Dice marshmallows. Boil water in bottom of a double boiler. Turn off heat. Place the milk chocolate in top of double boiler. Stir occasionally until melted. Line a tray with wax paper. Pour in ½ of melted chocolate. Cover with marshmallows and nuts. Pour rest of chocolate over this. When cooled, cut into squares.

Fannye Mae's Home Made Candy (Mississippi)

Ambrosia Crunch

Using the Holiday M&M's variety makes this a fun seasonal treat.

3 cups Rice Chex   **1 (12-ounce) bag plain M&M's**
3 cups Corn Chex   **1 (12-ounce) bag peanut M&M's**
3 cups Cheerios   **1 (12-ounce) bag white**
2 cups stick pretzels   **chocolate morsels**
2 cups peanuts

Mix all ingredients, except white chocolate, in a large bowl. Melt white chocolate according to package directions. Pour white chocolate over mixture and toss well to coat. Spread on wax paper and let sit until white chocolate hardens. Store in an airtight container.

Ambrosia (Mississippi)

Forever Amber

1 pound orange slice candy,
    cut up
2 (3½-ounce) cans flaked
    coconut
2 (14-ounce) cans sweetened
    condensed milk

1 cup chopped pecans
1 teaspoon orange extract
1 teaspoon vanilla extract
1 (1-pound) box powdered sugar

Preheat oven to 275°. Mix candy, coconut, milk, pecans, and extracts; place in a greased sheet cake pan. Bake 30 minutes. Remove from oven and stir in sugar, mix well. Drop by spoonfuls onto wax paper. Cool completely. Store tightly covered. Serves 8–10.

Recipes from the Heart (Mississippi)

Romantic Raspberry Chocolate Meringues

Versatile because of Jell-O base—try experimenting with other flavors.

3 egg whites
1½ ounces raspberry Jell-O
¾ cup sugar
⅛ teaspoon salt
1 teaspoon white vinegar

1 (6-ounce) package semisweet
    chocolate chips
½ cup finely chopped pecans or
    walnuts

Beat egg whites until they begin to get stiff. Add gelatin gradually, blending thoroughly. Add sugar a little at a time; beat until stiff peaks form. Beat in salt and vinegar. Fold in chocolate chips and nuts. Drop by half-full teaspoon on foil-lined baking sheets. Bake 20 minutes at 250°. Turn off heat and leave in oven 3 hours without opening door. To garnish, you may dip tops in a little melted chocolate, or before baking, add a little shaved chocolate or a chocolate chip to top of cookie. These will hold their shape. Makes approximately 80.

Hors d'Oeuvres Everybody Loves (Mississippi)

PIES and OTHER DESSERTS

PHOTO BY MICKEY P. WALLACE

Windsor, circa 1860, near Port Gibson, was one of the most grand antebellum mansions in Mississippi. It survived the Civil War, only to burn in 1890 at the hands of a careless smoker. The haunting Ruins of Windsor, with 23 remaining monolithic columns, has been filmed extensively.

Huntsville Chess Pie

1 (8-inch) unbaked pie crust
½ cup butter, softened
1 cup sugar
2 eggs, separated
1½ teaspoons white cornmeal
2 tablespoons heavy cream
½ teaspoon vanilla extract
Dash of salt

Bake pie crust in very hot oven (450°) until baked but not browned. Cream butter, sugar, and egg yolks together. Add cornmeal mixed with cream and vanilla. Fold in egg whites beaten with salt until stiff. Pour into baked shell and cook in hot (400°) oven for 5 minutes. Reduce heat to 350° and bake 1–2 minutes longer or until filling is just set. If top browns before filling is set, put a piece of aluminum foil over top and complete baking. Serve pie while slightly warm.

Cook with Nancy, Plain or Fancy (Alabama)

Down in Dixie Bourbon Pie

1 box chocolate wafers,
  crushed
¼ cup butter or margarine,
  melted
21 marshmallows
1 cup evaporated milk
1 cup heavy cream
3 tablespoons bourbon

Mix chocolate wafer crumbs and melted butter. Pat into bottom and sides of a 9-inch pie pan. Bake at 350° until set, about 15 minutes. In saucepan, heat marshmallows and milk until marshmallows melt and mixture is smooth. Do not boil. Remove from heat. Whip cream until stiff. Fold into marshmallow mixture. Add bourbon and pour into cooled chocolate crumb crust. Refrigerate 4 hours or until set. Additional whipped cream and chocolate crumbs make an attractive garnish. Yields 6–8 servings.

Vintage Vicksburg (Mississippi)

Mose's Buttermilk Pie

3 eggs
1 cup sugar
2 tablespoons flour
1 stick butter, melted

1 teaspoon vanilla
1 cup buttermilk
1 (9-inch) pie shell

Beat eggs. Add dry ingredients and mix well. Add butter, vanilla, and buttermilk. Pour into pie shell and bake at 350° for 30–45 minutes or until custard is set. Custard will continue to firm after baking.

Top O' the Morning (Alabama)

Apple Pie in Cheddar Cheese Pie Pastry

CHEDDAR CHEESE PASTRY:
4 cups flour
2 teaspoons salt
1⅓ cups shortening

½ cup cold water
32 ounces Cheddar cheese, grated

Process flour, salt, and shortening in a food processor until crumbly. Add cold water in a fine stream, processing constantly. Add Cheddar cheese, processing constantly to form a ball. Chill, covered, for up to 2 days. Yields enough for 2 pastries.

FILLING:
2 cups sugar
½ cup (1 stick) butter, melted
2 eggs, beaten

2 teaspoons cinnamon
1 teaspoon vanilla extract
4 large Granny Smith apples, peeled, sliced

Beat sugar, butter, and eggs in mixer bowl until blended. Beat in cinnamon and vanilla. Stir in apples. Divide pastry into 2 equal portions. Roll one portion into an 11-inch circle on a lightly-floured surface. Fit into a 9-inch pie plate sprayed with nonstick cooking spray. Fill with apple filling. Roll remaining pastry into a circle on a lightly floured surface. Cut into strips. Layer over top of pie to form a lattice. Trim and flute edges. Bake at 425° for 10 minutes. Reduce oven temperature to 350°. Bake until pastry is golden brown and pie filling is set. Yields 6–8 servings.

Celebrations (Alabama)

Strawberry Angel Pie

¾ cup plus 3 tablespoons
  sugar, divided
4 tablespoons cornstarch
1½ cups boiling water
3 egg whites, beaten well
1 teaspoon vanilla flavoring

1 (10-ounce) package frozen
  strawberries
10 individual tart shells or
  meringue shells, baked
1 cup whipping cream

Combine ¾ cup sugar and cornstarch. Bring water to a boil; stir sugar mixture into boiling water and cook, stirring constantly, until clear. Pour slowly into egg whites beaten with remaining 3 tablespoons sugar. Add vanilla. Fold in 2 tablespoons strawberries; pour mixture into baked tart shells or meringue shells. Cool. Serve with whipped cream and remaining strawberries. If fresh strawberries are in season, garnish each serving with one or two.

I Promised a Cookbook (Mississippi)

Strawberry Pie

1 quart fresh strawberries
¾ cup water
1 cup sugar
3 tablespoons cornstarch

1 teaspoon lemon juice
1 cup whipped cream
1 (9-inch) pastry shell, baked

Place all but 1 cup of berries in bottom of baked pastry shell. Spread out well, and set aside. In a saucepan, simmer the other cup of berries in ¾ cup water for 5 minutes. Add sugar and blend well. Add cornstarch. After mixture thickens, add lemon juice. Cook until clear. Pour sauce over berries in shell. Chill in refrigerator, and top with whipped cream.

The Encyclopedia of Cajun and Creole Cuisine (Louisiana)

Bayou Lafourche is known locally as the "Longest Street in the World." It connects communities that developed along its shores: Thibodaux, Raceland, Lockport, Larose, Cut Off, Galliano, Golden Meadow, Leeville, and Port Fourchon. It ends at Grand Isle, the only inhabited barrier island in Louisiana.

Homerline's Blueberry Pie

1 (8-ounce) package cream
  cheese, softened
2 cups powdered sugar
2 pie shells, baked
1 cup chopped pecans

1 (21-ounce) can blueberry pie
  filling
1 package Dream Whip,
  prepared

Combine cream cheese and powdered sugar. Spread evenly on
pie shells. Layer pecans over mix. Add blueberry pie filling and
top with prepared Dream Whip.

Note: May use Cool Whip instead of Dream Whip.

Recipe by comedian Jerry Clower
Mississippi Stars Cookbook (Mississippi)

Millionaire Pie

1 cup chopped pecans
1 (14-ounce) can sweetened
  condensed milk
½ cup lemon juice
1 cup flaked coconut

1 (8-ounce) can crushed
  pineapple, drained
1 (8-ounce) container Cool Whip
1 graham cracker pie shell

Mix all ingredients together and pour into pie shell. Chill and
serve.

Fiftieth Anniversary Cookbook (Louisiana)

Pineapple-Coconut Pie

1 stick butter
1½ cups sugar
4 eggs
1 (8-ounce) can crushed
  pineapple

1 cup shredded coconut
1 tablespoon vanilla
2 (8-inch) unbaked pie shells

Melt butter. Mix sugar and eggs and blend with cooled butter.
Mix in pineapple, coconut, and vanilla. Pour into pie shells. Bake
in 350° oven for 35 minutes or until done. Yields 2 pies.

Huntsville Entertains (Alabama)

My Favorite Coconut Cream Pie

2 tablespoons flour, heaping
1¼ cups sugar plus
  8 tablespoons, divided
2 cups milk, divided
4 eggs, separated

2 tablespoons butter
1 can flaked coconut
1 teaspoon vanilla
1 (9-inch) pie shell, baked

Put flour, 1¼ cups sugar, a little milk (about 3 tablespoons), and egg yolks in boiler. Mix well. Add butter, coconut, vanilla, and remaining milk, and cook until thick. Put in baked pie shell. Make meringue of the egg whites and 8 tablespoons sugar. Put on top of pie and bake meringue until golden brown.

A Collection of My Favorite Recipes (Mississippi)

Mile High Pie

ALMOND PIE SHELL:

¼ cup butter
¼ teaspoon salt
2 tablespoons sugar
1 egg yolk

¾ cup sifted flour
¼ cup finely chopped almonds
  or pecans

Cream butter, salt, and sugar. Add egg yolk; stir in flour and nuts. Press dough into a 9-inch pie plate. Refrigerate for 30 minutes. Bake at 350° for 15 minutes. Chill before pouring in Filling.

FILLING:

1 (10-ounce) package frozen
  strawberries
1 cup sugar
2 egg whites, at room
  temperature

1 tablespoon lemon juice
Pinch of salt
1 cup whipping cream
½ teaspoon almond extract

Thaw strawberries and reserve a few for garnish. In mixing bowl, combine berries, sugar, egg whites, lemon juice, and salt. Beat for 15 minutes or until stiff. Whip cream with almond extract. Fold into berry mixture. Mound in Almond Pie Shell and freeze until firm. Garnish with berries.

Golden Moments (Mississippi)

Chocolate-Covered Cherry Pie

1 (12-ounce) package
    semisweet chocolate morsels
1 (14-ounce) can sweetened
    condensed milk
1 (20-ounce) can cherry pie
    filling
1 (9-inch) graham cracker pie
    crust
1 (8-ounce) container frozen
    whipped topping, thawed

Combine chocolate morsels and milk in a large microwave-safe bowl and microwave about 2 minutes until melted, stirring twice. Add cherry pie filling and mix well. Pour mixture into graham cracker pie crust and top with whipped topping. Chill until ready to serve. Yields 8 servings.

Calling All Kids (Alabama)

Oreo Cookie Pie

1 (3-ounce) package vanilla
    instant pudding
1 cup water
1 (14-ounce) can condensed
    milk
1 (12-ounce) container Cool
    Whip
1 (8-ounce) package cream
    cheese, softened
Chocolate pie crust
6 Oreo cookies

Combine pudding, water, condensed milk, Cool Whip, and cream cheese; mix well. Pour ½ into pie crust; reserve remainder. Crush Oreo cookies (not too small) and put on top of first layer, then spoon remainder of filling on top. Refrigerate. Can freeze.

Barbara's Been Cookin' (Mississippi)

Greenville, Mississippi, is the birthplace of James Maury "Jim" Henson (September 24, 1936–May 16, 1990) the most widely known puppeteer in American television history. Henson was the leading force behind the long running television series *Sesame Street* and *The Muppet Show* and films such as *The Muppet Movie* (1979) and *The Dark Crystal* (1982). The prototype for his most famous character, Kermit The Frog, was created from a green coat that Henson's mother had thrown into a refuse bin, and two ping-pong balls for eyes.

Chocolate Pie

5 large eggs, separated	1 teaspoon vanilla
4 tablespoons cocoa	2 cups milk, scalded
1 cup sugar	1 (9-inch) deep-dish pie shell,
5 tablespoons cornstarch	baked
4 tablespoons margarine	

Mix egg yolks, cocoa, sugar, cornstarch, margarine, vanilla, and milk in top of double boiler and cook until thickened. Pour into pie shell. Top with Meringue. Bake 15 minutes at 350°.

MERINGUE:

5 egg whites	½ cup sugar
1 teaspoon vanilla	

Beat egg whites with vanilla until soft peaks form. Gradually add sugar, beating on high, until sugar dissolves and stiff peaks form. Spread on pie.

Bethany's Best Bites (Alabama)

Chocolate Chip Pie

1 cup sugar	1 teaspoon vanilla
½ cup flour	1 cup milk chocolate chips
2 eggs, well beaten	¾ cup pecans
1 stick butter, melted	1 unbaked deep-dish pie shell

Blend sugar, flour, eggs, butter, and vanilla well. Stir in chocolate chips and pecans. Pour into unbaked pie shell and bake at 350° for 30–35 minutes or until firm.

St. Philomena School 125th Anniversary (Louisiana)

Lottie's Pecan Chip Pies

1¼ cups sugar
¼ cup cornstarch
½ cup (1 stick) butter or
  margarine, softened
3 eggs, beaten

1 teaspoon vanilla extract
1 cup chopped pecans or
  walnuts
1 cup chocolate chips
2 unbaked (9-inch) pie shells

Combine sugar and cornstarch in a bowl and mix well. Add butter and eggs and mix well. Stir in vanilla. Add pecans and chocolate chips and mix well. Pour into pie shells. Bake at 350° for 35–45 minutes or until brown. Yields 12–16 servings.

Calling All Cooks, Four (Alabama)

The Best Pecan Pie

1 stick butter
1 cup light Karo
1 cup sugar
3 large eggs, beaten
½ teaspoon lemon juice

1 teaspoon vanilla
Dash of salt
1 cup pecans
1 (8- or 9-inch) unbaked pie
  shell

Brown butter in saucepan until it is golden brown; do not burn; let cool. In separate bowl, add ingredients in order listed; stir. Blend in browned butter well. Pour into unbaked pie shell and bake at 425° for 10 minutes, then lower to 325° for 40 minutes.

The Cotton Country Collection (Louisiana)

Mobile is widely known as the Azalea City, but the evergreen azaleas for which it is famous are not native to the area. These oriental plants with brilliant spring blooms were imported during the 1920s to create a tourist attraction known as the Azalea Trail. From the 1930s through the 1950s, tourists flocked to Mobile to see azaleas in bloom. Although the Azalea Trail's attraction to tourists has declined in the ensuing years, its legacy still can be seen at Bellingrath Gardens, in the rise of Mobile's horticulture industry, and at Mobile's annual Festival of Flowers held in March.

The Ultimate Pumpkin Pie

CRUST:

1¼ cups all-purpose flour
½ cup powdered sugar
½ cup (1 stick) chilled butter,
  cut into pieces

3 tablespoons whipping cream

Preheat oven to 350°. Blend first 3 ingredients in processor until mixture resembles coarse meal. Add cream and process until moist clumps form. Gather dough into ball; flatten into disk. Wrap in plastic; chill 15 minutes.

  Roll out dough on floured surface to 14-inch round. Transfer dough to 9-inch, glass pie dish. Line Crust with foil, pressing firmly. Bake until sides are set, about 10 minutes. Remove foil. Bake Crust until pale brown, about 10 minutes more. Reduce oven temperature to 325°.

FILLING:

¾ cup sugar
1 tablespoon packed golden
  brown sugar
1 tablespoon cornstarch
2 teaspoons ground cinnamon
¾ teaspoon ground ginger
¼ teaspoon (generous) salt

1 (16-ounce) can solid-pack
  pumpkin
¾ cup whipping cream
½ cup sour cream
3 large eggs, beaten
¼ cup apricot preserves

Using whisk, mix first 6 ingredients in bowl until no lumps remain. Blend in pumpkin, whipping cream, sour cream, and eggs. Spread preserves over Crust; pour in Filling. Bake until Filling puffs at edges and center is almost set, about 55 minutes. Cool on rack. Cover; chill until cold.

Note: Can be made a day ahead.

Golden Moments (Mississippi)

Eudora Welty, who was born and lived most of her life in Jackson, Mississippi, was a world-renowned novelist and short story writer. Among the many awards Ms. Welty received for her work are the Pulitzer Prize, six O. Henry Awards, the French Legion of Honor Medal, and the National Medal of Arts. Presidents Jimmy Carter and Ronald Reagan awarded her the Presidential Freedom Medal of Honor and the Presidential Medal of Arts, respectively. She was the only living writer to be included in the prestigious Library of America Series. Ms. Welty's family home in Jackson is on the National Historic Register.

Sweet Potato Pie

1 cup mashed sweet potatoes
2 cups sugar
1 stick butter, melted
3 eggs, beaten

1 cup evaporated milk
1 teaspoon vanilla
2 unbaked (8-inch) pie shells

Mix potatoes, sugar, butter, eggs, milk, and vanilla. Pour into unbaked pie shells. Bake one hour at 350°.

Bell's Best IV: The Next Generation (Mississippi)

Nanny's Caramel Pie

When Nanny went to the kitchen and pulled out that black iron skillet, we knew we were in for a treat!

1 cup plus 2 tablespoons sugar, divided
1 tablespoon flour
3 eggs (2 separated)
1¼ cups milk

Pinch of salt
1 tablespoon very hot water
1 teaspoon vanilla
1 tablespoon butter
1 (8-inch) pie crust, baked

Mix ½ cup sugar with flour. Beat 1 egg plus 2 egg yolks (save whites for meringue) and add to sugar mixture. Add milk and salt, beating well with wire whisk. Set aside.

Brown ½ cup sugar in a heavy pan. It is best to do this over medium heat, allowing sugar to melt slowly. When completely dissolved, continue to cook until syrup is a golden color. (Watch out—this will burn easily if overcooked.) When sugar is browned, add 1 tablespoon very hot water, whisking constantly. Continue whisking as you slowly pour egg-milk mixture into browned sugar. Cook until thickened. Remove from heat and add vanilla and butter. Pour into baked pie crust and top with meringue made from remaining egg whites and 1–2 tablespoons sugar. Bake in 350° oven until meringue is lightly browned. Cool before serving.

Family Secrets...the Best of the Delta (Mississippi)

Lazy Betty

2 (21-ounce) cans pie filling
  (your choice)
1 (18¼-ounce) package
  yellow cake mix
1 cup chopped nuts
2 sticks margarine, melted
Cool Whip

Pour pie filling into ungreased 9x13-inch baking dish. Smooth filling, sprinkle with cake mix, then with chopped nuts. Drizzle melted margarine over entire top. Bake at 375° for about 40 minutes. Serve topped with Cool Whip.

Cooking with Mr. "G" and Friends (Louisiana)

Peanut Butter Pie

½ (8-ounce) package cream
  cheese, softened
½ cup confectioners' sugar
1 cup peanut butter
½ cup milk
1 (8-ounce) tub nondairy
  whipped topping (optional)
1 (9-inch) chocolate cookie pie
  crust
Chocolate syrup (optional)

In a mixing bowl, beat cream cheese and sugar until creamy smooth, scraping sides often. Add peanut butter and milk; beat slowly until smooth, about 3 minutes. Blend in topping until no streaks appear. Pour into pie shell and freeze. May be topped with whipped cream and chocolate syrup, if desired. Yields 8 servings.

Dining Under the Magnolia (Alabama)

Apple Spoon-Ups

2 (21-ounce) cans apple pie
  filling
1 teaspoon cinnamon
1 (8-ounce) can crescent dinner
  rolls

1½ cups sour cream
1 cup brown sugar

Spread apple pie filling in a 9x13-inch pan. Sprinkle with cinnamon. Unroll crescent rolls and place over apples. Combine sour cream and brown sugar. Spread over rolls. Bake at 375° for 40–45 minutes. Serve warm.

The Pick of the Crop (Mississippi)

Best Ever Apple Cobbler

An all-time favorite, this swirled cobbler is moist and juicy, yet flaky on top.

½ cup (1 stick) butter
2 cups sugar
2 cups water
½ cup shortening

1½ cups sifted self-rising flour
⅓ cup milk
1 teaspoon cinnamon
2 cups finely chopped apples

Heat oven to 350°. Melt butter in 9x13-inch baking pan. In a saucepan, heat sugar and water till sugar melts. Meanwhile, cut shortening into flour until particles are like fine crumbs. Add milk and stir with fork only until dough leaves side of bowl. Turn out onto floured board, and knead until smooth. Roll dough into large rectangle about ¼ inch thick. Sprinkle cinnamon over apples, then sprinkle apples evenly over dough. Roll up dough like a jellyroll. Dampen the edge with a little water to seal. Slice dough into ½-inch thick slices. Place in pan of melted butter. Pour sugar syrup carefully around rolls. (This looks like too much liquid, but the crust will absorb it.) Bake 55–60 minutes.

Variation: This cobbler may be made with other fresh, frozen, or canned fruits, such as blackberries, blueberries, cherries, or peaches. If packed in liquid, drain and substitute for part of sugar syrup. Always use 2 cups liquid.

Auburn Entertains (Alabama)

Lazy Peach Cobbler

1 cup sugar
1 cup self-rising flour, sifted
1 cup milk
1 teaspoon vanilla
1 stick butter, melted
10 fresh peaches (about 1½ pounds), peeled, sliced

Mix all ingredients except peaches in greased, 9x13-inch casserole. Pour in peaches. Bake in 350° oven for 45–50 minutes. Crust will rise to the top.

Editor's Extra: Sprinkle top with sugar and drizzle on a little butter rum. Place back in oven for 5 minutes.

Devine Dishes (Mississippi)

Crusty Peach Cobbler

3 cups sliced fresh peaches
¼ cup sugar, divided
1 tablespoon lemon juice
1 teaspoon grated lemon peel
1 teaspoon almond extract

Arrange peaches in a greased 8-inch square baking pan. Sprinkle with a mixture of ¼ cup sugar, lemon juice, lemon peel, and almond extract. Heat in oven while preparing Shortcake.

SHORTCAKE:
1½ cups flour
½ teaspoon salt
3 teaspoons baking powder
3 tablespoons sugar, divided
⅓ cup shortening
½ cup milk
1 egg, well beaten

Sift together flour, salt, baking powder, and 1 tablespoon sugar, cut in shortening until mixture looks like coarse crumbs. Add milk and egg at once; stir just until flour is moistened. Spread dough over hot peaches. Sprinkle with remaining 2 tablespoons sugar. Bake in a 400° oven 40 minutes or until nicely browned.

Field O' Dreams Farm Cookbook II (Alabama)

 The phrase "stars fell on Alabama" refers to a meteor shower that was seen across Alabama in November 1833. In addition to being the title of a song and a book, the phrase has aptly come to refer to the many music stars with connections to Alabama.

Alabama "Blue Ribbon" Banana Pudding

¾ cup sugar
Dash of salt
¼ cup flour
3 egg yolks, beaten

1 tablespoon vanilla
2 cups half-and-half
15 vanilla wafers
2–4 bananas, sliced

Combine sugar, salt, and flour; add to egg yolk and vanilla in a double-boiler. Slowly add half-and-half, stirring frequently. Heat until it thickens. Layer wafers and banana slices in 1½-quart baking dish. Add pudding.

MERINGUE:
3 egg whites
2 dashes cream of tartar

6 tablespoons sugar
½ teaspoon vanilla

Beat egg whites and cream of tartar for 2 minutes. Slowly add sugar and vanilla and beat until very stiff. Spread over pudding and bake at 350° until Meringue is golden brown.

Capitol Cooking (Alabama)

Bananas Foster Bread Pudding

1 (12-ounce) loaf stale French bread, broken in small pieces
1 cup milk
4 cups half-and-half

2½ cups sugar
8 tablespoons butter, melted
4 eggs
2 tablespoons vanilla
3 bananas, sliced

Combine all ingredients; mixture should be very moist but not soupy. Pour into buttered 9x13-inch baking dish. Place on middle rack of cold oven. Bake in 350° oven for approximately 1 hour and 15 minutes, until top is golden brown. Serve warm with Bananas Foster Sauce.

BANANAS FOSTER SAUCE:
½ cup butter
2 cups dark brown sugar
4 ounces dark rum

2 ounces banana liqueur
2 bananas, cut in small pieces

Melt butter and add brown sugar to form a creamy paste. Stir in liquors until smooth sauce is formed. Add bananas and simmer 2 minutes. Serve warm over warm bread pudding.

Cooking New Orleans Style! (Louisiana)

Bread Pudding with Glazed Cream
(from Le Ruth's)

½ stick butter, softened
4 eggs
2½ cups sugar
1 quart milk
1 tablespoon vanilla

¼ teaspoon mace
¾ cup raisins
½ loaf stale poor boy bread,
    cut into slices 1-inch thick

Spread softened butter over 12-inch round baking pan. In a large bowl, mix eggs, sugar, milk, vanilla, and mace. Stir in raisins. Add bread and allow to soak 10 minutes. Pour into pan. Bake at 375° until pudding is almost firm. Remove from oven.

TOPPING:

½ cup whipping cream
⅓ cup sugar

½ stick butter

Increase oven temperature to 425°. Carefully pour liquid whipping cream over top (no substitutes) then sprinkle with sugar and pieces of butter. Return to oven and bake 10–15 minutes to allow cream to set. Serves 6–8.

Paul Naquin's French Collection II: Meats & Poultry (Louisiana)

Mary Mahoney's Bread Pudding

6 slices day-old bread
1 teaspoon cinnamon
½ cup seedless raisins
2 tablespoons butter, melted

4 eggs
2 tablespoons plus ½ cup sugar
2 cups milk
1 teaspoon vanilla extract

Break bread in small pieces in 1½-quart baking dish. Sprinkle cinnamon over bread and add raisins and melted butter. Lightly toast bread mixture in oven at about 350° (10–15 minutes or so). Then add mixture of eggs, sugar, milk, and vanilla after mixing well. Bake about 30 minutes or until solid. Traditionally served with rum sauce (whisk together butter, powdered sugar, and a little rum). Serves about 8.

Cooking on the Coast (Mississippi)

Hotel Natchez Bread Pudding
with Bourbon Sauce

The cooks of Natchez learned the secret of bread pudding—stale French bread and a good whiskey sauce. During the Yankee occupation of the city, many a Northern heart was stolen by this treat.

1 loaf French bread	3 tablespoons vanilla
1 quart milk	½ cup chopped pecans
3 eggs	1 cup raisins
2 cups sugar	1 tablespoon margarine

Soak bread in milk and work with back of a wooden spoon until it is well mixed. Add beaten eggs, sugar, vanilla, pecans, and raisins and combine well. Pour melted margarine in bottom of a heavy 7x11-inch oblong cake pan. Pour batter over butter. Bake at 350° for 1½ hours or until very firm. Cool. Slice into squares. Top with Bourbon Sauce.

BOURBON SAUCE:

½ cup butter, softened	1 egg
1 cup sugar	3 tablespoons bourbon whiskey

Cream butter and sugar together and cook in the top of a double boiler until mixture is very hot and sugar dissolves. Pour into a blender and add egg; blend at top speed so that egg doesn't scramble. Cool. Add bourbon just before serving. Spoon sauce over bread pudding. Heat under broiler. Serves 8–10.

Cook with a Natchez Native (Mississippi)

One of Mississippi's oldest cities, Natchez, was founded in 1716, predating the current capital city—Jackson—by more than a century. The city sits on a high bluff above the Mississippi River and in order to reach the riverbank one must travel down a steep road to the landing. Prior to the American Civil War, Natchez had the most millionaires per capita of any city in the United States, making it arguably the wealthiest city in the nation at the time. It was frequented by notables such as Aaron Burr, Henry Clay, Andrew Jackson, Zachary Taylor, and Jefferson Davis. Today the city boasts that it has more antebellum homes than anywhere else in the United States, partly due to the fact that during the war, Natchez was spared the destruction of many other Southern cities, such as Vicksburg to the north.

Chocolate and Peanut Butter Mousse

8 ounces semisweet chocolate, chopped
½ cup peanut butter, unsalted
3 eggs
¼ cup sugar

1 cup heavy cream, whipped
3 tablespoons chocolate curls
3 tablespoons roasted and chopped peanuts

Put chocolate and peanut butter in the top half of a double boiler. Place over medium-high heat, stirring occasionally until the chocolate has completely melted and blended with the peanut butter, about 8–10 minutes. While the chocolate melts, separate the eggs. Beat egg yolks and sugar until they hold a peak. Set aside. Remove melted chocolate mixture from heat; add yolk mixture and blend. The mixture will become stiff. Add the egg whites and stir until mixture becomes smooth. Fold in whipped cream. Spoon into serving cups and decorate with chocolate curls and chopped peanuts. Yields 4 servings.

Peanut Delights (Alabama)

Jeff Davis Custard

This was a favorite dessert at Christmastime.

1 quart milk, scalded (do not scorch!)
½ cup sugar
Pinch of salt

6 whole eggs
½ cup cold milk
¼ teaspoon vanilla or almond extract

Scald 1 quart milk; add sugar and a pinch of salt. Beat eggs, then add cold milk. Stir and add gradually to hot milk mixture. Cook in top of double boiler until custard coats the spoon. Allow to cool. When cold, add flavoring. Serve in dessert dishes. Top with a heaping tablespoon of whipped cream, peaked at the top, and add a red cherry to the side of the dish.

Loaves and Fishes (Alabama)

Pecan Slice Torte

CRUST:

1 cup flour   ½ cup butter

Mix to a paste the flour and butter. Press on bottom of a buttered 9x9-inch square pan. Bake 15 minutes at 350°, until a very light brown.

FILLING:

2 eggs, slightly beaten   2 tablespoons flour
1½ cups brown sugar   ¼ teaspoon baking powder
¾ cup flaked coconut   ½ teaspoon salt
1 cup chopped nuts   1 teaspoon vanilla

While Crust is baking, mix Filling ingredients in order given above. Pour Filling on the baked Crust and again bake at 350° for 20 minutes. Remove from oven and cool. When cool, spread with Icing.

ICING:

2 tablespoons butter   1 tablespoon lemon juice
1½ cups powdered sugar   ½ cup finely chopped nuts
3 tablespoons orange juice

Mix Icing ingredients. Spread on torte. Sprinkle top with nuts. Let this cool in the pan you bake it in. Cut in small squares to serve, as it is very rich and delicious. Makes 16 or more servings.

River Road Recipes II (Louisiana)

Lemon Chess Tarts

4 eggs, slightly beaten   1 tablespoon cornmeal
1½ cups sugar   ¾ teaspoon grated lemon rind
6 tablespoons butter, melted   1 tablespoon lemon juice
   and cooled   16 unbaked tart shells
¼ cup milk

In mixing bowl, combine eggs, sugar, butter, milk, cornmeal, lemon rind, and lemon juice, stirring well to distribute sugar. Place tart shells on cookie sheet and divide filling evenly among the 16 shells. Bake at 350° for 35–40 minutes or until knife inserted in center comes out clean. Cool on wire rack. Cover and chill to store.

Gran's Gems (Mississippi)

French Banana Éclair

This dessert is something to look at as well as delicious.

1 cup water	1 cup flour
½ cup butter	4 tablespoons sugar
½ teaspoon salt	4 eggs

Bring water, butter, and salt to boil in large saucepan over medium heat. Combine flour with sugar and add all at once, stirring vigorously with spoon until dough forms ball and leaves sides of pan. Remove from heat. Beat in eggs, one at a time, and continue beating until dough is stiff and glossy. Set aside about a third of dough for top. On greased 10x15x1-inch jellyroll pan, form remaining ⅔ of dough into one long oblong, about 7 inches wide. Spoon reserved dough into mounds along the top of the oblong. Bake at 400° for 30 minutes. Remove from oven. With a sharp knife, make slits along sides of éclair 2 inches apart to let steam escape. Return to oven and continue baking 10 minutes longer. Remove to cooling rack. Slice off top of éclair. Remove any soft dough inside. Cool thoroughly and fill.

FILLING:

4 cups whipping cream	6–8 bananas
4 tablespoons sugar	4 tablespoons crème de cacao

Whip cream in mixing bowl until soft peaks form. Gradually add sugar, whipping until stiff. Mash enough bananas to make about 2 cups. Add crème de cacao to mashed bananas and fold into whipped cream. Fill éclair shell with half of whipped cream and banana mixture. Slice remaining bananas over whipped cream. Cover sliced bananas with remaining whipped cream. Replace top of éclair and drizzle with Glaze.

GLAZE:

½ cup powdered sugar	1 teaspoon vanilla
2 tablespoons cocoa	6–8 tablespoons boiling water
2 tablespoons butter, melted	½ cup chopped pecans

Combine powdered sugar, cocoa, melted butter, and vanilla in small bowl. Stir in enough boiling water to make a thin glaze. Drizzle over filled éclair. Sprinkle with chopped pecans. Chill until serving time. Slice crosswise to serve; each slice may be cut in half. Yields 16–20 servings.

From a Louisiana Kitchen (Louisiana)

Chocolate Éclairs

1 cup water	4 large eggs
1 stick butter or margarine	1 (3-ounce) box vanilla pudding
1 cup all-purpose flour	(regular or instant)
¼ teaspoon salt	2 cups cold milk

Boil water in heavy pot; add butter and stir till melted. Add flour and salt all at once, stirring and cooking a minute or so till mixture forms soft ball that does not separate. Remove from heat; cool 10 minutes. Add eggs one at a time, beating vigorously after each.

Form 12–15 spoonfuls batter into smooth capsule shapes on a greased cookie sheet. Bake in 450° oven 15 minutes, then lower to 325° and bake another 25 minutes. While éclairs are baking, prepare and refrigerate pudding (package directions) and Chocolate Topping.

When éclairs are cool, slice top third off with sharp knife. Fill each èclair with about 2 tablespoons pudding. Replace top. Frost with Chocolate Topping. Refrigerate loosely covered with sheet of wax paper.

CHOCOLATE TOPPING:

2 (1-ounce) squares unsweetened baking chocolate	1¼ cups powdered sugar
	1 teaspoon vanilla
	2–3 tablespoons milk
3 tablespoons butter	

Melt chocolate in microwave on HIGH for 2 minutes (or over hot water on stovetop). Add butter; stir to melt. Add powdered sugar, vanilla, and milk for thin consistency. Beat with spoon till glossy.

Note: Easier than you imagined, I'll bet. Cream Puffs are similar, but round, and sprinkled with powdered sugar. Try chocolate or lemon filling or stiffly whipped cream.

The Little New Orleans Cookbook (Louisiana)

Death by Chocolate

This is great for a party or barbecue! Put in a pretty, clear glass dish so that you can see the different layers.

1 (18¼-ounce) box chocolate cake mix	2 (12-ounce) tubs whipped topping
1 cup Kahlúa coffee liqueur	6 chocolate-toffee candy bars, broken into small pieces
4 (3-ounce) boxes chocolate mousse mix	

Bake cake according to package directions for 9x13-inch cake. Prick top of baked cake with fork; pour Kahlúa over cake. Let this soak in (it can be left this way overnight). Make chocolate mousse according to package directions.

To assemble cake, crumble half the baked cake and place it on bottom of large glass bowl. Layer half of mousse, half of whipped topping, then half of the candy bar pieces. Repeat layers. Serves 18.

Family Secrets...the Best of the Delta (Mississippi)

Strawberries Over Snow

1 large angel food cake	1 (8-ounce) carton frozen whipped topping, thawed
1 (8-ounce) package cream cheese, softened	¾ cup milk

Trim crust from cake. Tear into chunks and place in 9x13-inch baking dish. Combine cream cheese, whipped topping, and milk, blending until smooth. Spread mixture over cake chunks. Chill.

GLAZE:

1 cup water	12 drops red food coloring
1 teaspoon lemon juice	2 pints strawberries, cut in halves
1 cup sugar	
2 tablespoons cornstarch	

Combine water, lemon juice, sugar, and cornstarch in saucepan. Bring to a boil; cook until thickened. Remove from heat. Add food coloring; mix well. Fold strawberries into Glaze. Let stand until cool. Pour Glaze over cake. Chill thoroughly. Serves 8–10.

Cane River's Louisiana Living (Louisiana)

Strawberry Pizza

CRUST:

2 sticks margarine
2 cups all-purpose flour

1 cup chopped nuts

Melt margarine with flour; press into 9x13-inch pan and add chopped nuts on top; press in. Bake at 350° until brown; cool completely.

FIRST LAYER:

1 (8-ounce) package cream
  cheese, softened

3 cups confectioners' sugar
1 (12-ounce) tub Cool Whip

Blend cream cheese and sugar until smooth; fold in Cool Whip. Layer over Crust. Peak up on sides so Top Layer won't run off.

TOP LAYER:

1 cup sugar
1 cup water
3 tablespoons cornstarch

1 (3-ounce) box strawberry
  Jell-O
2 pints strawberries, sliced

Mix first 3 ingredients in pan and bring to a boil; cook till clear. Cool a little. Add Jell-O; cool completely. Add strawberries and spread on top.

Calling All Cooks (Alabama)

Summer Trifle

1 (3-ounce) box vanilla
  pudding
1 (14-ounce) can condensed
  milk
1 cup water
1 (12-ounce) container Cool
  Whip

1 pound cake or large angel
  food cake, broken into large
  pieces
Fresh strawberries, halved
Fresh blueberries

Mix the pudding, condensed milk, and water with beaters. Refrigerate for 5 minutes. Fold in Cool Whip.

Layer in a glass bowl, such as trifle bowl, in the following order: cake, berries, sauce, cake, berries, sauce. Top with fresh berries before serving.

Give Us This Day Our Daily Bread (Mississippi)

Crêpes Suzette

1⅛ cups sifted flour	½ cup butter
4 tablespoons sugar	½ cup powdered sugar
Pinch of salt	1 teaspoon grated orange rind
3 eggs	Juice of 1 orange
1½ cups milk	¼ cup Grand Marnier or
1 tablespoon melted butter	Cointreau
1 tablespoon cognac	¼ cup brandy
1 teaspoon butter	

Sift together sifted flour, sugar, and salt. Combine eggs (beaten) and milk. Stir into dry ingredients until smooth. Stir in 1 tablespoon butter and cognac. Let stand for 2 hours.

In a frying pan, heat ½ cup butter. Pour in 1 tablespoon of batter to cover bottom of pan with a thin layer. Rotate pan to spread batter evenly. Cook one minute on each side. Stack crêpes one on top of the other, separated by wax paper.

Cream butter, powdered sugar, and orange rind. Add orange juice and Grand Marnier or Cointreau. Spread on crêpes and fold or roll them up. Arrange on hot serving dish. Sprinkle with sugar and warmed brandy. Ignite and serve flaming. Serves 6.

Recipes and Reminiscences of New Orleans I (Louisiana)

Cherry Jubilee Parfait

Nice for festive occasions; serve with cookies.

36 large black pitted cherries	Sugar cubes
2 tablespoons sugar	Lemon extract or orange extract
2 cups cherry brandy or plain	Vanilla ice cream
brandy	

Heat cherries and sugar till juice thickens slightly; cool; add brandy. Saturate sugar cubes with lemon or orange extract. Place ice cream in parfait glasses; pour some of syrup from cherries over ice cream. Place 4 or 5 cherries on top of ice cream; place sugar cube on a mound of ice cream among but not touching cherries. Hold tip of lighted match to cube to light just before serving. Serves 8–10.

Encore (Louisiana)

Banana Split Dessert

When you're ready to serve this treat, top it with chopped pecans, cherries, and a drizzle of chocolate syrup!

2 cups graham cracker crumbs	2 cups milk
6 tablespoons margarine, melted	3 bananas, sliced
2 (3-ounce) packages instant vanilla pudding mix	1 (20-ounce) can crushed pineapple, drained
	1 (12-ounce) container whipped topping

In a bowl, combine crumbs and margarine. Press mixture into an oblong baking dish and set aside. In another bowl, prepare pudding mix with milk according to package directions. Spread pudding over crumb mixture. Layer with banana slices, then pineapple, then whipped topping. Chill 3 hours or overnight. Cut into squares to serve. Yields 12 squares.

Tony Chachere's Second Helping (Louisiana)

Peach Buttermilk Ice Cream

1 tablespoon unflavored gelatin (1 envelope)	¼ teaspoon salt
1¼ cups sugar, divided	4 cups whipping cream
2 cups buttermilk	1 tablespoon vanilla extract
1 egg, beaten	2 cups mashed fresh peaches

In saucepan, combine gelatin, 1 cup sugar, and buttermilk. Dissolve gelatin mixture over low heat, stirring occasionally. Gradually add hot mixture to egg, stirring constantly. Stir in salt, cream, and vanilla. Combine mashed peaches and remaining ¼ cup sugar; add to mixture. Chill and churn-freeze. Yields approximately 3 quarts.

Note: If fresh peaches are not available, mashed, canned freestone peaches may be used. Do not add sugar to peaches. Regular milk may be substituted for buttermilk in the recipe.

Giant Houseparty Cookbook (Mississippi)

Praline Ice Cream Sauce

½ pound (about 22)
 marshmallows
1⅓ cups brown sugar
1 cup light cream
Dash of salt

4 tablespoons butter or
 margarine
1 teaspoon vanilla
⅓ cup broken pecans

Combine first 4 ingredients in 2½-quart saucepan. Heat and stir until mixture comes to a boil. Cook over medium heat about 10 minutes or to 224°. Remove from heat; add butter. Cool slightly; add vanilla and nuts. Serve warm. Makes 2 cups.

Pigging Out with the Cotton Patch Cooks (Louisiana)

Rice Ambrosia

1 cup crushed pineapple
1 cup Mandarin orange
 segments
2 cups cold cooked rice
1 cup flaked coconut

1 cup unpeeled chopped apples,
 or 12 halved maraschino
 cherries
1 cup whipped cream

Drain pineapple and orange segments. Add rice, coconut, and apples. Whip cream and fold into rice mixture. Chill before serving. Serves 6–8.

Between the Levees (Mississippi)

LIST of CONTRIBUTORS

PHOTO © LOUISIANA OFFICE OF TOURISM

The St. Charles streetcars in New Orleans, Louisiana, have been declared moving national historic landmarks. Streetcars have been running along St. Charles Avenue since 1835. It is the oldest continually operating street railway system in the world.

Listed below are the cookbooks that have contributed recipes to this book, along with copyright, author, publisher, city, and state, when applicable.

Absolutely à la Carte ©1999 Charlotte Walton Skelton, Cleveland, MS

Alabama, Rich in Flavor ©2005 Katherine Helms, Pennylane Press, Decatur, AL

The Alabama Heritage Cookbook ©1984 Heritage Publications, Birmingham, AL

Alabama's Historic Restaurants and Their Recipes ©1998 Gay N. Martin, 2nd Edition, John F. Blair, Publisher, Winston-Salem, NC

Aliant Cooks for Education ©2004 Morris Press Cookbooks, Aliant Bank, Alexander City, AL

Ambrosia ©1997 Junior Auxiliary of Vicksburg, MS

Another Taste of Alabaster, Friends of the Albert L. Scott Library, Alabaster, AL

Auburn Entertains ©1983, 1986 Aurburn Entertains, Helen Baggett, Jeanne Blackwell, and Lucy Littleton, Rutledge Hill Press, Nashville, TN

Barbara's Been Cookin', Barbara Buckley, Edwards, MS

Bay Tables ©1999 Junior League of Mobile, AL

Bell's Best ©1981 Telephone Pioneers of America-Mississippi Chapter #36, Jackson, MS

Bell's Best II ©1982 Telephone Pioneers of America-Mississippi Chapter #36, Jackson, MS

Bell's Best III: Savory Classics ©1992 Telephone Pioneers of America, MS Chapter #36, Jackson, MS

Bell's Best IV: The Next Generation ©2001 Telephone Pioneers of America, MS Chapter 36, Jackson, MS

Best of Bayou Cuisine ©1997 St. Stephens Episcopal Church, Quail Ridge Press, Inc., Brandon, MS

The Best of South Louisiana Cooking ©1983 Bootsie John Landry, Lafayette, LA

Bethany's Best Bites, Bethany Baptist Church, Andalusia, AL

Between the Levees ©1994 Delta Rice Promotions, Cleveland, MS

Beyond the Grill ©1997 D.D. Publishing, Debbye Dabbs, Jackson, MS

Beyond Cotton Country ©1999 Junior League of Morgan County, Decatur, AL

Big Mama's Old Black Pot Recipes ©1987 Stoke Gabriel Enterprises, Alexandria, LA

Blue Mountain College Cookbook ©2000 Blue Mountain College National Alumnae Association, Blue Mountain, MS

Bountiful Blessings, Dumas Baptist Church, Dumas, MS

Bouquet Garni ©1983 Pascagoula-Moss Point Mississippi Junior Auxiliary, Pascagoula, MS

A Bouquet of Recipes, Home Flower and Garden Club, Homer, LA

Bravo! Applaudable Recipes ©1977 Mobile Opera Guild, Mobile, AL

Breaking Bread Together, Touching Hands, Meridian, MS

Bully's Best Bites ©1996 Junior Auxiliary of Starkville, MS

Cajun Cookin', Franklin Golden Age Club, Franklin, LA

Cajun Cooking ©1996 Acadian House Publishing, Lafayette, LA

Cajun Cooking for Beginners ©1996 Acadian House Publishing, Marcelle Bienvenu, Lafayette, LA

Cajun Cuisine ©1985 Beau Bayou Publishing Company, Acadian House Publishing, Layfayette, LA

Cajun Men Cook ©1994 Beaver Club of Lafayette, Beaver Club of Lafayette, LA

Calling All Cooks ©1982 Telephone Pioneers of America, Alabama Chapter #34, Birmingham, AL

Calling All Cooks, Two ©1988 Telephone Pioneers of America, Alabama Chapter #34, Birmingham, AL

Calling All Cooks, Four ©2000 Telephone Pioneers of America, Alabama Chapter #34, Birmingham, AL

Calling All Kids ©2002 Telephone Pioneers of America, Alabama Chapter #34, Birmingham, AL

Cane River's Louisiana Living ©1994 The Service League of Natchitoches, LA

Capitol Cooking, Alabama Legislative Club, Clanton, AL

Celebrations ©1999 Telephone Pioneers of America, Alabama Chapter #34, Birmingham, AL

A Collection of My Favorite Recipes, Deette Daniels, Meadville, MS

Come and Dine ©1986 Naomi Fonville, Lumberton, MS

Come and Get It! ©1990 Junior Welfare League of Talladega, AL

The Complete Venison Cookbook ©1996 Harold W. Webster, Jr., Quail Ridge Press, Brandon, MS

Cook with a Natchez Native ©1977 Myrtle Bank Publishers, Bethany Ewald Bultman, Natchez, MS

Cook with Nancy, Plain or Fancy, Nancy Holliman, Huntsville, AL

Cooking & Gardening with Dianne ©1996 Dianne Cage, Monroe, LA

Cooking for Love and Life ©1979 Recipes for Life, Inc., Lafayette, LA

Cooking New Orleans Style! ©1991 Episcopal Churchwomen of All Saints, Inc., River Ridge, LA

Cooking on the Coast ©1994 Rose Annette O'Keefe, Ocean Springs, MS

Cooking Wild Game & Fish Southern Style ©2000 Billy Joe Cross, Brandon, MS

Cooking with Friends, Rena Lara Volunteers, Alligator, MS

Cooking with Gilmore, Gilmore Memorial Hospital Foundation, Amory, MS

Cooking with Mr. "G" and Friends, Kevin Grevemberg, Anacoco, LA

The Cook's Book, Alabama Association of Women's Clubs, Inc., Tuscaloosa, AL

The Cook's Book ©1972 Calvary Episcopal Church, Cleveland, MS

A Cook's Tour of Shreveport ©1964 The Junior League of Shreveport, LA

Cooks and Company ©1988 Muscle Shoals District Service League, Sheffield, AL

The Cotton Country Collection ©1972 Junior Charity League, Monroe, LA

Cotton Country Cooking ©1972 The Decatur Junior Service League, Inc., Decatur, AL

The Country Gourmet ©1982 Mississippi Animal Rescue League, Jackson, MS

The Country Mouse ©1983 Quail Ridge Press, Inc., Sally Walton and Faye Wilkinson, Brandon, MS

Critic's Choice, The Guild of Corinth Theatre-Arts, Corinth, MS

Devine Dishes, Greater Mt. Calvary Baptist Church, Jackson, MS

Dining Under the Magnolia ©1984 Scott Wilson, Grove Hill, AL

Dinner on the Ground ©1990 Stoke Gabriel Enterprises, Alexandria, LA

Dixie Dining ©1982 Mississippi Federation of Women's Clubs, Inc., GFWC, Jackson, MS

Down Home Dining in Mississippi ©1999 Mississippi Homemaker Volunteers, Inc., Water Valley, MS

DOWN HOME in High Style ©2004 Jack DeLoney, Jack DeLoney Art Gallery, Ozark, AL

Easy Hospitality ©1996 Downhome Publications, Inc., Patty Roper, Jackson, MS

Encore, Shreveport Symphony Women's Guild, Shreveport, LA

Encore! Encore! ©1999 Gulf Coast Symphony Orchestra Guild, Gulfport, MS

The Encyclopedia of Cajun and Creole Cuisine ©1983 The Encyclopedia Cookbook Committee, Inc., John D. Folse, Lafitte's Landing Restaurant, Baton Rouge, LA

Extra! Extra! Read All About It! ©1995 Corinne H. Cook, Baton Rouge, LA

Family Favorites, Catholic Daughters of the Americas #2388, Westlake, LA

Family Secrets ©1985 The William Henry Thomas Family, Thomas Family Memorial Association, Cartersville, GA

Family Secrets...the Best of the Delta ©1990 Lee Academy, Clarksdale, MS

Family Traditions, Esta White Freeland, Mer Rouge, LA

Fannye Mae's Home Made Candy, Fannye Mae Gibbons, Jackson, MS

Favorite Flavors of First ©2002 UMW Circle One, First United Methodist Church, Mountain Brook, AL

Favorite Recipes, Baptist Health System Senior Housing, Centre, AL

Favorite Recipes from First Baptist Church of Columbiana, First Baptist Church of Columbiana, AL

Feeding His Flock, Decatur United Methodist Church Women, Decatur, MS

Festival Cookbook ©1983 Humphreys Academy Patrons, Belzoni, MS

Field O' Dreams Farm Cookbook I ©1993 LaVa Publications, Ann Varnum and Martha Lavallet, Webb, AL

Field O' Dreams Farm Cookbook II ©1996 LaVa Publications, Ann Varnum and Martha Lavallet, Webb, AL

Fiftieth Anniversary Cookbook, Northeast Louisiana Telephone Co., Inc., Collinston, LA

Fine Dining Mississippi Style ©1999 John M. Bailey, Quail Ridge Press, Brandon, MS

The Five Star Family Book of Recipes, Five Star Credit Union, Dothan, AL

Food for Thought ©1995 Junior League of Birmingham, AL

Foods à la Louisiane ©1980 Louisiana Farm Bureau Women, Baton Rouge, LA

From a Louisiana Kitchen ©1982 Holly Berkowitz Clegg, Baton Rouge, LA

From Mama to Me, Anita G. Guidry, Church Point, LA

From the Firehouse to Your House, Don and Sue Griffith, Jackson, MS

Gardener's Gourmet ©1985 Garden Clubs of Mississippi, Inc., Yazoo City, MS

Giant Houseparty Cookbook, Philadelphia-Neshoba County Chamber of Commerce, Philadelphia, MS

Gibson/Goree Family Favorites, Gibson/Goree Family of Choctaw, Birmingham, AL

The Gift of Gracious Meals, First Baptist Church of Louisville, MS

Give Us This Day Our Daily Bread, Parishioners Family and Friends of St. Helen Catholic Church, Amory, MS

Going Wild in Mississippi ©1995 Mississippi Telephone Pioneers, Jackson, MS

Golden Moments ©1996 Arlene Giesel Koehn, Golden Moments Publishing, West Point, MS

Gone with the Fat ©1994 Cookbook Resources, Jen Bays Avis and Kathy F. Ward, West Monroe, LA

Gourmet of the Delta ©1964 St. John's Women's Auxiliary and St. Paul's Women's Auxiliary, Leland and Hollandale, MS

Gran's Gems, Jane Rayburn Hardin, Birmingham, AL

Great American Recipes from Southern 'n' Cajun Cook'n', James S. Gwaltney, Sr., Florence, MS

The Great American Writer's Cookbook ©1981 Dean Faulkner Wells, Yoknapatawpha Press, Oxford, MS

Great Flavors of Mississippi ©1986 Southern Flavors, Inc., Pine Bluff, AR

Great Performances ©1990 The Symphony League of Tupelo, MS

Grits 'n Greens and Mississippi Things ©2002 Parlance Publishing, Sylvia Higginbotham, Columbus, MS

The Gulf Gourmet ©1979 Westminster Academy Mothers Club, Gulfport, MS

Hallmark's Collection of Home Tested Recipes, Freeda Rogers Hallmark, Tuscaloosa, AL

Heart & Soul Cookbook ©2004 Women's Ministries, Greenville, AL

Heart of the Home, East Baton Rouge Extension Homemaker's Council, Inc., Baton Rouge, LA

Hearthside at Christmas, Patricia Edington, Mobile, AL

Heavenly Hostess, St. John's Episcopal Church Women, Monroeville, AL

Heavenly Manna, First United Methodist Church Women, Fort Payne, AL

Heirlooms from the Kitchen ©1985 Joan Hutson, Huntsville, AL

Hope in the Kitchen, Hope Sunday School Class, Ridgecrest Baptist Church, Madison, MS

Hors D'Oeuvres Everybody Loves ©1983 Quail Ridge Press, Inc., Mary Leigh Furrh and Jo Barksdale, Brandon, MS

Hospitality Heirlooms, South Jackson Civic League, Jackson, MS

The Hungry Hog ©1995 Phil D. Mayers, Lafayette, LA

Huntsville Entertains ©1983 Historic Huntsville Foundation, Huntsville, AL

I Promised a Cookbook, Josephine M. Conner, Sioux Falls, SD

In the Pink, Beauregard Memorial Hospital Auxiliary, DeRidder, LA

Incredible Edibles: A Gardner's Cookbook ©2003 DeKalb County Master Gardeners, Fort Payne, AL

Inverness Cook Book ©1963 All Saints Episcopal Guild, Inverness, MS

Irondale Cafe Original WhistleStop Cookbook ©1995 Mary Jo Smith McMichael, Original WhistleStop Cafe, Irondale, AL

Iuka Masonic Lodge Cookbook, Iuka, MS

Jambalaya ©1983 Junior League of New Orleans, Inc., New Orleans, LA

Just for Kids, Jen Bays Avis and Kathy F. Ward, West Monroe, LA

Kay Ewing's Cooking School Cookbook ©1994 Kay Ewing, Kay Ewing, Baton Rouge, LA

Kitchen Delights ©2001 The Tylertown Times, Tylertown, MS

Kitchen Keepsakes ©2000 First United Methodist Church, Heritage Committee, Dothan, AL

Kitchen Sampler ©1985 The Bessemer Junior Service League, Bessemer, AL

Kooking with the Krewe, Twin Cities' Krewe of Janus, Monroe, LA

Kum' Ona' Granny's Table, Senior Citizens Retirement Facility, Montgomery, AL

L'Heritage Du Bayou Lafourche, Lafourche Assn. for Family & Community Education, Lockport, LA

La Bonne Cuisine ©1980, 1981 Episcopal Churchwomen of All Saints, Inc., New Orleans, LA

Lake Guntersville Bed & Breakfast Cookbook, Carol Dravis, Lake Guntersville Bed & Breakfast, Guntersville, AL

Le Bon Temps ©1982 Young Women's Christian Organization, Baton Rouge, LA

Let's Get Together ©2001 Junior Auxiliary of Clinton, MS

Let's Say Grace Cookbook, Order of the Eastern Star, State of Alabama, Mobile, AL

The Little Gumbo Book ©1986 Quail Ridge Press, Gwen McKee, Brandon, MS

The Little New Orleans Cookbook ©1991 Quail Ridge Press, Inc., Gwen McKee, Brandon, MS

Loaves and Fishes ©1984 The Episcopal Churchwomen, St. Paul's Episcopal Church, Daphne, AL

Louisiana Entertains ©1978, 1983 Rapides Symphony Guild, Alexandria, LA

Louisiana Keepsake ©1982 Lillie Petit Gallagher, Petit Press, Baton Rouge, LA

Louisiana LEGACY ©1982 The Thibodeaux Service League, Inc., Thibodeaux, LA

Louisiana's Original Creole Seafood Recipes, Tony Chachere, Creole Foods of Opelousas, LA

Madison County Cookery ©1980 Madison County Chamber of Commerce, Canton, MS

Magic ©1982 The Junior League of Birmingham, AL

Mama Couldn't Cook ©2005 Mama Couldn't Cook Cookbook, The Oliver Girls, Trussville, AL

The Mississippi Cookbook ©1972 University Press of Mississippi, Jackson, MS

Mississippi Stars Cookbook, South Pontotoc Attendance Center PTO, Pontotoc, MS

More Cultured Country Cooking ©2000 The Columbiana Culture Club, Columbiana, AL

More Fiddling with Food, First Baptist Church of Mobile, AL

Mountain Laurel Inn and Mentone Memories, Mountain Laurel Inn, Mentone, AL

Munchin' with the Methodists ©2001 Carolina United Methodist Women, Booneville, MS

Natchez Notebook of Cooking ©1986 Trinity Episcopal Day School, Natchez, MS

Nun Better ©1996 St. Cecilia School, St. Cecilia School of Sacred Heart Parish, Broussard, LA

Offerings for Your Plate ©1989 Junior League of Monroe, LA

Old Mobile Recipes ©1956 St. Paul's Episcopal Church, Mobile, AL

Once Upon a Stove ©1986 Birmingham Children's Theatre, Birmingham, AL

One of a Kind ©1981 Junior League of Mobile, AL

Pass the Meatballs, Please! ©1996 Michael Cannatella, Port Allen, LA

Paul Naquin's French Collection I: Louisiana Seafood ©1978 Paul Naquin, Baton Rouge, LA

Paul Naquin's French Collection II: Meats & Poultry ©1980 Paul Naquin, Baton Rouge, LA

Paul Naquin's French Collection III: Louisiana Wild Game ©1984 Paul Naquin, Baton Rouge, LA

Peanut Delights, National Peanut Festival Association, Dothan, AL

The Pick of the Crop ©1978 North Sunflower PTA, Drew, MS

Picnic in the Park, Mantachie Playground Committee, Mantachie, MS

Pigging Out with the Cotton Patch Cooks, Audrey Lee McCollum, Mer Rouge, LA

The Pilgrimage Garden Club Antiques Forum Cookbook ©1986 Pilgrimage Garden Club, Natchez, MS

A Pinch of Rose & A Cup of Charm ©1998 Rose Dorchuck, Kosciusko, MS

Pineapple Gold ©1983 Joann Hulett Dobbins, Meridian, MS

The Plantation Cookbook ©1972 Junior League of New Orleans, LA

Prime Meridian ©2001 Lamar Foundation, Lamar School, Meridian, MS

Quickies for Singles ©1980 Quail Ridge Press, Inc., Fellowship Church, Baton Rouge, LA

Recipes & Remembrances ©2004 Morris Press Cookbooks, Arab First United Methodist Church, Arab, AL

Recipes and Reminiscences of New Orleans I ©1971 Parents Club of Ursuline Academy, Inc., Metairie, LA

Recipes from the Heart, Stitches of Love, Columbia, MS

Recipes from the Heart of Branch, Branch Baptist Church Youth, Morton, MS

Recipes from Bayou Pierre Country, Mildred Rachel Norris, Gorum, LA

Revel ©1980 Junior League of Shreveport, LA

River Road Recipes II ©1976 The Junior League of Baton Rouge, LA

River Road Recipes III ©1994 The Junior League of Baton Rouge, LA

Roger's Lite Cajun Cookbook ©1989 Vernon Roger, Baton Rouge, LA

A Salad a Day ©1980 Quail Ridge Press, Inc., Ruth Moorman and Lalla Williams, Brandon, MS

A Samford Celebration Cookbook, Samford University Auxiliary, Birmingham, AL

Savor the Spirit ©2002 Alabama Society, United States Daughters of 1812, Birmingham, AL

Scents from Heaven, Trinity United Methodist Church, Alexander City, AL

Seasoned with Love Too ©1986 Barbara Page, Brandon, MS

Secrets of The Original Don's Seafood & Steakhouse ©1996 Don's Seafood & Steakhouse of Louisiana, Inc., The Original Don's Seafood & Steakhouse, Lafayette, LA.

Shared Treasures, First Baptist Church, Monroe, LA

Sharing Our Best ©2003 Morris Press Cookbooks, United Methodist Women, First United Methodist Church, Bay Minette, AL

A Shower of Roses ©1996 St. Therese Catholic Church, Abbeville, LA

Simple Pleasures from Our Table to Yours ©1998 Arab Mother's Club, Arab, AL

Simply Southern, Linda and Bob Brown, Picayune, MS

Simply Southern ©1998 Alagasco, Chef Clayton Sherrod, Arab, AL

Sisters' Secrets, Beta Sigma Phi, Ville Platte, LA

Sofilthy's Vittles Cookbook, Barbara White, Bay Springs, MS

Southern But Lite ©1994 Cookbook Resources, Jen Bays Avis and Kathy F. Ward, West Monroe, LA

The Southern Cook's Handbook ©2001 Quail Ridge Press, Inc., Courtney Taylor and Bonnie Carter Travis, Brandon, MS

Southern Generations ©2002 Junior Auxiliary of Starkville, MS

Southern Scrumptious: How to Cater Your Own Party ©2002 Betty Brandon Sims, Decatur, AL

Southern Scrumptious Entertains ©2002 Betty Brandon Sims, Decatur, AL

Southern Settings ©1996 Decatur General Foundation, Decatur, AL

Southern Sideboards ©1978 Junior League of Jackson, MS

St. Philomena School 125th Anniversary, St. Philomena Home & School Association, Labadieville, LA

Sterling Service ©1996 Dothan Service League, Dothan, AL

Straight from the Galley Past & Present, Ladies Auxiliary of Bay Waveland Yacht Club, Bay St. Louis, MS

Sumpthn' Yummy, Nan Dessert, Sara Engelhardt, and Betsy Plummer, Montgomery, AL

Take Five, A Cookbook ©1993 D.D. Publishing, Debbye Dabbs, Jackson, MS

Talk About Good II ©1979 Junior League of Lafayette, LA

Taste of the South ©1984 The Symphony League of Jackson, MS

Tasteful Treasures, First Baptist Church of Ridgeland, MS

The Tastes & Traditions of Troy State University ©1994 Troy State University Foundation, Troy, AL

The Tastes & Traditions of Troy State University II ©2000 Troy State University Foundation, Troy, AL

Tasting Tea Treasures ©1984 Greenville Junior Woman's Club, Greenville, MS

Temptations ©1986 Presbyterian Day School, Cleveland, MS

'Tiger Bait' Recipes ©1976 LSU Alumni Federation, Baton Rouge, LA

Tony Chachere's Cajun Country Cookbook, Tony Chachere, Creole Foods of Opelousas, LA

Tony Chachere's Second Helping ©1995 Tony Chachere, Creole Foods of Opelousas, LA

Too Good To Be True ©1992 Chet Beckwith, Baton Rouge, LA

Top O' the Morning ©1992 Alabama Gas Corporation, Chef Clayton Sherrod, Alagasco, Birmingham, AL

Top Rankin Recipes ©1986 Rankin General Hospital Auxiliary, Brandon, MS

Tout de Suite à la Microwave II ©1980 Jean K. Durkee, Lafayette, LA

Treasured Favorites ©2001 Disciple Women First Christian Church, Montgomery, AL

Treasured Tastes ©1986 Mobile College, Daphne, AL

Treasures from Our Kitchen ©2001 United Methodist Women, Waynesboro, MS

Trim & Terrific American Favorites ©1996 Holly B. Clegg, Baton Rouge, LA

Try Me ©1984 Arthritis Volunteer Action Committee, Arthritis Foundation, Mobile, AL

Turnip Greens in the Bathtub ©1981 Genie Taylor Harrison, Baton Rouge, LA

The Twelve Days of Christmas Cookbook ©1978 Quail Ridge Press, Inc., Ruth Moorman and Lalla Williams, Brandon, MS

Vintage Vicksburg ©1985 Vicksburg Junior Auxiliary, Inc., Vicksburg, MS

Waddad's Kitchen ©1982 Waddad Habeeb Buttross, Natchez, MS

When Dinnerbells Ring ©1978 Junior Welfare League of Talladega, AL

Who's Your Mama, Are You Catholic, and Can You Make a Roux? ©1991 Marcelle Bienvenu, The Times of Acadiana, Lafayette, LA

Why Gather in the Kitchen? ©2001 Sybil H. Powell, Ridgeland, MS

With Special Distinction ©1993 Mississippi College Cookbook, Clinton, MS

INDEX

Blount County is Alabama's Covered Bridge Capital and home of the Covered Bridge Festival each fall. Horton Mill Bridge, located five miles north of Oneonta on Highway 75, is seventy feet above Black Warrior River, making it the nation's highest covered bridge above water.

INDEX

INDEX

INDEX

INDEX

INDEX

INDEX